Effective Media
Planning

Effective Media Planning

*A Guide to Help
Advertisers and Agencies
Develop Plans That Work*

by
August B. Priemer

Lexington Books
D.C. Heath and Company/Lexington, Massachusetts/Toronto

Library of Congress Cataloging-in-Publication Data

Priemer, August B.
Effective media planning : a guide to help advertisers and agencies
develop plans that work / by August B. Priemer.
p.   cm.
Includes index.
ISBN 0-669-20808-6 (alk. paper)
1. Advertising media planning. I. Title.
HF5826.5.P75   1989
659.1'11—dc19   89-30940
CIP

Copyright © 1989 by Lexington Books

All rights reserved. No part of this publication may be reproduced or
transmitted in any form or by any means, electronic or mechanical,
including photocopy, recording, or any information storage
or retrieval system, without permission in writing
from the publisher.

Published simultaneously in Canada
Printed in the United States of America
International Standard Book Number: 0-669-20808-6
Library of Congress Catalog Card Number: 89-30940

The paper used in this publication meets the minimum requirements
of American National Standard for Information Sciences—Permanence
of Paper for Printed Library Materials, ANSI Z39.48-1984.

Year and number of this printing:

89 90 91 92 8 7 6 5 4 3 2 1

Contents

Introduction

T his book is an epilogue to my long career as something of a media maverick. Like my career, the book itself can be summarized as being an intellectual assault on the bad thinking, the lazy thinking, and the nonthinking that have kept media planning, and its related advertising functions, from being significantly improved during the last quarter of a century. Its contents should be useful to anyone ready to become more professional than the advertising business asks its people to be, or even allows them to be. After spending almost four decades wandering mass-market advertising's labyrinth of thought-process dead ends, I've tried to mark a trail so that others can travel more swiftly than I did.

I'm certain that many media people will profit from reading this book. It was written by one of their own kind, primarily for their benefit, and from the way they see the advertising process. But its material isn't only for media people. It can help most advertising people think more professionally than they do now. For marketing people, there are constructive insights into media planning, into how their advertising works, into how to get better advertising research, and even, perhaps, suggestions on how they can get better copy for their brands. Product managers who use, proactively, the material in this book, will most certainly become more skilled managers of the advertising process.

During my career, I spent as much, or more, time with marketing people as I did with my media coworkers. I learned to understand, and work around, their conflicting career needs. On one hand, they are expected to advance the business of their brands, and their companies; on the other hand, they are tugged by the need for personal advancement, which is frequently more power-ful. During my thirty-seven years in media management, I worked with the marketing people responsible for many of this country's best-known package-goods trademarks: Tide, Cheer, Ivory, Spic 'n Span, Clorox, Camay, Zest, Crest, Gleem, Secret, Prell, Head & Shoulders, Crisco, Duncan Hines, Raid, Off!, Glade, Pledge, Shout, Edge, and a host of others. Some of these marketing peo-ple have since become chairman or president of one of this coun-try's large corporations. Others have founded their own profitable companies. A few weren't equal to the performance of their famous brands, as you may infer from my examples of how badly some things are sometimes done even in a good marketing or advertis-ing organization.

I worked only at arm's length with the advertising agency ac-count people who interacted with these marketing managers. But I learned that they, too, have conflicting needs. They are expected to advance the business of their client, the advertiser; but usually there is a more powerful need to advance the business of their adver-tising agency, which is the source of their personal advancement. This book offers account managers the opportunity to set higher standards for the thought process they bring to media planning, and to advertising in general. Even the occasionally Machiavellian account managers (who have always been upset by my thinking) may find the book's insights worthwhile, if only to counter, more effectively, what I say, as they try to maintain a profitable status quo for their employers and for themselves.

The serious student of advertising should find this book inter-esting, if only because it contains insights that won't be found else-where. People in the business of advertising, those who know it well enough to criticize it, do not write very critically about advertis-ing. People who are not in the business, but who write critically about advertising, really don't know enough about it to criticize.

My career in media was uninterrupted for thirty-seven years, but I was blessed with other responsibilities during many of them. A marketing research department reported to me for five of these years. During this period, I learned enough about copy testing to believe I could do it better than it was being done by others, most of whom could never reach a consensus with their peers on the correct testing technique. I also discovered that the results of copy testing could be an unexpected source of new insights on media planning and advertising theory.

After relinquishing my marketing research responsibilities, for the next fifteen years I continued to test finished commercials and ads. Although I worked without any research staff, I ultimately tested about six hundred TV commercials, one hundred print ads, and a dozen or so radio commercials. One of the beneficial by-products of this hands-on involvement with advertising research was that I learned how to create a low-cost tracking system that produced discriminating response curves for advertising campaigns. Throughout the book, the reader will discover insights from this learning.

I mention these nonmedia skills because they were crucial to my being able to escape the traditional role of the media man who "knows his place" and does only what he's told to do. If he or she is to help create an effective advertising campaign, the media professional must be able to ask probing copy questions, precise research questions, and, certainly, strategic marketing questions. Too often, media people are asked to put together media plans with little direction, or bad direction, from the nonstrategic thinking of marketing or account management. Copy that is badly timed, or totally lacking in real benefit for consumers, too often condemns a media plan to failure. These failures are rarely measured. The advertising industry's most effective powers of persuasion have been used to convince themselves that good research on the consumer's response to advertising is either too expensive to conduct, nonactionable by the time results are available, or simply impossible to develop in a way that will capture the effects of an advertising campaign.

If this sounds critical, it's because I think that most of the people responsible for advertising need to work a lot harder in order to earn our respect. There's nothing more public than advertising. Like celebrities and public officials, advertising often deserves to be criticized for its visible lack of professionalism. Of course, everyone makes mistakes. Certainly all of us are novices at the beginning of each new endeavor. But should novices be paid hundreds of thousands of dollars a year? Although successful, well-compensated advertising people see themselves as experts, not novices, their incomplete skills, or conflicting economic interests, often prevent them from being productive and efficient.

Unlikely as it may seem after reading these words, the book, in its entirety, may still be viewed as positive. Granted, it does begin destructively. But so does some of the most effective advertising. A classic advertising technique first shows a consumer that her current brand doesn't perform as well as the advertised brand. A consumer fully satisfied with her current brand isn't likely to switch to one that offers parity performance. A practitioner of advertising is no different from the consumer. If he thinks he knows what he's doing, and thinks he is doing it well, he has no incentive to learn how to do it differently. Until we admit to being ignorant of something, we have neither reason nor incentive to learn what we don't know.

Young people, the confessed novices, are usually open to new and better ideas. That's because they have no vested interest in the status quo. They have no false expertise to defend. The group I've always found most resistant to being helped are those with more than ten or fifteen years of advertising or marketing experience. These are the men and women who have reached positions of middle-management, or higher, and are using their "expertise" to manage the advertising process. These people tend to be reluctant to admit that their advertising experience is ill-founded, and that much of what they think they know is either myth or mistake. Their reluctance to learn is understandable. Many of them are action-oriented people, and decisiveness is dependent on confidence in one's own knowledge. When these men and women are confronted with ideas that threaten the confidence they have in their own knowledge, their decisiveness is weakened. For managers whose style of management is based on keeping control, destruction of their knowledge base is an obvious threat to their ability to control.

I hope some of these mature managers will review and challenge the erroneous beliefs they label their "experience." If they do, progress toward effective and more efficient advertising will be achieved more quickly. If they don't, the enlightened young will have to wait until they themselves move into positions of authority, where they will be able to make advertising as professional as it ought to be.

1
Advertising:
More Often a Problem
Than a Solution

During the second half of the 1980s, business and industry in these United States have discovered that their marketplace has become far more competitive than it was in the good old days. Companies have been buying other companies, as an easier way to achieve growth. Other companies have been selling off badly digested acquisitions; these acquisitions were intended to provide profitable growth, but they didn't grow, and weren't profitable. Many companies, after years of introducing unprofitable new products, have conceded that sales growth isn't always the easiest way to increase profits.

Instead, these companies are now choosing to reduce expenses, which makes their current sales base more profitable. Many of their most highly paid employees have been offered early retirement, and a multitude of ambitious young men and women are being kept out by hiring freezes. Production of sentimental but unprofitable old brands is finally being discontinued. Obsolete manufacturing facilities, incapable of producing efficiently enough to survive in this more competitive marketplace, are being closed down. Reorganization and new management groups are expected to find more profit in their current consumer franchises by making their organizations more "lean and mean." (Dare we ask how much longer the corporate world can afford to remain sentimental about unproductive buzz words such as these, which are still with us long after unproductive practices and obsolete facilities have been abandoned?)

Unless business becomes easier and more profitable, the status quo will remain under pressure to change. Even some advertising budgets are being reduced, despite pressure from the advertising industry to increase the advertising budget in hard times. "Evidence" has been offered that companies that increase advertising budgets during a recession fare better, in the long run, than those which reduce them to protect their profitability. (A skeptic might observe that any company strong enough to continue spending through a recession would be more likely to fare better than one that couldn't.) I've never seen anyone challenge this self-serving evidence, so we shouldn't be surprised to find that many decision makers have accepted it at face value. Many of them seem possessed by a blind faith in the power of advertising to accomplish marketing miracles. They show, by their choice of alternatives, how reluctant they are to cut advertising budgets. Some have chosen to retire their most skilled and experienced employees, in order to fund the airing of a 30-second TV commercial, which they think will "really make things happen" in the marketplace.

But how often does a TV commercial really make something happen in the marketplace? They rarely know. Few of us ever know what happens in the marketplace as a result of advertising (other than direct-response or sale-price advertising). We don't know how, when, or why our advertising works in the marketplace. The advertising industry itself doesn't know. The following are the opening words of a stimulating handbook, written in 1979 by Dick Vaughn, of Foote, Cone & Belding Communications (FCB) (then and now one of the largest advertising agencies in the world): "The advertising industry has long been challenged to explain how advertising works. That it does work is not an issue. But how it works, and why it works, are critical concerns still unresolved."[1]

This admission of ignorance isn't an indictment of FCB as an advertising agency. If anything, it shows that FCB is one of a tiny elite able to recognize, or willing to admit to, its own ignorance. Most of the advertising industry has yet to confront how its advertising—its only reason to exist—actually works! Paradoxically, the agency that has confessed its ignorance is the one that may be closest to understanding how advertising does work. By admitting its ignorance, it seems to be questioning much of what passes for knowledge in the business of advertising. By this admission, it tells us that FCB seems to be more aware than other agencies of how much it needs to learn. Not surprisingly, FCB works much harder than most agencies to learn how advertising does work.

But hold on. Perhaps I praise FCB a bit too much. Notice how they qualified their admission of ignorance with the statement, "That it does work is not an issue." In other words, even they take for granted that advertising, in general, "works." They omitted the key word *when* from their confession of ignorance. The implication is that advertising always works, even though nobody knows how or why. I contend that if we don't know how and why advertising works, we don't know when it works, either. We just don't want to admit it.

The advertising industry uses great skill in hiding its ignorance from itself, and from others. Ironically, people in advertising could learn what they need to know if they would only admit that they don't already know it. There are enough very intelligent men and women working in advertising to move the art of advertising ahead by decades, which would bring it to where other intelligent people have already moved the technologies of medicine, computers, space exploration, and a host of other intellectual achievements.

But how can an industry that spends billions of someone else's money admit to being ignorant of how its product—advertising— really works? Has the advertising industry waited too long, claimed too much knowledge and expertise, to confess, now, that it really doesn't know? What a terrible Catch-22! This continued pretense guarantees that knowledge and understanding will never be acquired, because we never pursue what we think is already firmly in our grasp.

Advertisers have provided no incentive for advertising agencies to learn more about what they do, or how to do it better. For decades, advertisers have lazily accepted a system of compensation that penalizes their agencies for becoming more efficient producers. For example, if an efficient agency can get a four-million-dollar job done for only three million, its compensation is reduced by a fourth. Quite logically, the industry has learned to set the spending of advertising budgets as its goal. That's why "efficient" spending, not the achievement of consumer response, defined in sales terms, long ago became the standard measure of performance for the work of people in advertising.

Thanks to this commission system of compensation, the advertising industry has always managed to visualize advertising tasks requiring spending levels higher than the amount of money the advertiser has available to spend. In this way, an ad agency avoids the danger of losing a source of revenue: the advertiser always spends its total advertising budget. Years ago, when dollars bought more, budgets were as fully expended as they are today, when dollars buy far less. Small brands may spend little, but they spend all they have. Large brands in the same product category spend much more, but they too spend all they have. The large brands have a much smaller target of "non-triers," but they spend all they have on this smaller target. When the target of new triers becomes too small, or when everyone has tried the brand, the target is likely to be redefined as "users." The advertising now is supposed to stimulate users to keep using the product.

In the early 1980s, the industry displayed its creativity by coming up with the term "re-trial," which is defined as a repurchase that occurs so long after the consumer's last use that it's like trying it all over again. (A chauvinistic analogy would be a woman's regaining her virginity after a long period of celibacy.) The one goal that the industry keeps constant for a brand, from its introduction to its last sale, is that its advertising budget must be completely spent.

The hearsay support for spending all you can afford to spend on advertising has so institutionalized the belief that we never hear it challenged. Continued support comes in the form of pronouncements such as, "Media have become fragmented, and much more expensive to use effectively"; "Consumer marketing has become more targeted, and targeted media are more expensive"; "Marketing is more local, where it is more expensive to advertise"; "Ethnic groups need their own marketing programs, and these carry a cost premium," and so on. Because of this continued reinforcement of the basic premise, major advertisers usually spend all they can afford to spend on advertising, and still return a profit that satisfies their management or stockholders.

The foregoing phrase reveals the other disincentive for the advertising business to learn more about how it works. If advertiser clients are already spending all they can afford to spend on advertising, new knowledge about how advertising works can't increase ad budgets (and agency revenues). New information can only keep budgets at the same level, or reduce them. Imagine a young man in an advertising agency. He rushes into the president's office and announces: "I've just discovered how to accomplish the advertising goals of all our clients at half the cost of what they're now spending!" Is this young man immediately promoted? Is he given an enormous raise in salary? Or will someone suggest sending him on a one-way cruise to the middle of the nearest large body of water, with cement in his luggage?

Paradoxical as it seems, while the advertiser is trying to produce the best product at the lowest cost, one of the company's major expenses is being managed in the opposite direction by his external advertising support group. But the problem isn't only external. Somebody in the advertiser's company probably benefits from its spending more, rather than less, for the same advertising effect. Where there's an advertising manager or director, his compensation will be greater if he is managing a large budget rather than a small one. He'll have a larger group of people working for him, which gives him more status in the company. He gets more "points" on the salary guide, so he earns more money. Rarely does he have profit responsibilities that might otherwise discourage advertising waste.

The product-manager system of marketing management also benefits from higher ad budgets. A big-budget brand is likely to have more contact with the top of the organization than brands with small budgets. Product managers are promoted from small brands to big ones. Big brands are the step below promotion to the next level of marketing management. On the other side of the coin, the product manager who skillfully manages an unadvertised, but usually profitable, smaller brand, can be a corporate nonentity. Like the advertising director, the product manager rarely has profit responsibilities. His goal is higher sales and a higher market share. If high levels of advertising don't lead to higher sales, they at least protect him from being faulted for being timid with his marketing efforts when his brand has a sales problem.

So both sides of the advertising process—the advertiser's own people and his advertising agency—have biases that pressure them to spend as much money as they can get their hands on. Effectiveness of advertising is implied by the spending advantage one brand has over another; we say it has a higher "share of voice." Higher-spending tests are implemented regularly, even though it's widely known that virtually none has ever paid out. These extra-spending tests are rarely in response to a known consumer need for more communication from the testing brand. Their managers simply assume that "more is bound to be better than less."

With no financial incentive to learn more about what its advertising does, and with its efficient spending of money accepted as proof-of-performance for advertising effectiveness, the industry shouldn't surprise us with how little it knows about how its advertising works. But what should surprise us is that so many intelligent people have been involved in the process of advertising for the last three or four decades, and no more than a handful of them have asked questions that challenge the competence of the system. A rational mind can't be exposed for long to the inner workings of this business without concluding that much of what is being said and done makes no sense at all. It isn't the healthy, accepted ignorance that precedes all learning. It's self-delusion; it's "Let's pretend that all this jargon and all these numbers really mean something." In a way, the best sale made by advertising has been to its own people. With little substantiation, advertising has convinced its practitioners that they really know what they're doing.

This self-directed campaign by the people in advertising assures them that their work is producing commercials with good "persuasion," commercials that "impact" their clients' business by "reaching" target consumers with "effective frequency" as viewers watch "quality" TV shows; that they "sustain" their clients' business with the "continuity" of this advertising; that their budgeting is accurately based on an "advertising-to-sales ratio," which provides an effective "share of voice" in each brand's product category; and that despite extremely high media costs, "flighting" their "intrusive" commercials allows them to penetrate the "clutter" and achieve a "meaningful competitive presence." The words in quotes are probably those most often used by people in the business of advertising. But these words are no better than fantasy food. They have become a form of civilized incantation, the genetic offspring of industry jargon and some macho buzz words. I call them "verbal narcotics."

Their users don't understand them, but they use them—and abuse them. The words imply a mastery over the intellectual crafts of advertising, a false mastery. Advertising people are convinced that they know what they're doing. But they don't. And they never will, until they try to find out how to do what they think they're already doing.

In the pages that follow, I will try to show the reader the results of this sort of thinking. If this part of my "commercial" is successful, the reader will be as disillusioned with the conventional thought processes of advertising as consumers have been with the products that leave a ring around their collars, or waxy yellow build-up on their floors. Once the reader has become disillusioned, perhaps he will "buy" the solutions I offer in the later pages of this book. If I've done my job well, if my "advertising" has been effective, and has led to a sale, the reader should react to an occasional stinging sensation with no more than a "Thanks, I needed that."

2
The Consumer
Can Be Served,
but Not Controlled

E ffective advertising copy is created by men and women who
understand that their role is to serve consumers, not try to
control them. These men and women ask themselves: "What can
I put into this advertising that will make it beneficial, not for my
brand, but for the consumer?" These are the ones who understand
that their advertising must do this for the consumer in order to
do anything constructive for their brand.

Effective media planning is accomplished by people who under
stand their role in similar terms. The consumer's communication
needs, when understood and satisfied by a team of insightful media
and creative people, guide the development of an advertising campaign on its rocky road to effectiveness. When we ignore her needs,
and depend instead on our own preferences, prejudices, and preconceived notions, we betray a desire to control, not to serve, the
consumer. That's when our creative product, our media planning,
or both, becomes off-strategy, off-target, and just plain wasteful
of time, money, and marketing opportunity.

The importance of advertising's being guided by the communication needs of consumers appears to have been best understood
by the industry in the development of its creative executions. More
than a decade ago, I listened to the creative director of a leading
advertising agency tell the Association of National Advertisers
(ANA) that a good TV commercial speaks person to person with
a single consumer, and is not unlike talking to a friend. A decade

earlier, I had listened to the patriarchal creative head of another leading agency as he encouraged our marketing management to use "woman talk" in the commercials for our household products used by women. He was concerned because manufacturing people expected copy to be written in their idiom, while agency people wanted copy to be written in theirs, and because neither listened to how consumers talk about a product in their own language.

In the early seventies, Lehn & Fink put a conventional floor wax, of ordinary quality, into a squeeze bottle. Then, in a simple side-by-side demonstration, their TV commercial showed consumers how much easier floor care would be if they, like "the woman in Apartment B," used the new product, called Mop & Glo, to clean and shine their kitchen floor. Brilliantly guided by the advertiser's understanding of the consumer's desire to see herself cleaning and shining her floor with no more effort than the woman in the introductory TV commercial, Mop & Glo became the first successful one-step floor wax. In the process, Lehn & Fink's brand took over the number-one position in the floor-wax category, and retained that leadership position for many profitable years.

However, despite these examples of creative insight into advertising's fundamental obligation to serve the consumer, they may be the exceptions rather than the rule. This is true even in the area of copy development, where the consumers are often physically involved throughout the creative process, from concept testing to the testing of finished commercials and print ads. Think, for example, of the basis on which the industry each year awards itself Clios. Like the Oscars of the film industry, these awards are given for what pleases industry insiders, not for commercials that have proved to be capable of obtaining a buying response from consumers. It's likely that many Clio-winning commercials have never been consumer-tested. Those I have seen have had much in common with the commercials on my reels of test failures, which I put together periodically to show product-manager trainees what not to do if they want to communicate successfully with consumers.

The Myopic Eye of the Beholder

The agency that advocated talking person-to-person in advertising, also created and produced a "beautiful" air-freshener commercial for our company. Their commercial used the eight-year-old Brooke Shields to bring herbs from the garden to her mother. The distinctive voice of Tammy Grimes narrated, in an intimate manner, the names of the herbs whose fragrances were suggested by the new Fresh Herbal air freshener. The commercial was soft-focus, the beautiful characters were in lacy summer dresses, and the cinematography could have been inspired by the paintings of Renoir. The commercial went beyond beautiful. It was exquisite, an obvious candidate for a Clio award. How successful was it? Only 6 percent of the women who saw it on a prime-time TV program could remember any part of it the next day. This was the lowest recall score ever, not just for the brand, but for the company itself.

Did the agency and brand-management team welcome the consumer feedback obtained in the copy test? Of course not. They retested the commercial. They were certain that the low test score was one of these occasional aberrations suffered outside the 95 percent confidence level of an advertising research sample. But it wasn't. A retest score of 7 percent proved that the first test had given them a statistically perfect score (of the wrong kind, unfortunately). Did the agency and the brand-management people accept, and learn from, what the consumer was trying to tell them, that is, that they couldn't reach her with this kind of advertising? That they were only talking to themselves? Not really. They chose instead to tinker with the commercial. They all believed that it was beautiful, and that a beautiful commercial was right for this brand. They were determined to find a way to get those unresponsive consumers to pay attention to it!

The agency rearranged the pieces of the commercial a little bit. They didn't want to change it too much, because then it would have ceased being the beautiful commercial they had fallen in love with. They brought the package, and the brand name, forward—to the beginning of the commercial, and hoped that this would improve what the industry refers to as "brand-name registration."

Anyone who has tried fixing creative failures will be able to guess the result of the third test. It was the same as the second, which had been statistically the same as the first: another single-digit recall score. A communication disaster!

The advertising agency and brand-management people finally gave in to consumers, and reluctantly dropped their beloved commercial into the trash bin. The beautiful, eight-year-old Brooke Shields was seen in this commercial by only a handful of people, and remembered by far fewer. But that's not the end of the story. Further insult was yet to be added to the injury already suffered by the creative and managerial egos which had been so emphatically rebuked by consumers—to whom they had disdained to address in their own language.

Several years later, as guest lecturer to an advertising class at one of the University of Wisconsin campuses, I spoke to students on the subject of how and why advertisers should test their commercials under realistic viewing conditions. I used a reel of commercials that included successes and failures, as measured by the day-after-recall technique. The students were asked to evaluate each commercial as good, bad, or average; then they were shown how wrong they usually were in their judgments. The point I was trying to make was this: What looks good or bad to a person given the task of evaluating a commercial can be considered just the opposite by consumers when watching television programs under normal viewing conditions.

Because it was such a good example of disguised "badness," the Fresh Herbal commercial soon found a place among the nine ads on the reel of commercials I used for teaching. The commercials were shown consecutively, with a ten-second pause between them, to allow the students to record their judgments on a worksheet. I waited for the end of the showing by pacing back and forth, on one side of the projection screen. I was rehearsing my comments, and not really paying attention to which commercial was being shown on the screen. My back was to the audience when, during the Fresh Herbal commercial, the entire audience exploded in laughter. What had happened? I asked my secretary, who had assisted me in handing out the worksheets. Had anything happened in the auditorium while my back was turned? She had seen nothing. What was on the screen when the audience began laughing?

The voice of Tammy Grimes had been narrating the list of herbs evoked by the fragrance of this new product: "sage, chamomile, lemongrass. . . ." Lemongrass! The phrase had struck this group of students, who were of the marijuana generation, as enormously funny! The commercial, with its soft-focus and intimate voice-over, which were intended to create a beautiful mood, was nothing more than a "laugher" for these young men and women. And as consumers, they were expected to take it seriously enough to want to buy it!

A unique example? Not really. I have other examples that amply illustrate that advertising people, in general, think they know what's right for their audiences, without bothering to consult consumers on the subject. Remember the agency whose creative head understood how important it was to learn how women talk about products in their own language? At one time this agency was looking for the "right" presenter to help introduce a new, relatively upscale, floor-care product.

Carol Channing, On Her Knees, Waxing?

Someone in the advertising agency had recently seen Carol Channing, then at her peak of popularity, in a broadway musical. The chemistry we call "creativity" began its mysterious process, and Carol Channing became the recommended presenter. But one of our midwestern marketing managers wasn't as taken with Ms. Channing's broadway talent as was the agency. He asked if she was really the right kind of person to represent a new acrylic floor finish (or floor wax, to use "woman talk"). The agency said, yes, they believed she was. They were very confident of their choice. But to verify it for their unconvinced client, they conducted a small research study among one hundred women who took care of their own floors, and who lived in and around Chicago, including some of the better residential suburbs.

The research was structured to learn Ms. Channing's name awareness, picture recognition, potential dislikes, and suitability as presenter for a new floor-care product. For comparative purposes, the same information was obtained from consumers for Ed McMahon (well established as an announcer on the "Tonight Show"), Rose Marie (supporting comedienne on the original "Dick Van Dyke Show"), Penny Singleton (who played Blondie in the film series based on the cartoon strip), and Betsy Palmer (an established TV personality).

Was Ms. Channing the best choice? Well, she had the highest photo recognition of the five. Her name recognition was a close second to Ed McMahon's. So much for the good news. Now for the bad. Something about Ms. Channing's personality was disliked by more women than the combined number of women disliking all four other personalities! Even worse, she was judged by more consumers to be more unsuitable for presenting a floor-care product than the other four personalities combined. Forty-three percent of the research sample told the advertising agency that its choice of personality was blatantly wrong, that Carol Channing was obviously not their "language."

How could some of the most skilled professional communicators be so wrong in their choice of how to communicate with consumers? Simple. They instictively substituted their own atypical preference of personality for the consumers'. They were prepared to impose their own taste on their consumers. They assumed the role of master, not servant. Fortunately, they conducted—and got slapped down by—objective research. They never were allowed to execute their mistake, but only because someone in the client's management thought more like a consumer than like a manager. It doesn't happen this way very often.

The advertiser certainly isn't always the good guy, who knows the consumer better than the ad agency, and who keeps the agency from making a big mistake. Advertisers can be as arrogant and as thoughtless about consumers as any advertising agency. Let's go back to the introduction of Lemon Pledge furniture polish, and look at what I think is a classic example of a consumer put-down, done for the "benefit" of one of the most successful brands that has been sitting proudly on supermarket shelves for the last three decades.

The Lemon Pledge Mystique

When the Drackett Company introduced Behold furniture polish, the first major lemon-scented furniture polish in aerosol form, our company had a very high market share of all the furniture polish sold. About eight months later, as a defensive measure, we introduced Favor, our own lemon-scented aerosol polish. Simultaneously, we were developing a new lemon formula for Pledge (more Pledge was then being sold than all other brands combined). The new lemon product was shipped to the retail trade less than six months after our introduction of Favor.

To help introduce Lemon Pledge, the marketing group acquired rights to use the famous song, "Lemon Tree." A ballet-like TV commercial was produced. The commercial showed a beautiful young woman, in a pale-blue chiffon evening dress, moving gracefully around a very upscale living room, dusting the furniture with Lemon Pledge. The "Lemon Tree" song, with its words rewritten to include Lemon Pledge, played in the background.

As the blond young woman, in semi-slow motion, rounded a grand piano, she arched her shoulders backward, displaying an abundant bosom beneath her chiffon dress. The commercial was written, scored, and produced to capture what was referred to as the "mystique" of Pledge (a quality that consumers couldn't describe in research interviews, but which marketing people believed was their real reason for buying more Pledge than all other brands combined).

This beautiful commercial, which everyone felt had captured the mystique of Pledge, was tested before airing, using a theater-viewing research technique. Among the measuring devices were positive and negative checklists, by which consumers could describe, in qualitative terms, their reaction to the commercial they had just seen. There was also a dial for each viewer to hold in her hand while she watched the commercials being tested. The dial was to be turned to the right (thumbs up) when she saw something she particularly liked, or to the left (thumbs down) when something displeased her. These responses were graphed, second by second, to capture the flow of consumer reaction as the commercial was being viewed.

The reaction of women in the research sample was a surprise to those who had created and approved this commercial. Of the thirty-nine commercials tested for us by this research technique, this newest one was perceived as "silly" by the highest percentage of viewers. It was considered "unbelievable" by more viewers than all but five of the other thirty-eight commercials. Viewers thought it was the least "informative," and the third "least interesting" of all thirty-nine commercials tested. The pre-post score (which is now called *persuasion*) was less than half the average of our ten commercials that had tested least interesting to consumers.

Even more of a surprise was what happened next. The commercial was put on the air, and allowed to run for years! It was even pooled out into similar executions, using the same "Lemon Tree" song and stylized cinematography which had been chosen to capture on film the brand's mystique. Not surprising, however, was the consistency of negative test results that welcomed these pool-outs.

One of these later commercials accidentally provided a second source to confirm the consistent negative reaction of consumers. The commercial was a 30-second pool-out of the original Lemon Tree commercial. It showed the same actress, with her hair styled in a new way, and this time well-dressed—probably for afternoon shopping in an upscale department store. She was dusting her beautiful furniture in a Spanish-contemporary ranch house, again to the background music of the "Lemon Tree" song.

The commercial's on-air recall score was less than half the norm, which signified a commercial's being average. But everyone involved in its creation felt it was too good to discard. They decided to fix it by making it "more intrusive," and by "strengthening the brand-name registration." To accomplish this, they added five seconds to both the beginning and the end of the 30-second voice-over commercial. In these added segments, the woman in the commercial spoke directly to the audience about Lemon Pledge. The hope was to snap viewers to attention at the beginning of the commercial, and to "burn in" the brand's benefit claim by repeating it at the end.

What had now become a 40-second commercial was retested. It got the identical low recall score obtained by its 30-second version.

This time the commercial was junked. Nobody really liked the 40-second hybrid. It had lost whatever "mystique" it had had, by trying to improve its communication to consumers. The agency went back to the drawing board, and created a totally new fantasy. In this commercial, a young woman in the woods was pulled up a tree by a vine, and into a beautiful tree house, where she dusted the furniture with Lemon Pledge. This commercial didn't test particularly well, either, but it was better than its predecessor. A decision was made to air it on network TV.

The rejected hybrid, called California House, was put on my educational reel of original-versus-improved commercials. These were the test failures that their agency had attempted to improve. All these improvements received test scores that were virtually identical to the scores received by their originals, demonstrating that communication failures were not likely to be improved in their ability to communicate with consumers. I had occasion to show this reel to about thirty research people at Burke Marketing Research, as part of a training session. (Burke did all the on-air testing of our commercials at the time.) Most of the thirty people in the room were women, the target of all the advertising on my reel.

I had my back turned to the audience while the film was running, just as I had done during my presentation of ads, including the air-freshener commercial, to students at the University of Wisconsin. This group also exploded into laughter! This time, the laughs occurred during California House, when the camera went to semi-slow motion to capture the ballet-like grace of the woman drawing a dust cloth along the top of her buffet. This was the portion of the commercial that was supposed to be the embodiment of the Pledge mystique. But the tears in the eyes of these women were not from heart-tugging emotion. The tears were from laughing at the absurdity of a woman making such moves while dusting furniture.

By now you may have already asked yourself one of these important questions: Why was this star-crossed campaign approved in the first place? Why did it remain approved after consistent negative feedback from the consumers, who meant life or death to the business of this brand? How could a brand with the stature of Pledge be allowed to embarrass itself in this way?

Well, the brand was doing just fine in the marketplace. Much of its lost market share was quickly regained from Behold and Favor. These two lemon polishes had gathered in more than one-third of the market by the time Lemon Pledge was ready to be shipped to its retail customers. It should be noted, however, that Lemon Pledge began selling well as soon as it appeared on store shelves, even before the advertising began. If Pledge without lemon was a wonderful product, according to consumers, and if lemon was a strong positive addition to the brand, why shouldn't Lemon Pledge sell well without advertising?

But the real answer to why Pledge was allowed to embarrass itself by this advertising was found, and ignored, in the theater test of its introductory commercial. The answer was in the results of the thumbs-up, thumbs-down dial turning of the viewers of that original commercial. While women were dialing their second-by-second response to the Lemon Pledge commercial, so were a like number of men. They were not our target audience but were in the auditorium for another commercial being tested in the same research session. When the actress in the Lemon Pledge commercial slow-motioned her way around the grand piano, thrusting out her magnificent bosom, the men's response curve went up sharply, and the women's went down sharply! Figure 2–1 shows exactly what happened.

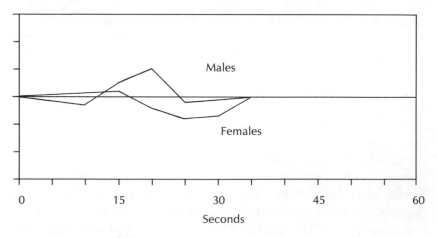

Figure 2–1. *Flow of Response to Lemon Pledge Commercial*

The conclusion to be drawn is obvious: the men who were responsible for approving this commercial reacted like the men in the research session. And what's wrong with that? Aren't men supposed to react like men? Not when they're managers, they shouldn't! This commercial was made for women, not for men. The male managers didn't act like advertising managers, but like any red-blooded man on the street, that is, like the ones who walked into the research session. They ignored the response of the woman consumer, and allowed many millions of dollars to be spent on communication that worked against the brand rather than for it.

Times Change, but Not the Mistakes

The preceding stories aren't new ones, but they serve as good teaching tools. And things haven't really changed much in the years since then. Only a few years ago, our marketing vice president convened his managers to review a cassette of TV commercials that had been put together by an organization that helps advertising agencies solicit new business. On this cassette were what we assumed to be the "showcase" creative product of several advertising agencies. We watched these commercials very closely. We knew our manager was going to ask us to evaluate the soliciting agencies on these examples of their talent.

At one point in the tape, all we saw, for perhaps the first thirty or forty seconds of a long commercial, was a car traveling along scenic mountain roads. The only audio was background music. We all tried to guess what product was being advertised. The car? Canadian tourism? High-mileage gasoline? All wrong. It was for a car-rental agency!

We fast-forwarded through the rest of that agency's reel of commercials. One of what they considered to be their best commercials had failed to communicate to eight car-rental prospects, all staring intently at the commercial in the quiet of a conference room. This agency obviously hadn't done much to understand the communication needs of its client's consumers. They had given us what they wanted to give us, and they seemed to be proud of trying to stuff it down the consumers' throats! They had enough arrogance to try to impress us with contempt for their audience. But they paid the price for it. We wrote them off as a contender, immediately. And yet, if that commercial was used on TV, their client paid an even higher price for its agency's lack of professionalism.

Writing the Consumer out of Media Plans

So much for how badly consumers' communication needs can be routinely ignored during the creative process. Let's now examine how those who put together media strategies and plans are guilty of the same kind of negligence. We quickly discover that almost all media thinking flows from the perspective of what the advertiser and his advertising agency want to do, not from the consumer's communication needs. Effective copy, that which talks person-to-person with a consumer, can't "half talk" to this consumer. Yet someone presenting a media plan is likely to tell you that your brand averages 2.5 exposures of your commercial to 50 percent of its target audience. Not a single consumer will be talked to, person-to-person, an average of 2.5 times. A media plan may average this number of commercial exposures, but media plans are a means of communicating between advertising people; they don't communicate with consumers. Individual, whole exposures of advertising copy do. And a certain number, or specific timing, of these whole exposures are required for effective communication to take place between brand and consumer.

But media planners don't begin their planning with a consumer in mind. Real people are rarely, if ever, discussed in media planning. Consumers have been abstracted into demographics, psychographics, and life-style-target audiences of gargantuan proportions. They are called "narrow, well-defined target audiences," but there are always millions of them. How can anyone plan an effective pattern of advertising exposures for millions of consumers (who encompass a wide variety of living scenarios) without first figuring out an effective pattern for only one of them?

The answer is that he can't—but he can pretend to. And he can disguise this pretense with the overwhelming components of a mass-media plan. There is so much to grasp in a media plan that planners must, by necessity, abstract and generalize. As it is done now, the real consumer, the only person who can buy the product, is completely hidden and ignored in patterns of *reach, frequency, continuity,* and all the other abstractions used in an attempt to master him or her. If, however, a planner were to pretend that he has created an effective media schedule for a single consumer, the pretense would soon collapse under the probing questions of just about anyone. It's easy to visualize a single consumer's interaction with advertising. It's easy to ask the questions that will challenge its logic.

For example, we could start by asking whether or not a brand's target consumer needs more than one exposure to process, and respond to, the urging of the advertising. If the answer is "no, only one is necessary," we can ask how long it will be before the response decays to inactionability. In other words, how long will it take for the consumer to execute her internal response in tangible product form (buy it, use it, use more of it, use it differently, and so on)? Beyond this presumed duration of the advertising's effectiveness, another one exposure will be needed, not because it comes as the second exposure of a sequence (no sequence was judged necessary), but because the independent working of any advertising exposure must have a time limit put on its effective life.

Let's now assume that the answer to the question was yes, that the consumer needs more than one exposure to be able to process and respond to the urging of what is said in the advertising. When must exposure two occur? Here we confront a *sequence,* a dependent relationship between exposures one and two. Timing, in terms of the interval between exposures, is critical. Should it be a minute, an hour, a day, a week, a month, a year? How much time and other stimuli (other advertising and other events in the consumer's life) can be allowed to take place before the sequence loses its cohesion, making the second commercial, in effect, a new exposure number one once again?

The magic exposure, number three, appears extensively in advertising strategies. Our next question should be obvious. If a consumer requires a sequence of three exposures, when must exposure number two occur? How much time can be allowed to pass between this exposure and exposure number one? When must exposure number three occur? And must these three exposures be identical messages? Or can one be a TV exposure and the others magazines, or radio, or newspaper, or in-store? If all exposures must be in the same medium, can shorter/smaller messages be mixed in the exposure sequence? If they can, exactly how is all this supposed to work, in order to allow a consumer to process the advertising material, and then take the actions she or he would otherwise not have taken without benefit of exposure to the advertising?

These questions are all very logical, and easy to understand. Their answers are essential to the preparation of a consumer-oriented media strategy and plan. But the industry's standard approach to media strategy and planning fails to pose these questions. Why? First, because they're very difficult questions to answer. But more importantly, they're ignored because the industry can get by without answering them. It's much easier, and quite satisfactory, to mix together a lot of mystical numbers, in a symmetrical pattern, and present the resultant document—with an elaborate introduction of industry jargon and buzz words. Few clients are able to find fault with it. The words and comments heard in media meetings are likely to be something like these: "It looks like a good plan to me. Doesn't it to you?"

If it does, it certainly shouldn't. I see most media plans as being the product of a stereotyped advertising ritual. Those that try to look different are just that: media plans trying to look different. They do not address or satisfy the communication needs of a flesh-and-blood consumer. And the irony is that consumers are paying for this advertising that fails to satisfy their ignored communication needs. The costs of the army of people who create and manage this advertising, the costs of buying time on TV, and space in magazines—all are charged to consumers, in the form of the price paid for the products they use.

But it's not only the financial cost to the consumer that indicts the process; it's the terrible waste. Consumers must sit through all those self-indulgent TV commercials that have been created with no consideration of their communication needs. It's those media plans that have been created without any regard for his or her ability, or opportunity, to process this advertising material. And it's the consumer who pays, in money for the products and in time spent watching this advertising, for this unprofessional work of so many advertising people. (Without doubt, the advertiser is also penalized—by lower profits—for this waste. But the advertiser should know better. After all, this is his business. Shed no tears for the advertiser who abdicates responsibility for getting effective advertising in return for money that would otherwise go to employees or stockholders.)

Let's look in detail at some things that are wrong with media strategies and plans. We can start by examining some of the words that are used to make both the advertiser and the advertising agency feel good about meaningless media strategies, ineffective media plans, empty TV commercials, and whatever else tries to pass as evidence of advertising competence. I call these words "verbal narcotics." They are so destructive to professionalism in advertising that they deserve to be given a chapter of their own.

3
Verbal Narcotics

I 've coined the term "verbal narcotics" to describe words or phrases that make us feel good without any tangible evidence that we should. These are words that let us escape responsibility for hard thinking, words that allow us to fantasize that we already know the answers. Many of them, such as *presence* and *impact* are so abstract that they can't be pinned down to any specific meaning at all. But they do imply accomplishment, and in a business where real accomplishments (measured in business results) are hard to come by, the weakest of implications can often make us feel good.

Other words, such as *reach* and *effective frequency*, have very specific meanings; they can be expressed in hard numbers. But the numbers usually represent unreality trying to prove itself real through quantification. The numbers, seen on paper, make us feel good. They may be instrumental in getting approval for spending an advertising budget, which pays the salaries and rent of the advertising agency. They may also preserve the job of whoever is responsible, on the advertiser's side, for getting his commercials on the air, or his ads into print.

Some words, such as *continuity* and *flighting*, are misunderstood by their users because their media thought process isn't oriented toward consumers but toward themselves. These words are used because they imply power that could never be claimed if the consumer were part of this thinking.

Some verbal narcotics are very specific words and concrete terms, such as *people meters*, which, instinctively, are hyped out of scale in order to fill a subconscious power gap, and to make the user feel good. The first electronic diary was quickly labeled a people meter, even though it merely upgraded a paper diary to an electronic diary. It didn't meter people's viewing of TV in the same way as the meter on a TV set monitors the use of the TV. But calling it a people meter gave it a quick (undeserved) boost to the status of ultimate technology, and gave an increased sense of power to its users.

People involved with advertising like verbal narcotics. They need them, even more than they need cocktails at lunch. Take away these magic words and we leave them having to answer more questions than they would ever dream existed. Account managers at advertising agencies would be tongue-tied, or perhaps tongue weary, from talking around the subject in meetings with their advertiser clients. Agency media people wouldn't be able to communicate with either their own account management or with the advertiser. Without some of these words, marketing people would be unable to communicate with each other, up and down the marketing chain of command. This is a terrible scenario! Do we dare to examine these verbal narcotics? Are we opening a Pandora's box that will release a wind that might blow away all advertising?

The Macho Myth of *Reach*

Several decades ago, someone labeled a set of audience numbers *reach*. Today, the same mentality has produced the *people meter*. *Reach* is not, and never was, what advertising people say it is, or think it is, or hope it is. When we say we can reach something, it means we can touch it. When we say we can reach someone, it means we can touch that person. But when a media plan is said to reach 60 percent of its targeted audience it hardly ever means that it will touch, or make actual contact with, that 60 percent. Many of those 60 percent never will have an opportunity to see the advertiser's TV commercial or print ad, or hear his radio commercial. Many of them aren't even in the living room when his brand's TV commercial appears at the break in a program these viewers are watching. Many of the 60 percent will skip the page on which the brand's magazine ad is positioned. Many of the 60 percent are out of hearing range of his radio commercial, or are talking to someone while his commercial plays.

The audience supposedly reached by TV used to be a "household." Meters on TV sets accurately measured the tuning of those sets to the channel carrying commercial TV programs. But households, per se, don't buy anything. People do. Subsequently, diaries were kept, more or less accurately, by viewers in households where TV usage wasn't measured by meters. This "people" information from the diaries was blended with set-usage information of the meters, and came up with what the industry felt was the most accurate measurement of viewing of TV programs. It's important to remember that the enormous mass of TV viewing information collected during the last four decades has been about program viewing, not about the viewing of commercials. And the two audience definitions are far from the same.

During the fifties and sixties, individual studies were conducted to learn how many people actually watched TV programs, or were even in the room and physically able to see commercials. In 1956, a leading advertising agency conducted a telephone-coincidental study, to find out what women were doing while the TV set was on in their home at the time the telephone rang. They discovered that at the time of the call, more than 40 percent of the women they contacted during evening hours were out of the room while the TV set was on. They also discovered that a lesser number, somewhere in the high 30-percent range, were out of the room in the daytime while the set was on. (If this finding conflicts with your preconception regarding attentiveness to daytime versus nighttime programs, don't let it. More family members are at home in the evening; a program turned on in the evening is less likely to be the choice of the household's adult female than it is in the daytime, when the choice of programs is more likely to be hers.)

Despite these early insights, advertising has allowed decades to pass without adjusting counts of commercial audiences to realistic size. The reason generally offered is that there is no accurate way to adjust the program-viewing numbers. And that's true. But the unadjusted audience numbers are not accurate either! Any modest downward adjustment makes the TV audience numbers less inaccurate. Perhaps the real reason is that nobody in this business likes to see small numbers. Given the choice between a known inaccurate high number and a more accurate estimate, but in the form of a lower number, the high has almost always won. Additionally, an estimated number must be supported, and sometimes defended. The inaccurate, but accepted, number is a safe way out for those who want to conserve their supply of courage for encounters of greater import to their careers.

The irony is that the advertising industry has always had access to some reasonably good information on how many program viewers are unavailable to the TV commercials carried by these programs. For more than three decades, Burke Marketing Research of Cincinnati, Ohio, has conducted day-after-recall research to measure how well TV commercials communicate to their audiences, under normal viewing conditions. Burke's technique requires that they measure precisely how many viewers are actually exposed to the test commercials. These commercial viewers become the denominator in a recall percentage, where the numerator is the number of viewers able to recall something from the test commercial. Without having an accurate denominator, the percentage of those remembering the test commercial would be an erroneous fraction, or "recall score." Year after year, Burke's interviewers have found that almost one-third of the women who claimed to have watched a prime-time program weren't in the room watching the TV set when the test commercial was shown.[1] These numbers are in the same range as an extrapolation of the 1956 agency study of tuning versus viewing mentioned earlier. They're also in the range of what you or I might estimate them to be, in the absence of any research.

Let's see if this last statement is correct. We know that few viewers, if any, sit through an entire evening of prime-time viewing without leaving the room. About how often would you guess people leave the room while watching TV? (We really shouldn't have to guess; it would be easy for anyone to keep track of this in one's own home.) My guess is that it would average more than once an hour, but less than once every half hour. Is your guess different? More often? Less often? Whatever your guess, overlay it on a schedule of prime-time TV, and calculate what percent of the commercial breaks are missed by a consumer leaving the room this often. My estimate of leaving the room has the average viewer missing about one out of three commercial breaks—right in line with Burke's numbers. What about your estimate?

Up to now, we've been trying to quantify advertising's failure to reach people at all, even once. Most advertising is said—rightly or wrongly—to need more than one exposure to be effective. If an advertiser decides that two or more exposures are needed for consumers to be reached effectively, he must reduce the audience reached by his advertising to a number below the number he has already reduced it to, in order to account for people being out of the room, or, in the case of magazines, for readers not opening to his ad. If a program reaches 20 percent of an advertiser's target audience, his commercial reaches only a little more than 13 percent. But if viewers need more than one exposure to be reached effectively, *nobody* has really been reached by the advertiser on this first program of his TV campaign. Even when the overlapping of media audiences provides multiple exposures for many of those actually reached by the advertiser's message, some will be contacted only once. And once—in this advertiser's definition of effectiveness—is not enough to count.

While knowing all this, and making no real effort to get out of the corner into which it has painted itself, the advertising industry continues to use the big, unreal *reach* numbers. Why? Well, it feels good. It certainly feels better than when the numbers are cut down to their real size. That's when a lot of people get tense, excited, and even angry over numbers that are lower than they used to be, or lower than they "should be" (whatever that means!). If we point out to these people that they can't sell to someone they haven't reached effectively, or haven't reached at all, they become even more upset. These are the classic symptoms of withdrawal from the drugging effect of the verbal narcotic, "reach."

Frequency: Effective, Plain, or with Decimals?

Prior to the seventies, *frequency* was little more than a number obtained by dividing gross audience contacts by net audience reached. If your gross media audience was 180 percent of your target (or 180 gross rating points), and your net audience (or reach) was 60 percent, your average frequency of contact was three times. But most numbers weren't this even. Your brand was more likely to reach 58 percent of your target, an average of 3.1 times. Look through old media plans and you'll always find decimal points in frequency numbers. Nobody ever seemed to reach people with whole messages.

Here we discover the first unreality caused by using the verbal narcotic *frequency*, which envelops us in a cloud of mind-drugging smoke. Advertising is only effective when the consumer sees or hears it, not when it appears in our media plans. Fragments of frequencies (3.1, 3.5, 3.7, and so on) appear in media plans, but not in the consumer's living room. The consumer sees one, two, three, or some other whole number of exposures of a brand's advertising. Prior to the mid 1970s, advertising decision makers were likely to choose a plan that gave them a frequency of 3.7 over one with a frequency of 3.5 because it gave them "more frequency." The plan with lower average frequency could very well have totaled more people reached with a specific frequency of exposure they believed to be effective. But these advertising decision makers couldn't have known it. They weren't asked, or told, which specific level of frequency was effective and which one wasn't.

Sometimes advertising and product managers of earlier years would "trade off some frequency for reach." Of course, they didn't know that the reach number in their plan wasn't real. For them, a reach of 60 percent was higher than 58 percent, just as a frequency of 3.1 was lower than a frequency of 3.2. Their decisions were difficult only when alternatives offered them the same gross audience, but with slightly different patterns of reach and frequency (58 percent/2.7 times versus 56 percent/2.8 times).

In the second half of the seventies, there developed an interest in the distribution of message frequency among target audiences. Advertising people discovered that two average frequencies of 4.6 could have significantly different patterns of message distribution. For example, though providing the same total reach, one frequency of 4.6 could be reaching more people three or four times than the other frequency of 4.6. Managers were asked to make a decision as to whether a frequency of three or four exposures was important to the advertising's being effective. And they did, even though they weren't yet working with exposures of their advertising; they were working with exposure to the media vehicles carrying this advertising. Their decision became known as *effective frequency*, a verbal narcotic with the tranquilizing effect of Valium.

After searching among the numbers for an appropriate choice of effective frequency, advertising finally decided on the number "three," a number with religious overtones, and certainly the low number most people tend to select. "Two" and "four" are even numbers; they have an awkwardness about them. "One" is an odd number, but it is too small ("one is never enough"). "Five" seems too high a number to manage. The brilliant Herbert Krugman, who contributed so many psychological insights while working at the General Electric Co., liked three exposures to a TV commercial.[2] He envisioned the consumer responding to number one with: "What is it?"; to number two with: "What of it?"; and to number three with response through action. Krugman said that the third exposure was a psychological third, and that it would occur when the consumer was ready to take action. This means that the consumer's third exposure could be the twenty third time he or she sees the advertising, having ignored the twenty exposures between number two and readiness to take action. However, a good verbal narcotic is not thought provoking. Thus, Krugman is generally quoted as saying only that three exposures are enough.

As recently as the summer of 1988, I was shown a media plan which stated that the agency subscribed to the "accepted industry standard for effective frequency" of three exposures in a four-week period. Reading further, I discovered that these were media-vehicle exposures, not consumer exposure to commercials. Nor was there any standard established for the distance between these exposures. So long as all three were confined within a four-week period, and allowed to fall randomly during this period, they were assumed to be effective. The product's purchase cycle wasn't four weeks, nor was its use cycle.

The often cited study of the effects of frequency, by Colin McDonald of the British Market Research Bureau, concluded that two exposures in a purchase cycle were the frequency most effective for positive brand switching.[3] Three exposures were found to be no more effective than two, and one exposure was found to be less effective than none at all. Elaborate reasoning was offered to explain this last, and seemingly illogical, conclusion; I don't think it merits repetition here. Many advertisers will have difficulty using McDonald's findings, especially when they market brands with radically different purchase cycles. How can two exposures in two weeks, for a brand with a two-week purchase cycle, be as effective as two exposures in two months for a brand with a two-month purchase cycle, or as effective as two every six months for a brand with twice-a-year purchasing, and so on?

The subject of effective frequency becomes confusing whenever we pause to analyze it. Mike Naples, then director of Marketing Research of Lever Brothers Company, tried to draw stable conclusions in his book *Effective Frequency: The Relationship Between Frequency and Advertising Effectiveness*.[4] But his cases are so few, relative to the thousands of campaigns that took place during the period covered by his study, that his findings are not very convincing. This isn't surprising. In the final analysis, the word *frequency* has such different meanings in the context of a communication strategy that there may never be anything that we can accurately label *effective frequency*.

Frequency can mean a sequence of repetitions designed to teach something that can't be learned through a single statement (commercial or ad). A sequence probably requires that exposures be spaced close together, so that each repetition (of exposure to advertising material) builds on an earlier one. But frequency can also be used to mean multiple exposures of an instantly learned selling statement, spaced some distance apart in order to catch different consumers when they are susceptible to being sold the kind of product being advertised. Both these examples will be explored in detail later in this book. Suffice it to say here that nothing called *effective frequency* can ever be simply defined as a pure number of advertising exposures.

Conjuring Up *Presence*

I've been justly accused of carrying logic to the point of being obnoxious about it. My zeal for being rational has surfaced as overt hostility toward parapsychologists, seance holders, and believers of miracles, whether religious or secular. Not surprisingly, I betray intellectual pain through hostile behavior whenever an advertising person tries to intoxicate my brain with the *presence* attributed to a brand in his or her recommended media plan. I've had to leave the room, mentally, when told that another brand needed "a meaningful competitive presence."

Can anyone define this utopian condition that advertising people of all levels of experience refer to as *presence*? To me, a "presence" is something unseen and unheard, except by the spiritualist who has conjured it up in a seance for a group of gullibles sitting around a table holding hands. Or it might be something you feel when entering a dark room after you've come home late at night after seeing a Dracula movie. How did this nonsense word get into advertising?

Let's try to take the word seriously for a moment. As it's used in advertising, presence sounds like a form of awareness. But awareness is quantified; we say that a certain percentage of a brand's target audience, perhaps 46 percent, has become aware of the brand. There is such a thing as good awareness, that is, when awareness reaches a higher percentage than might otherwise be expected; and there's poor awareness, when the percentage of awareness is lower than expected. But presence doesn't stoop to numbers. It always seems to be an absolute: your brand either has or doesn't have presence. And "competitive presence" is a double absolute: without naming specific competitors, and without the use of supporting numbers, your agency will often state that your brand has competitive presence (or hasn't, and needs it).

The only quantification of *presence* I've ever heard was one of implied smallness. No numbers were given, nor were any adjectives used to help understand the word. But advertising people have often said that at a given point in time, a brand needs "some presence." This dainty verbal offering suggests that the brand doesn't need a lot of anything, but that it needs "some," and that it does not have any at this time. It still sounds like awareness, but the brands supposedly needing this presence were not without awareness. Some of them even had good awareness. But apparently no presence.

How does a brand get presence? By advertising, of course. I guess a little advertising gives a brand "some presence." Perhaps a lot of advertising gives a brand "meaningful competitive presence." You have to "guess" and "perhaps" a lot when dealing with something that has the same dimension as the dark interior of your bedroom after a Dracula movie. You also have to wonder a lot. You wonder why an industry that generates three hundred zillion numbers every workday of the year can't put a single one of them against the word presence. You wonder why so many managers allow their companies to put hundreds of millions of dollars into the hands of people who for years stay high on this verbal narcotic, who verbally fly through their careers like Peter Pan, and never really come down to earth to confront their business responsibilities.

IMPACT!: Presence Raised to the Nth Power

Advertising people who believe in *presence*, but who aren't satisfied with it, seem to be the same ones who look for *impact*. Perhaps there's a presence even stronger than a "meaningful competitive presence." *Impact* fits the description pretty well. So if a brand needs much more than "some presence," this brand can do something different from the ordinary, it can advertise to reach beyond a meaningful competitive presence, and get itself lots of presence. This brand can raise presence to the Nth power. It can achieve *IMPACT!*

When I hear the word *IMPACT!*, I, with my literal, logical mind, see a car slamming into a tree, or a falling piano just missing someone and crashing onto the sidewalk; or I see Rocky beating up a side of beef. Am I really looking at advertising effectiveness and not recognizing it? Women are the target of most advertising. Does effective advertising (*IMPACT!*) have something to do with beating up women? Or could it mean slamming a product into a woman's face? Or could it be dropping the product from a rooftop and have it just miss her, so that she doesn't ignore it? (I may be confusing the last example with being *intrusive*, another potent verbal narcotic.)

The advertising business is engaged in making and selling images of nonexistent beautiful people, happy people, excited people, satisfied people. The real men and women who are in the advertising business have developed great skill in making and selling these images. They prove it in many ways, but ironically, never more thoroughly than with the images of the nonexistent results and effectiveness of their own efforts. Impact is advertising's own mental image of great happenings. In a sense, advertising people have used their greatest skills to create, within themselves, the self-portrait of a nonexistent powerful person.

Any product that has been given a specific advertising goal doesn't need anything as abstract as impact. The advertising people responsible for this product will try to achieve something specific; they don't need to substitute a mental rainbow for the real object of its advertising. But specific advertising goals aren't easy to come by. Advertising people who aren't willing to make the extra effort needed to find these goals must come up with something in their place. If it's in capital letters, is followed by an exclamation mark, and sounds macho, these advertising people may be able to pass it off as a legitimate advertising goal. They can, too often, when the word is *IMPACT!*

Continuity. A Nonexistent Dichotomy

In the days before so many women were liberated from the shackles of their home, a common saying was "a woman's work is never done." This condition also applied to advertising, where the work also never seemed to be done. Now advertising retains exclusive claim to the saying. It certainly makes economic sense for advertising's work never to be done. Payment stops when work stops, so advertising can't stop working without severe damage to its economic foundation.

Most people are paid for getting something done. You pay a builder for having your house built, not for swinging a hammer or pushing a saw while building it. You wouldn't allow your builder to make a career out of coming to your house with his hammer and saw every day for the next ten or twenty years. Building your house is a task; when the task is done, the builder gets paid, goes away, and builds another house for somebody else (completes another task).

But let's suppose the task of your new brand's advertising is to find the 20 percent of the population that you know have a use, a need or a desire for it, and then to communicate to this 20 percent in a way that will get them to try it. What happens when the task has been finished, when all 20 percent have tried your brand? You've paid well for the advertising. Can you now stop paying for more advertising? Of course not.

Advertising will create a new task for itself, so that it can continue to serve the brand and get paid for it ("sustain" is the word most used).

It's no wonder that the advertising industry, which is maintained economically by the practice of doing, rather than by getting things done, likes the verbal narcotic *continuity*. The continuation of a client's advertising is its very life blood. There is a Darwinian compulsion in most successful advertising men and women to learn and use the word *continuity*. Small wonder that it appears so often in advertising plans, or that it is used so often in meetings where advertising strategy is discussed. But like all verbal narcotics, it's liked so much by its users that they use it where it doesn't belong, where it fills a void left by what should be a meaningful point of strategy or execution. It gives everyone a false sense of security. Advertising people think thay have said something meaningful when they've used the word *continuity*, but they really haven't.

A family-owned corporation can have continuity of family control for several generations of the same family. This means that there is never a break in the line of family control; every day, some member of the same family controls the corporation. But when the word *continuity* is used to describe a product's TV advertising during a budget year, it becomes the verbal narcotic that fills its users head with the wishful thoughts of things happening— somewhere, somehow—continuously. Of course it isn't so. There is no such thing as an unbroken bond between any advertising and any consumer. Exposures to advertising are occasional interruptions in the life of a consumer. The only people for whom advertising might be a continuous experience would be those men and women working in the business of advertising itself, and few of them. Only the workaholics, who live their job day and night, might be said to experience advertising continuously.

People who use *continuity* to describe advertising lack a consumer orientation to their business. They focus on how to fill in all

the boxes on a fifty-two-week calendar with some kind of advertising. Perhaps they've recommended three TV commercials each
week—for a "continuity" effect. Some consumer will certainly see
the product's advertising each week. This proves that the advertiser is doing something each week, but each individual consumer
may see the product's advertising as infrequently as once a month,
or less often. What the consumer needs (expressed as an effective
pattern of advertising exposures) has never been addressed by the
user of continuity. The two items—pattern of exposure and the
word *continuity*—are not even compatible: the first is a real com-
ponent of responsible advertising strategies; the second is just an
incantation.

Ironically, advertising people who use the word *continuity* make
no effort to conceal its lack of meaning from those to whom they
offer it. If a product can afford only a small amount of advertising each month, then monthly advertising becomes *continuity*. If
the product can afford some advertising each week, this weekly
advertising defines *continuity*. Thus, in its most flagrant adapta-
tion to whatever meaning the user chooses to give it, continuity
becomes a nonexistent dichotomy: it is something that can be more
or less continuous, without being broken! (It may have been inspired by the magician's trick of cutting a rope into small pieces,
and then pulling the uncut rope out of his closed hand.)

Clutter: Advertising's Red Herring

If *continuity* did exist, what is said to be *clutter* would be its mortal enemy. Clutter would also be the mortal enemy of *presence*
and *IMPACT!*, if they existed. Clutter is reputed to be a monstrous
barrier to effective advertising, so we must search until we find
something specific to put in its way. There is, of course, the possibility that clutter itself doesn't exist. But if it doesn't, we can still
put it on the negative plane of nonexistence, along with presence,
impact, and continuity. Now, nonexistent "clutter" can operate as
a barrier to all those other nonexistent things.

Of course, clutter might really exist. What would it be if it
did? I've searched the face of my TV tube for clutter during the

past ten years. I had heard, at least that long ago, that TV had become "horribly cluttered." I'm still looking for the clutter. In the last ten years, only twice has more than one commercial ever appeared on the face of my TV set at the same time. Once was when a cable problem put "ghosts" on my screen; the other was when the screen split in two, and had different things happening on the left and right sides. So, almost never has clutter interferred with a TV commercial while it was being shown on my TV set. My living room itself has often been cluttered during a commercial. I remember one time in particular. The bell rang, the dog barked, an infant niece threw up on the rug, and we all ran into each other trying to respond at the same time. The commercial obviously didn't break through this real clutter, nor will any commercial ever be able to.

Advertising people frequently use *clutter* to describe a cluster of five or more consecutive commercials, during which one of their commercials will appear. On paper, this looks cluttered to them. They think that their commercial will have to compete for the attention of the TV viewer against more rather than few, commercials. But this is nonsense. When their commercial is shown, nothing on the screen competes for the viewer's attention. They get their exclusive thirty seconds to communicate. If they have something to say, and say it well, the consumer will pay attention. If they have nothing to say, or say something badly, the consumer will ignore them. They can try to blame clutter, but only their advertising (and/or their product) is to blame. Clutter is an easy excuse for advertising failures. Clutter is an easy excuse to ask for a bigger ad budget. Clutter is a red herring, something to distract from real advertising problems.

Burke Marketing Research has obtained day-after recall data for the TV commercials of advertiser clients since the 1950s. Over the years, they have examined this large volume of test data for general findings on variables that might affect their testing technique. One of their documented conclusions is that commercials tested in a chain of up to eight consecutive commercials have produced recall scores statistically the same as those for commercials tested alone, or in small groups of commercials.[5]

Too many commercials in a row, in too long a commercial break, give TV viewers the time and the incentive to leave the room to do something else. Burke Marketing Research has documented that slightly higher levels of defection do occur during long commercial breaks. Another point is that too many commercials might make viewers decide to tape programs in order to screen out these numerous commercials, or rent videotapes which have no commercials. All such evasive activity by consumers would certainly be negative for advertising. But it won't be the *clutter* that everyone in advertising talks about "penetrating," or "breaking through." If consumers aren't there, no commercial can break through to them. So we still don't know what the industry means when it talks about *clutter* that can be broken through.

Some advertising people seem to believe that excessive numbers of commercials on TV, and ads in magazines, clutter the consumer's mind with too much advertising. As they see it, their advertising needs to find a place for itself in the cluttered space of the consumer's mind. This is supposed to be accomplished by an "impactful" commercial, and/or by "effective frequency." I think, however, that they give themselves and their peers credit for too much skill in establishing a clutter of commercials in the mind of consumers. I think they also underestimate the consumer's ability to screen out much of the irrelevant product information in the advertising she sees, always allowing enough room in her mind for something she considers relevant and important.

If a consumer ignores product information that does not interest her, and if most commercials do not interest her, she brings a relatively uncluttered mind to the viewing of TV commercials. Doubling the number of "non-interesting" commercials doesn't create increased clutter. "A non-interest" commercial has no value, or zero value. Two times zero is still zero. You can't dispute the math. You can only argue with my assumption that most commercials fail to interest the average TV viewer in the product being advertised.

To argue this assumption, you'll have to throw out two decades of consistent findings by day-after-recall research. For example, only half the women who sat through your commercial last night will remember having seen it; even if you were to call them today, and give them a good description of the commercial they sat through. Without a description, fewer than one-fourth of viewers can remember anything at all about a commercial. Even fewer remember any of the selling points in your commercial. And this is day-after-recall—which may be weeks, or even months, prior to this consumer's next purchase occasion for the kind of product your advertising is trying to sell! How can we imagine that this consumer's mind will ever be cluttered with advertising?

Some laboratory research on clutter has been done for the benefit of curious advertisers. By comparing the recall of commercials in a normal program environment with one in which the commercial load was doubled, the researchers concluded that more commercials led to lower recall. They were correct, but only on a percentage basis. The average commercial was recalled by fewer people when there were more commercials. But each respondent remembered the same number of commercials, which was about four. This number of recalled items coincides with the number that people can retrieve from short-term memory in an exposure-response situation. In other words, the number of recalled items (or commercials) is normative; when the base is changed, the percentage changes, even though the number of items recalled is constant.

But more important, think of the implications of any significant number of consumer responses to commercials in a single TV show. How many responses would this add up to in a week of normal TV viewing? And, in an average week, how many times do you think a consumer really responds to TV advertising? Add up how many times you yourself have responded in a week. How many product-image modifications have taken place in your mind in the last seven days? Ten modifications? Twenty? Thirty? (You'll have to keep going much higher to match a projection from four modifications per hour of TV viewing.) For some of us, the answer is none.

There's plenty of room in the consumer's mind for new and relevant information, but there may be "clutter" in the consumer's physical experience with brands of the products regularly used. Most consumers have tried several brands, in every product category they use, with some degree of regularity. It's difficult to offer an experienced consumer something that strikes him or her as really new and appealing. So perhaps it's the product that has to break through product clutter. Advertising men and women would probably leap to this challenge, saying, "But advertising can add value to a product; we can make a so-so product into something exciting—with the added value of our breakthrough advertising." Maybe. But with the legal restrictions now placed on advertising content, one can't lie about a product (add a value that doesn't exist) as some advertisers used to do.

Intrusiveness: A Case of Mental Rape

Intrusiveness is a quality that contemporary advertising aspires to. Intrusiveness is considered by many to be a critical ingredient in effective advertising. But to be intrusive, advertising must intrude— force itself without invitation, without right, or without welcome— into the mind of a consumer. (If this definition sounds too terrible to be true, read your dictionary. This is a dictionary definition, not mine.) What I have just described is nothing short of mental rape.

Widespread use of the word intrusive, as related to advertising, gives us a clue as to how unimportant or unattractive the content of this advertising must appear to its creators. A rapist dominates his victim with a display of power, he has no self-respect or feelings of confidence in himself as a human being. He has to prove self-worth by dominating the weak and powerless. Advertising betrays its lack of confidence in its own worth by thinking like an unwelcome guest, by forcing its way into a consumer's mind, by assuming the role of a mental rapist.

The word *intrusiveness* came into the advertising vocabulary primarily to fill the need established by another verbal narcotic— *clutter*. Acceptance of *clutter* made it necessary to break through it with something *intrusive*. *Intrusiveness* is also felt to be needed by advertising for low-involvement or low-interest products. Advertising people correctly assume that a woman doesn't devote much thought or emotion to selecting a brand of detergent, furniture polish, or toilet paper. They believe that a certain kind, or quality, of commercial or media plan is needed to allow them to intrude into the mind of the woman who is presumed to be indifferent to the advertising of these products. They use what they believe to be the successful example of Wisk detergent ("ring around the collar") and Charmin bathroom tissue (Mr. Whipple's "please don't squeeze the Charmin"). There is research data showing that both campaigns stimulated a negative attitudinal reaction in women, yet both products were successful while these ads were used. Is this another case of "in-spite-of" rather than "because-of?" Or can a woman's mind be successfully and profitably raped by a TV commercial? The failure of a multitude of other products whose advertisers have tried this technique leads me to believe that Wisk and Charmin were "in-spite-of's." But even if these products were successful as a result of their advertising, the overwhelming number of failures leaves us with terrible odds against success in future attempts to overcome consumers by means of mental rape.

Preoccupation with intrusiveness leads media people to perform heroic deeds in an attempt to vanquish the giant windmill they are told awaits them over the next hill. TV commercials have been scheduled in "impact units," that is, where the same commercial ends one break in the entertainment and opens the next commercial break. This impact unit is supposed to intrude upon the consumer's presumed inattentiveness to the household product being advertised. The idea is said to have originated in conjunction with media planning for the products of the Lever Brothers Company, makers of detergents, toothpaste, margarines, and other low-involvement products.

Most recently, pop-ups, gatefolds, and other mechanical configurations of magazine advertising are being used by the advertisers of many products; they apparently believe that the content of their on-page advertising is not intrusive enough. In the advertising industry, many of these creative media devices are admired. But when I think of advertising's effectiveness being dependent on its ability to woo the consumer's mind, not to take it by force, I don't expect these devices to be very successful. They appear to be little more than a disguised assault, rather than a courtship.

Persuasion: As Easy as Taking a NAP

Persuasion is another example of how one segment of the advertising industry hypes a word, in order to give it more meaning than it deserves. (Other examples are *reach* and *people meters*.) Prior to the 1970s, *persuasion* was called a "pre-post score." Now the same pre-post shift in the consumer's choice of brands (after exposure to the test commercial) is being promoted as the degree of persuasiveness that the commercial can exert on its audience. The irony is that most of the persuasion numbers generated in tests for established products appear to be influenced less by the test commercials than by the composition of the test samples.

A serious flaw in the laboratory testing of TV commercials for persuasion is that research samples can't be matched in the elements that will make them equally knowledgeable about, and interested in, the different brands that test their commercials this way. If a brand that is testing its commercial has already achieved 50 percent awareness among users of its product category, an invited research sample may be either more or less than 50 percent aware of the brand (perhaps 65 percent or 35 percent). Research can't screen for awareness of this brand without injecting a cuing bias into the test.

Let's say that what is being tested are two new commercials for a brand that offers the same product benefit to consumers, or, as some say, "is written to the same positioning in the brand's product category." Let's assume that 20 percent of category users are interested in this benefit, and would try the brand if available and if the price were competitive with other major brands in the product category. Sample A has 65 percent awareness of the brand, which means that 35 percent are not aware of it. Sample A, therefore, has an automatic +7 percent *persuasion* available to whatever commercial is being tested. How? As 35 percent become aware of the brand, the 20 percent interested in the product benefit make their symbolic purchase. (In the test offering, the product has been made fully available, and is priced free, as an alternative to a free container of the consumer's usual brand or brands.)

Now let's look at Sample B. Here the test brand has only 35 percent aware of it, which means that 65 percent will be made aware by any commercial the brand has chosen to test (as long as it communicates the same positioning). When 20 percent of this 65 percent make their symbolic purchase, the commercial registers a *persuasion* score of 13 percent. (This could even be the same commercial that was tested in Sample A.) The commercial tested in Sample B was not proved more persuasive than the one tested in Sample A (certainly not if it was the same commercial). Each commercial simply moved 20 percent of its non-awares to action. The difference in the persuasion scores resulted entirely from the different potential for pre-post gain that Sample B contained in its higher number of non-awares. This non-awares potential in samples used for persuasion tests makes an appropriate acronym: NAP—which is what researchers seem to be taking when they accept all persuasion numbers at face value.

If nobody knows anything about Brand X, a consumer's first exposure to it in the form of a TV commercial is essentially a concept test. What the concept test asks the consumer, in offering her a choice of brands in the same product category, is "How interested are you in the benefits Brand X is offering you in its commercial?" Variations in response to different commercials, written to the same product positioning, are most likely nothing more than variations in the research samples, not in the effectiveness of these commercials. A new floor-care product was launched with a commercial that scored the higher *persuasion* of two introductory commercials. But just before the introduction, the two commercials were retested, and the scores reversed their original position. When the persuasion from the two tests was averaged, the commercials were found to be equal. The commercial for a new toiletry product was retested, and its persuasion dropped from 11.2 percent to 4.8 percent. Three subsequent retests produced scores of 9.4 percent, 8.1 percent, and 9.4 percent. Average the high and low scores, and you'll find them to be about the same as the average of the next three.

When you average several postexposure scores (not the pre-post scores) for various commercials of the same brand, you'll have a number that should roughly correspond to the brand's true concept score. You can verify this by comparing it to the percent of aware consumers who actually try the brand in the marketplace (referred to in marketing-research jargon as the trial/awareness conversion ratio). Figure 3–1 shows a chart (using actual *persuasion* tests) which correlates the percentage of category users who have chosen the testing brand after exposure to its commercial (the postexposure score) with the percentage

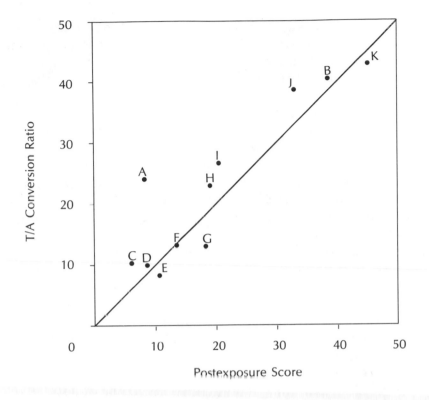

Figure 3–1. *Correlation of Postexposure Scores with Trial/Awareness Conversion Ratios*

of brand-aware category users found to have actually purchased the brand in the marketplace (trial/awareness conversion ratio). Most points in the graph represent an average of three to seven tests; multiple tests reduce or eliminate the sample variations from a true-concept score.

The diagonal line represents a perfect correlation between postexposure scores and conversion ratio. The one large variance from the diagonal line, for Brand A, actually reinforces the positive findings of this analysis. The deviant brand had been the market leader, but was made obsolete when new Brand B, with a superior formula and packaging, directly competed with it. The test of Brand A's commercial was conducted after Brand B had taken away most of the older brand's market share. Therefore, we were comparing trial numbers (obtained when Brand A had no direct competition) with a concept score registered after the brand and its concept had been made obsolete by product and packaging superiority.

The scores for several other new products are also shown in figure 3–1. What should be understood, in the scores of these new products, is that their postexposure score is the same as their pre-post (or persuasion) score, since their "pre" is normally a statistical zero. Some researchers have become excited when they have found a correlation between their persuasion scores and actual trial results in the marketplace. This correlation does occur, but only for new brands, where there is no pre score. It doesn't take researcher skills to understand that if the only time a pre-post score correlates with numbers in the real world is when there is no pre-score, it isn't the pre-post number that correlates. It's obviously the post-score itself that correlates.

When advertisers don't understand the numbers generated by copy tests, their response to these numbers can be damaging to people as well as to products. Let's look at an example of how misunderstood pre-post scores were used by an advertiser to create widespread job tension and unproductivity in one of its advertising agencies. The testing brand was new, and very different from other brands in the product category it was about to enter. Its agency tested six introductory commercials to find the best way to show consumers the brand's unique product positioning. The results of the brand's pre-post testing are shown in table 3–1.

Table 3–1

Commercial	Pre/Post Score
A	+21
B	+20
C	+15
D	+14
E	+13
F	+13
Average	+16

Since the test was for a new brand, the pre-scores were statistical zeroes. Thus, the pre-post score was also the post-score. (This observation is critical if you are to understand why the users of the test results misunderstood the implication of these tests and subsequent copy testing.) The product was launched with Commercial A; the advertiser wasn't yet aware of the variations that could result from differences between invited test samples, and he took all the numbers at their face value.

During the launch period, the advertising agency worked diligently on new commercials that would be used after the brand's introductory period. Two new commercials were produced in rough form, for testing. Much to the dismay of both agency and advertiser, the new commercials had pre-post test scores of only +7 percent and +9 percent, respectively, as shown in table 3–2. The agency was severely criticized and told to do better—or else! They were confused. They had been confident that the new commercials were at least as good as the original ones they had produced, and which had good results when tested.

I was looking through the research data for clues to why the new commercials had failed, when I discovered something that intrigued me. The postexposure scores of the two new commercials were identical with the average postexposure score of the six commercials tested prior to the brand's introduction. But during the time between the two series of tests, the brand had been launched nationally, and had developed a base of aware consumers, of buyers, and of those intending to buy. The two new commercials entered their test situation not with pre-scores of zero, but of 7 percent and 9 percent, respectively. Although the original commercials had a non-aware potential of 100 percent, the new ones, as shown in table 3–3, had exactly half that potential!

Table 3–2

	Pre/Post Score
Original Average	+16%
New Commercial A	+ 7%
New Commercial B	+ 9%

Table 3–3

	Pre	Post	Difference
Original Commercial	0	16	+16
New Commercial A	9	16	+ 7
New Commercial B	7	16	+ 9

This brand's test results are not on the correlation chart shown in figure 3–1, because the numbers come from two different testing services. The results are very much the same, however, which reinforces the conclusion that many, or most, *persuasion* tests are really *concept* tests, and do not measure true differences in the ability of different commercials to persuade. In this case, the agency was unjustly criticized for producing results identical with those that had earlier pleased their client. But nobody understood the results, because nobody really understood the technique. Even the testing service seemed not to understand how their own technique worked. In response to my asking whether the scores for the two new commercials were really as bad as their pre-post numbers suggested, they replied that pre-levels under 20 percent don't inhibit switching, thus ignoring that this brand couldn't achieve more than 20 percent in its postexposure levels, because this was the percentage of category users interested in its product concept.

Isn't it terrible to think that the work of men and women with creative talent can be given direction by sample variances? Isn't it terrible to think that advertising agencies may be losing clients because they produce low persuasion scores for brands that really can't achieve significant scores because their awareness is so high that there are no "non-awares" to respond to their offering of product benefits? Isn't it terrible to think that advertisers of hundreds of established products are accepting as evidence of effectiveness numbers that come from making consumers aware of them only in a research sample, the same consumers who have resisted the attempt of all prior advertising to make them aware of these products outside the research room? But the most terrible thought of all is that this has been happening for more than two decades, and will continue to happen for as long as the unconcerned users of advertising research will allow. Who wants to change? Not the research companies who are selling "persuasion" scores. Not the advertisers, who often are more concerned with making decisions easier rather than better. Not the advertising agencies who are getting automatic persuasion scores of some sort from their brands' "non-aware" potentials.

As one marketing manager said to me in candor several years ago: "I know my information is no good, but there isn't anything better. I've got to use it. I can't get a commercial approved for airing without a test score."

Only Effective Commercials Can *Wear Out*

My discussion of *persuasion* was lengthier than I would have liked it to be. However, the better you understand the dynamics of these pre-post numbers, the better you'll understand that popular verbal narcotic: *wearout*. An advertising person's first reaction to hearing the word *wearout* probably isn't the euphoria we associate with the use of verbal narcotics. But it soon becomes just that.

In order to wear out, advertising must be "working." Things wear out from overuse, not from nonuse. Advertising that raises concerns about its wearout is assumed to have been effective advertising. In most cases, there never was any proof that a specific commercial ever was working. That's because few advertising people, if any at all, know how advertising works. If we don't know *how* advertising works, we can never be sure that it's working at all. But by concerning ourselves with a commercial's wearout, we've avoided the difficult job of proving that it's working. We have simply implied that the commercial was effective, and have accepted that implication as all the proof we need; then we become anxious about when it will stop working. I'm sure there's no dishonest intent in this intellectual sleight of hand that many advertising people perform for their own benefit. After all, they did accept one anxiety ("Is it wearing out?") to avoid the other ("Is the advertising effective?").

Anxiety may be too strong a word for so therapeutic and constructive an idea as *wearout*. Commercial wearout has many economic benefits beyond proving that its commercials are working. Here are some of them:

1. Advertising agencies are given more creative assignments; they can justify a higher level of compensation than if their clients used the same commercials months or years longer than they do now.

2. Commercial-production houses have more commercials to produce, more revenue from these commercials.

3. Commercial testing services have more commercials to test, more revenue from this testing.

4. Product managers are more visible within own companies if they make commercials to replace those made by their predecessors (during each manager's short tenure).

5. Impatient corporate management, easily bored with the pace at which their commercials change, are satisfied that "something is happening" with their advertising.

For all its apparent benefits, *wearout* fogs the minds of advertising people, and works in the same way as other verbal narcotics: it keeps the advertising industry in its primitive state of self-understanding, and at a continued high level of inefficiency. Advertising people should, but don't, ask themselves probing, analytical questions, such as, "Exactly *what* is wearing out? Is it the commercial itself, the campaign that has included many commercials, or the basic benefit promised to consumers in the brand's advertising?" To use an example recognized by many of us: Did consumers turn off to the last execution of Charmin's Mr. Whipple campaign; did they turn off to the campaign in any execution, or have all women interested in a squeezably soft toilet tissue tried Charmin and taken a fixed position on its performance? Or has another toilet tissue made claims that make obsolete the idea of "squeezably soft?"

The images transmitted to the TV screen by a commercial are the same on its first and one hundred and first airing; any change that takes place occurs in the consumer's reaction to the commercial. So it would be more accurate for us to say that the consumer's response wears out, not the commercial. We could also say that the *task* of this particular commercial has been completed or has "worn out". In this case, we wouldn't replace the commercial with a pool-out, or with a related execution on the same creative strategy. We would first replace the task of the advertising, and then write a totally different commercial to address this new task. Creativity that responds with reflex action to the word *wearout* can be 180 degrees off-target if it's the task of the advertising and not the execution of the commercial that needs replacement.

Here's the point at which *persuasion*-testing sheds some constructive light on *wearout*. Let's assume that the function of a new brand's commercial is to generate awareness and trial of 20 percent of category users; and that research has accurately measured the trial potential of this new brand at 20 percent of current category users. As the new brand's commercial progressively develops awareness and trial, from zero to 20 percent, it is technically wearing out. When all 20 percent have tried the product, the brand's commercial could be said to be "all worn out." But is this what we should say when a commercial has fully achieved its advertising goal? We had better not, or we'll make the mistake of replacing the commercial before we select a new advertising goal for which to develop a new commercial.

The commercial that launched one of the new products we introduced had a *persuasion* score of +14.9 percent. Eleven months later, the same commercial was retested; it received a score of +8.4 percent, a loss of more than 40 percent of its original persuasion. Because of this loss, you might conclude that the commercial was in the process of "wearing out." But if you looked at the postexposure scores from the two tests, you would see a higher absolute number, not a lower one, for the second test—but statistically, probably the same score. (See table 3–4.)

About as many of the women who were made aware by the retested commercial chose our brand over the other products offered. But during those eleven months, the commercial had been

Table 3–4

	Pre	Post	Difference
Before Intro	4.0	18.9	+ 14.9
After Intro	13.4	21.8	+ 8.4

working to build awareness of this brand. Now, many of the women in the research sample were already aware of the brand, and would have chosen it before they were shown the commercial. The non-aware potential had been progressively reduced during these eleven months. The persuasion number, being dependent on the size of this non-aware potential, had to go down. But since persuasion was unrelated to the commercial itself, the commercial could still elicit choice of the brand from about 20 percent of the women who became aware of it. The commercial was working exactly as it had done on its first exposure. But now, after eleven months, its advertising task had been reduced by its success in building awareness.

Ironic, isn't it? Commercials are retired because they're thought to be wearing out, and these may be the only commercials that show evidence of having been "working". Until advertising people know exactly what each of their commercials is supposed to do, they will misread research, putting on the air commercials that don't deserve to be aired, and taking off the air those that are still working for them.

Quality Trips Lightly From the Tongue

In the absence of test data, a good commercial is defined by the judgment of the highest person on the totem pole of advertising decision makers. Most of these people, however, didn't get promoted to power because of their ability to choose good commercials rather than bad ones. It may be foolhardy to do, but it's easy to prove that often they don't know which are their best and which are their worst commercials. All you need do is collect about a dozen commercials that have been tested so thoroughly that no doubt exists as to their relative ability to communicate to consumers. The dozen should include a representation of very good, average, and very bad commercials.

Show these commercials to your decision maker and ask him or her to indicate whether each commercial is good, bad, or average. You would find, after completing this test, that the results are quite random. Any other group of laymen or laywomen would do almost as well in judging commercials. The advertising expertise of decision makers is not in predicting how well their commercials will communicate with consumers; their expertise is in arbitrarily deciding what is good or bad. The expertise of these people is in the exercise of power, not of judgment.

The arbitrary designation of *quality* isn't confined to TV commercials or print ads. As number-intensive as the media function is, even a media choice increases or decreases in *quality* after it receives the benediction of an advertising decision maker. My favorite of all time is the *quality* designation for high-rated TV programs. One marketing manager would always ask me the same question: "How many of my commercials are in the top twenty TV shows?"

Over the years, we provided this manager with enough factual material to disabuse him of his top-twenty reflex. We showed him data from recall tests which proved that recall of commercials was no higher on top-twenty shows than on the bottom twenty. We explained to him that the people watching the top-rated shows were, over time, the same people as those watching the low-rated shows; that more of them happened to be watching the higher-rated shows at the same time. We showed him a Burke Marketing Research special study of commercial recall by people who claimed that the show carrying the test commercial was "one of their favorites," versus recall by people who found the test show to be "not very interesting." As expected, there were no significant differences in overall recall-score effect.[6]

We warned him that demand for winning shows was always higher than for losers, and that this drove up the price per person watching the winners. He always listened. He always asked questions that indicated he heard what we were saying. And then he always asked: "But how many of my commercials are in the top-twenty TV shows?" He was determined not to let anyone, or any information, deprive him of his power to give a *quality* value to TV programs rated in the top twenty.

Another marketing manager was, and still may be, obsessed with "prime time." Whenever presented with a media recommendation, she always would demand: "I want more prime time." This manager didn't consider late evening TV viewers to be as valuable

as those watching prime-time TV. We pointed out to her that
viewers have fewer distractions later in the evening. During the early
hours of prime time, small children are still up, demanding attention; the telephone rings; dinner clean-up and the evening
newspaper compete with the consumer's TV viewing. We explained
that consumers give up sleep to watch a TV program at midnight.
It seems foolish to say that a consumer is less interested and less
attentive than at 8:00 P.M., in the middle of family activity. We
showed this manager the attentiveness data, collected over two
decades, which revealed no support for the designation of "prime"
to the evening hours so named. We even produced recall scores
which affirmed that commercials were recalled as well when tested
on late-evening, nonnews programs as when tested on prime-time
programs.

Our mistake was in thinking that we were trying to help someone to make a better informed decision. We were, unknowingly,
trying to strip a manager of her power to bestow her own value
on a major segment of advertising media. We failed, of course.
And so, the next time we present her with a media plan, I'm sure
we'll hear: "I want more prime time."

Other managers have relegated syndicated TV programs to
third-class status. Why they've done this isn't fully clear to me.
Perhaps the sound of "syndicated" conjurs up a mafiosa image in
heads muddled by over-use of verbal narcotics. The television
viewer has no way of knowing how the program is being delivered
to his local station. He watches what he wants to watch. How it
got to him—whether by network feed or by cassette from a
syndicator—is totally irrelevant. If the production values of some
syndicated TV programs are inferior to those of most network programs, the audience watching these syndicated programs is probably less concerned with production values than with entertainment values.

The weekly tabloid publications, such as the *National Enquirer*
and the *Star*, don't have the production values of *Life* magazine.
But their readers number far more than *Life*'s, and these readers
obviously have their own definition of "quality." So do the viewers
of low-budget syndicated TV shows. The imperious decision maker
has no authority over consumers; consumers make the final decision

on what, for them, is quality media. The advertising decision maker who ignores the chain of command in the real world is likely to be one who tries—unsuccessfully—to market products while assuming this imperious (manufacturer's) point of view.

Some decision makers also say that the content of TV programs influences the effectiveness of their commercials. They think that glamorous commercials communicate better in the environment of a glamorous, prime-time soap opera. They think that humorous or lighthearted commercials communicate better in situation comedies. Their commercials might do better in compatible programs if these commercials were actually part of the programs that carry them, but of course they're not.

Their commercials are part of the interruption of these programs by a cluster of commercials, and these interruptions set their own programming environment. An advertiser's shampoo commercial will sometimes follow (and could be assumed to be part of) a segment of the glamorous soap opera that carries it. But four out of five times it will follow another commercial. If we assume that the advertiser's shampoo commercial would become part of the program simply by following one of its segments, then we should assume that his shampoo commercial would just as easily become part of these other commercials, which it follows 80 percent of the time. The advertiser's shampoo commercial, in this way, could become part of the commercial for a toilet bowl cleaner, or upset-stomach remedy, or dripping-sinus medicine, or a montage of all three. Does the viewer fail to respond to the mood of these other commercials and stay with her soap-opera mood? If the viewer does resist these other commercials, what makes the advertising decision maker think she will respond, selectively, to his commercial? The answer is simple: he doesn't think. The only way an intelligent person can continue to make unintelligent decisions is to avoid thinking before making them.

There is no doubt that there is a negative form of quality in certain programs, for certain commercials. The classic example is a documentary on the extermination of Jews in the gas chambers of Auschwitz. The scheduled sponsor of the series of documentaries was the American Gas Association. Fortunately, the content of this documentary was learned in time to prevent a disastrous pairing of sponsor and program. On a lesser scale, a commercial for Raid's Mouse and Rat Killer was removed from the "Ed Sullivan Show" at the request of CBS: the entertaining mouse, Topo Gigio, was scheduled to appear on the same episode. A furniture polish commercial was moved from one episode of the Carol Burnett Show to another: it had been scheduled to appear following a skit in which Carol sprayed a chest of drawers with an aerosol furniture polish, and the chest, immediately after the spraying, collapsed. But how these understandably negative program environments lead advertising decision makers to their stand on positive environments is a tortuous mental path that I've never been able to follow.

Nor have I been able to understand the reasoning of those who decide that network stations are superior to independent stations for their local TV spots. Many independent stations now carry programs that were on the national networks a few years earlier. Some syndicated programs are carried simultaneously across the country, on network and independent stations alike. It seems illogical that one should buy a local spot on "Jeopardy," which might be carried by a network station in Peoria, but reject a local spot on "Jeopardy" in Davenport, just because an independent station carries it. Perhaps this *quality* bias carries over from years ago, when independent stations had lower ratings than they have now. Low ratings have always been anathema for many decision makers; they have written buying policies prohibiting the purchase of local spots below a certain rating level, say 3 percent. But many of these same decision makers have urged the purchase of cable programs, which may average ratings of only 1 percent or 2 percent in their limited coverage areas. Does this make sense? Yes, if someone has attached a *quality* label to cable viewers. Maybe those of us who don't understand all this are merely envious of the power that we don't have, power to decide what is and isn't *quality*.

Share-of-Voice, or Is It Silent Symmetry?

Every brand's marketing situation is unqiue. Some brands are growing, some are declining, some are constant in their sales patterns. Some have high consumer awareness and high trial, some are still low in consumer awareness and trial. Some have great strength of distribution, others have distribution weaknesses. Some brands have better advertising copy than others do, other brands have better promotions than brands with superior advertising copy. Some have more sophisticated media plans, or better media buying than competing brands in the category. The single, unassailable conclusion we can draw about any product category is that a dollar spent on advertising has a different value for each of the brands in it.

Yet every day, somewhere in this strange business of advertising, people choose to ignore this unassailable conclusion. They must ignore it, because otherwise they couldn't use *share-of-voice* to support conclusions on advertising effectiveness, or for recommending levels of advertising budgets. Share-of-voice compares the advertising expenditures of all brands in a category, and draws conclusions as to whether Brand A's share-of-voice is good, which usually means that its share of spending is as high as its share of market; or that it's not good, which means that its share of ad spending lags behind its share of market. The first conclusion usually defends the current advertising budget; the other supports a recommendation to raise the budget.

For share-of-voice to be anything other than a verbal narcotic, everything said earlier must be wrong, all brands in the product category must have identical marketing situations. All copy must be equal; all media planning and execution be equal; all sales patterns, awareness, and trial must be comparable; and all nonadvertising influences must be constant for all brands. Additionally, advertising response for brands in this category must be linear; that is, each advertising exposure a consumer receives must produce the same kind of response as its predecessor, be it the first or one hundred and first exposure. Is all this possible? No. Is share-of-voice plausible? No. Then why is it so widely used to reach conclusions on advertising budget levels, and to support advertising budget decisions?

Like primitive man, who resorted to symmetry before his brain had learned a better way to handle the unknown, the modern advertising man must not know what else to do. How much money other brands are spending on advertising is irrelevant if we don't know the specific task their advertising is supposed to perform, and how well their advertising is performing this task. My brand's advertising budget may be half or twice what is needed to perform its only legitimate advertising task. If I know what that task is, I shouldn't be looking at what other brands spend to accomplish their tasks—which I don't know anything about, and about which my competitors will certainly tell me nothing. If I don't know what my brand's advertising task is, or how much advertising is needed to accomplish its task, I should try to find out. I shouldn't substitute a formula based on other people's budgets for other brand tasks. Using the phrase *share-of-voice* is an implicit admission of incompetence on the part of the user. The user of this symmetrical nonsense is trying to cover up his inability to set real advertising goals, and an accurate budget to achieve them.

Share-of-voice can be seen as an absurd proposition by anyone who has had exposure to the consistent failure of extra-spending tests. For share-of-voice to be meaningful, there must be a consistent relationship between advertsing expenditures and sales. For example, if I say that my brand's share-of-voice (spending) is 20 percent, and that I judge it to be good because my brand has a 20 percent market share, there must be some relationship of effect between the two 20 percents. But there isn't. If I increase my brand's share-of-voice to 40 percent (in a test situation), little or no change will occur in my brand's case share. This is what almost all market tests have shown. Since I don't know what effect any specific level of advertising will have on my brand's market share, I can only view share-of-voice as a series of meaningless numbers, designed to lead me to false conclusions, and probably to action that will be worthless, or perhaps even detrimental to my brand's total marketing effort.

The A/S Ratio: For Marketing Accountants Only

Anyone who uses an *advertising-to-sales ratio* to establish budgets and strategies for his advertising is probably an accountant who wandered into marketing by mistake. Both sides of his strategic ledger must balance: 8.5 percent of sales on one side, 8.5 percent of advertising on the other. If the company's chairman is a career financial person, use of the A/S ratio may be highly acceptable, or even welcomed. If consumer response to the advertising of this company's brands is linear, with 20 percent more advertising in Milwaukee consistently producing 20 percent more sales per household than it does in Columbus, then the A/S ratio is the most legitimate basis for establishing an advertising budget.

But if a brand's advertising does produce response in linear relation to its spending, it is a rarity—the exception, not the rule. Thousands of unsuccessful extra-spending tests have conclusively proved the generality that advertising response is not linear. If response to advertising is not linear, the A/S ratio is a worthless pair of numbers for budgeting and strategic purposes. It could be even worse than worthless; it could be counterproductive for a brand. For example, if a below-average market share was caused by slow distribution at the time of introductory advertising, this market share may be kept low by budgeting down for it after distribution has caught up to other areas. Some brands use the equivalent of a reverse A/S ratio when setting advertising budgets and strategy. They look at areas where they have the most business to gain, which often will be where their market share is weakest, and will budget aggressively to build their business in these areas.

My exposure to people who use A/S ratios as their primary strategic tool has led me to conclude that they are better accountants than marketers. They assure that profitability is constant everywhere. On paper, this looks good. In the dynamic marketplace where brands compete for consumer purchases, this mentality would probably be about as successful as the Maginot Line was for the French military tacticians during World War II.

Even more dangerous are the accountants who are made reckless by the swashbuckling atmosphere of marketing. They look retrospectively at the sales and advertising histories of brands that have used long-term A/S ratios, and they draw conclusions. Spending on these brands has been raised after higher sales triggered their A/S ratio to recommend more advertising. Or advertising has been reduced on these brands after sales declined, and when their A/S ratio required them to spend less. Our reckless observer has not seen which came first, the sales or the advertising. He has exclaimed: "Eureka! These brands prove that a linear response to advertising does exist! See, as they increase advertising, their sales increase. And look at these other brands. As they reduce advertising, their sales go down. There you have it: proof positive!" Proof positive, indeed. Proof that our business is staffed with people whose enthusiasm is second only to their carelessness in drawing bad conclusions from good data.

Thirty-seven years of observing the workings of the advertising business has left me with at least one unshakeable conclusion: sales produce advertising. If a brand has a large sales base, it can usually afford a large advertising budget. A brand with a small sales base can usually afford only a small advertising budget. If sales decline, advertising budgets usually are reduced. If a brand's sales go up, its advertising budget usually can be raised. So sales *do* produce advertising—almost always. I wish I could say that advertising almost always produces sales. But I can't. Because it doesn't.

4

Abuse of Advertising's Young and Innocent

W hy are the men and women of advertising so addicted to
verbal narcotics? Why do so many of these intelligent people believe the fairy tales and Bunyanesque legends of their own
business? Perhaps the learning process that operates in advertising is similar to that which allows intelligent children to accept
the adult fabrications of Santa Claus, the Easter Bunny, and the
Tooth Fairy. Children believe these adult fantasies because (1) they
are told them by trusted adults, (2) they want to believe them, and
(3) they have neither sought nor discovered conflicting data.

The young people of advertising have been told mythical things
by their trusted predecessors and leaders; they want to believe the
right things about their business, beliefs that will foster their own
success and advancement; and they don't pay serious attention to
conflicting data. As pointed out earlier, someone who has reached
a position of authority and obligatory respect has great difficulty
admitting that his knowledge base has been assembled from mis-
conceptions. In the world of children, the power position of adults
is never threatened by a child's ultimate rejection of the three
cultural fantasies he has been taught to believe. In the adult hier-
archy of power, rejection of a superior's fantasies is a clear threat
to his power, and can do permanent damage to one's career, in
advertising and everywhere else.

During the early years of an advertising career, a person usually
lacks the knowledge base to distinguish fact from fantasy. A young
person wants to learn whatever successful people are willing to
share with him. He wants to become as successful as his teachers.

In his enthusiasm, he gobbles up fiction and fantasy as he feeds from what he thinks is the tree of knowledge. Those who are politically driven will even knowingly accept and promote myth as fact, if convinced that this is the price of success. And sometimes it is.

Failure to See any Conflict Between Paired "Facts"

But the ultimate barrier to escape from the fantasies of advertising is our inability or unwillingness to pay attention to the conflicts that appear between pairings of what are, or what claim to be, facts. For many years, my most frequently used presentation slide has been one that shows how many hours women, in the age group twenty-five to fifty-four, watch TV each week during the month of November. This slide has five vertical bars on it, comparing least-viewing hours with most-viewing hours, and distributed into the five groups, which we in media know as the "audience quintiles by frequency of viewing." Nonadvertising people are overwhelmed by the "most-viewing" bar, which shows that 20 percent of these women watch TV an average of seventy hours each week. I also compute for them the average number of TV commercials actually seen, during this November week, by the women in the first three groups, that is, the 60 percent who account for about 85 percent of all TV viewing. By "actually seen," I mean that I've reduced program audiences by more than one-third in order to approximate physical exposure of women to TV commercials, not just to the programs carrying the commercials. The average number of commercials actually seen by these women (whose 85 percent of total viewing make them virtually the medium itself, for most mass-marketers) is about thirty thousand commercials a year. And this number was computed before 15-second commercials came into use!

These numbers won't startle or even impress most people in the business of advertising. Most of them know it already. In fact, most of them have seen even higher numbers, numbers used by those who haven't discounted program viewing for people who behave like the human beings they are—such as occasionally rising from their chairs during their seventy hours of TV viewing. Over the years, the reporting of the highest possible number of commercials has been used by writers trying to make a dramatic point about how "commercial" people's lives have become since the advent of television. No, advertising people are not surprised by how many TV commercials consumers actually sit and watch. But you and I should be surprised at how little they use this insight to chase Easter Bunnies and Tooth Fairies from their place of business.

Here is one of my favorite incongruities. The longest enduring creative format in TV commercials has been the presenter, otherwise known as a salesperson, or pitchman. Advertising agencies will probably dispute the use of "creative" to describe these presenter commercials. They're usually not creative at all; they seem more like "a last resort when all else fails." They're often dismissed as a manufacturer-ordered format. But, since the beginning of TV, they have persisted (and if you want to trace their roots back far enough, you'll find them to have been street peddlers in biblical times). The appeal of these TV commercials to manufacturers is found in one of their earliest descriptions of them: "A [presenter] TV commercial is like sending a salesman for your product right into the consumer's living room."

Isn't this a compelling way to think about the power of TV commercials? It appears to have influenced an enormous number of advertising people, who believe that use of TV guarantees making a sale to those millions of relaxed, off-guard people in their living rooms. But hold on there! Didn't we just discuss a slide that showed us that the people for whom advertisers buy TV commercials, those 60 percent who watch 85 percent of all TV programs (and commercials), see an average of thirty thousand TV commercials each year? Obviously, something doesn't make sense. The idea of thirty thousand sales people, marching in and out of Susan O'Grady's living room each year, is about as credible as an overweight Santa Claus climbing down my sooty chimney with thirty cubic feet of Christmas boxes in a bag over his shoulder. Susan O'Grady isn't going to respond to thirty thousand sales pitches every year, or any year! If she sits through this many commercials—and she still does— she has to change them in her mind from what the manufacturer wants them to be (effective sales pitches), to what she wants them to be (generally innocuous interruptions in the TV program she has chosen to watch). Every advertiser expects consumers to react enthusiastically to his brand's commercial, but he probably doesn't consider that every other advertiser is sitting behind a desk with the same expectations for his brand's commercial. Isn't the idea of thirty thousand emotional responses per year laughable, even grotesque? And I haven't included her tens of thousands of additional exposures to radio commercials, print ads, and out-of-home media!

Selecting the Research Technique that Helps Commercials Perform

Some advertisers try hard to make their commercials as unlike sales pitches as they can. You've seen commercials that made you laugh, or smile, or sit entranced for almost the entire thirty seconds. If you're like the people who give me a description of the impressive commercial they saw on TV last night, you don't remember the name of the brand advertised in most of these commercials; you sometimes don't even remember the product category that was being advertised. But you've welcomed these commercials into your living room. Well, you've welcomed them as much as you welcome any interruption in the program you've chosen to watch.

The trend toward more entertainment, in terms of humor, special effects, and lavish production values, appears to have coincided with a move away from realistic, on-air testing of commercials, and toward increased use of invited audiences to test these commercials. A commercial that blends well with the entertainment portion of the program is less likely to be seen as a commercial than is the hard-sell presenter, or other obvious commercial breaks in the entertainment. The blending-in commercials are less likely to be remembered the next day, when research calls are made to test how well the commercial was remembered and understood by consumers who had been watching TV in their normal way. On the other hand, when consumers are brought into a room to watch a program not of their choosing, they are no longer "normal TV viewers." They are "test viewers," and see things differently than they would in their natural viewing environment.

When women are called shortly after watching a TV commercial in their normal way at home, only about one-third of them can tell us anything about it. When brought into a research situation and shown the same commercial, virtually all women exposed to it can remember the commercial shortly after having viewed it. In fact, almost a third of these invited viewers can still remember the commercial when called three days later, a time when few normal viewers will be able to remember it. Here's a typical example, from my own experience.

What was destined to be a beautiful commercial for a new shampoo was tested in its rough form; women were brought into a room, where they watched it with other viewers. A normative number of women remembered the commercial three days later, when they were called at home. The commercial was finished, and then tested under natural viewing conditions. Here, it was remembered by 30 percent less than the normative number of viewers. More bluntly, it flunked its test. It was quickly tested again, this time using the laboratory technique used in testing its rough version. As the commercial did in its rough version, it again performed up to the norm. The results of the natural-viewing test were discarded and the commercial was judged to be a success. It was successful in the laboratory, but not in the real world. However, the marketing manager wanted to believe in the effectiveness of his commercial (just as children want to believe in Santa). Had he not obtained satisfactory results the second time, he would probably have found another way to test it. He had become a believer more than a manager. (The four-hundred thousand dollar-cost of this commercial may have strengthened his belief.)

Never Believe Isolated Examples of Proof

Now that I've given you my first example to prove a point, I must warn you that acceptance of a single example to prove something about advertising is why this business has come to believe all the nonsense it now does. One example can prove anything it wants to prove. So can a dozen. Perhaps even thirty or forty examples can be found for every conflicting viewpoint in advertising. Whenever we see a presentation, or read a paper on the findings from advertising research or testing, we must ask someone: "From how many total cases were these examples selected?"

We read in the newspapers about jackpot winners in Las Vegas. If you collect all the newspaper stories about winners and losers in Las Vegas (or Atlantic City), you will learn that "everybody" who goes there to gamble wins a lot of money. An analysis of newspaper stories will "prove" that there are no losers. The same is true of people who invest in the stock market. Based on verbal reports of my friends' stock-market activity, it's difficult not to make money. I hear, constantly, about someone selling at a profit. We all know that people lose more than they win in Las Vegas and Atlantic City. We all know that an investor is as likely to sell at a loss as at a gain. We know *these* are the facts, despite the selectivity of the information we receive to the contrary. We have learned to see gambling and stock-market investing in perspective. We see a bigger picture than we are presented with by those who want to lead us to a self-serving conclusion. Why don't we in advertising have the same perspective on the business that clothes and feeds us?

During the last twenty years, national advertising campaigns number in the hundreds of thosuands, or more. How many success stories have you heard? How many examples support all the self-serving conclusions of presenters and writers of articles and books? In the absence of a hard number, can we say "a handful?" Whenever someone takes your arm and asks you to leap with him (and his friend, Faith) to a conclusion that doesn't really make sense, ask first: "From how many total cases were these selected?"

Shall We Do What We Believe, or Believe What We Do?

In this business of advertising, who should we trust? Whose word can we believe? Who will not amuse himself, at our expense, by filling our heads with Santas, and Bunnies, and Fairies? Am I, even now, amusing myself at your expense? If your boss tells you just the opposite of what you've read in these pages, will you believe him or me? Do you really have a choice? Your belief is what you do, not what you say, or even what you think. If your boss believes in "persuasion," you won't get his signature on a recommendation for a copy test that doesn't give you a persuasion score. If he likes "share-of-voice," your advertising plan will be bounced back without a signature when you don't supply the numbers that make up your share of voice. You may have to recommend three exposures in a four-week period, or not get your media plan approved. You may have to talk to your boss in a language laced with verbal narcotics. He may only understand words like *continuity, presence, impact, synergy,* and *quality.* He may not want to understand anything else.

In the Valley of the Blind, the man with one eye is king. In advertising's Valley of Ignorance, the person with power is sage. When a new marketing manager is brought in, the established creative thinking for his or her brands may be reversed; hard-sell may replace life-style advertising, or vice versa; simple product demonstrations may replace the commercial equivalent of 30-second Broadway musicals, or vice versa; personalitites may replace real people, or vice versa. A new market research manager may replace real-world recall testing with laboratory "persuasion" testing, or vice versa. A new media manager may replace low-cost, opportunistic buying of TV programs with more expensive "quality" programs, or vice versa; reasons may be found for converting some TV advertising to magazine advertising, or vice versa. During my last twenty-two years as media director, there were six different heads of Marketing Research. During these years, there were six different heads of Marketing, plus a final split of the job into four divisional marketing heads! In only a few cases did these managers have any influence in the choice of their replacement. Over the years, I tried to steer a steady media course while I watched a lot of vice-versa-ing taking place in marketing and marketing research.

Short Careers, Shortsightedness, Narrow Perspective

Most people in marketing have a career of short-time assignments. They learn to have a successful short-term stint during each of these assignments. Success in each cycle is necessary if they are to move into the next stage of their development. Many learn to think in terms of short segments of their brand's life cycle, as well as their own. Everything begins and ends annually. Plans are for a year, and the best plan is created for each individual year. Usually ignored is this: what is best for one year is not necessarily the best for the second year. When we think in terms of brand life, as opposed to budgeting cycles, we can plan so that our use of media can be optimal for a number of budgeting periods. With long-range vision, we can see that our ideal one-year plan, repeated twice, will not necessarily become an ideal three-year plan.

Shortsightedness, or lack of the perspective needed to see the conflict between some of their strongly held beliefs, keeps many career advertising and marketing people childlike in these beliefs. For example, most marketing and advertising people believe that a free sample of a product is a much more powerful form of "communication" than a TV commercial or a print ad. But they fail to understand, or to accept, that people receive powerful "communication" when using the products they purchase regularly. If a brand is lightly advertised, they'll tell you that it has weak communication, and is vulnerable to competitive advertising. But even a nonadvertised brand may be communicating, loudly and clearly, to its regular users.

In 1985, I prepared a detailed estimate of how much communication product usage provided for a nonadvertised furniture polish. I took a weekly 15-minute dusting/polishing usage and gave it a value of four 30-second TV commercials. Why four? Because research shows that only one of four viewers can remember anything about a TV commercial when called on to do so the next day, but all women remember having polished their furniture the day before. And perhaps more importantly: the sensory impressions received while using the product are infinitely higher than when watching images flicker across a TV screen. My cost projection? Using the lowest-cost TV (daytime network), an advertised brand would have spent 55 million dollars to equal the effect of usage of a nonadvertised brand *in only half the user households!* And consider this: total reported advertising for the furniture-polish category that year was only 26 million dollars.

If I had equated a single TV commercial to a weekly polishing ritual, the highest-spending advertised brand ($8 million) would not have matched the effect of product usage in half the user households of any nonadvertised brand.

This furniture-polish example is an additional piece of evidence to prove that share-of-voice is a senseless game of meaningless numbers. In it, the unadvertised brand, with no share-of-voice, completely dominates the communication channel to its users. This example may also help to explain why brands in most categories fail to lose share when one of their competitors dramatically increases its level of advertising. Though increasing its advertising, it may have done little to increase its share of the total communication, including product use, which consumers receive from the brands in this category. But the example shows, clearly, that people fail to examine, with a critical eye, their own clashing beliefs (the assumed value of a free sample versus the assumed nonvalue of the same product when purchased by its user).

Another Failed Test of Logic: The 15-Second Commercial

The 15-second TV commercial has given the men and women of advertising yet another opportunity to demonstrate how well they can ignore the conflict between two points of their own logic. Here's a 1987 dialogue between an advertiser's media director and the account supervisor of a large advertising agency:

Media Director: I notice that you're recommending thirty-second TV commercials for the first two weeks of the year, then all fifteens thereafter. What's the logic of that?

Account Supervisor: We have a real good fifteen-second commercial. It tested at 85 percent of our thirty.

Media Director: I understand the fifteens. But why the thirties if the fifteens are that good?

Account Supervisor: The brand will have been out of advertising four months before it comes back in. We think we need to come back in as strong as we can. So we're recommending that we start off with the thirty.

Media Director: But you said you have a real good fifteen.

Account Supervisor: Yes we do, but the thirty is stronger.

Media Director: Is it twice as strong?

Account Supervisor: No, it isn't. We have a good fifteen.

Media Director: Then why don't you just run more fifteens at the beginning of the year? If your fifteens are worth 85 percent as much as your thirty, and cost only 50 percent as much, the brand will get more total advertising effect from the same dollars spent on fifteens.

Account Supervisor: Well . . . but the thirty has more sell in it. We think we need this extra sell after being out of advertising for over four months.

Media Director: Doesn't the fifteen sell? How did the copy points come through in testing?

Account Supervisor: Oh, the fifteen is good. It's just that we feel more confident about the thirty, especially when we've been off the air for so long.

Media Director: According to your numbers, only one out of four targeted consumers will be reached effectively with the thirty. This means that most of your advertising effect for the year will be contributed exclusively by the fifteen-second commercial. Women who see only the fifteen, and see it halfway through the year, are almost a year removed from their last exposure to your thirty-second commercial. If you think that the fifteen can't stand alone at any time during the year, even at the beginning, maybe you should consider using more thirties, or even all thirties.

Account Supervisor: [*Pause.*] Maybe we should just forget the thirties. We all think the fifteen is a solid commercial. Let's just run all fifteens. What does everyone else think?

The media plan was approved after another ten minutes of discussion. There were no thirties in the plan. Was this the right decision? Not necessarily. But it was a consistent decision. Perhaps the brand's fifteens don't sell anyone at all. But then again, perhaps the thirties don't either. The decision to use all fifteens was at least consistent with the data available to the decision makers. The mixture of thirties and fifteens, as originally proposed, had no logic to support it. Qualms about the shorter commercial could logically have led to use of nothing but thirties, but this would not have led to the use of thirties for the one-time benefit of a small minority of the brand's target audience.

Disrespectful Doubt:
The First Step Toward Professionalism

From the few examples just cited, perhaps we can begin to discover clues that ultimately may lead us away from advertising's fairy tales. Perhaps we can take our first steps toward the professionalism that we claim to have but cannot yet substantiate. After a child has asked his parents enough questions about Santa Claus, the Easter Bunny, and the Tooth Fairy, the parents are forced to answer with responses acceptable to an intelligent child. Once we professionals begin to ask "disrespectful" questions during the development of advertising copy and media plans, the users of verbal narcotics will be pushed to answer in a manner befitting the intelligent adults they are. They will no longer treat us like naive children.

Just as the child must, at some point, decide to begin expressing his doubt, so must we in advertising choose our point in time to reject the role of believer, and to adopt the posture of doubter. It's not easy for a child to let go of innocence. Imagine how embarrassed he must feel when he remembers how completely he believed in things which now seem so illogical and absurd. And it is not easy for us to step out of the role of believer, and to suffer the embarrassment of confessing that so many of our advertising beliefs no longer make sense. But we must, in order to grow in our profession. The longer we allow ourselves to pretend, the longer the myths of advertising will prevail over knowledge and understanding.

5
One Man's Loss
of Innocence

My own innocence began to unravel about twenty-seven years ago. At the time, I was working in the media department of the Procter & Gamble Co. Then, as now, P&G was one of the finest marketing organizations in the world. Over the years, its brands have continued to set quality standards for their product categories. Many of them have been important contributors to the health, hygiene, or well-being of the American consumer (Crest toothpaste, Head & Shoulders shampoo, Pampers disposable diapers, and so on). Their media department, too, was an early leader of advertiser media departments. But over the years, this staff group has not been regarded as highly as the parent company itself. Perhaps an experience I had while working there will suggest reasons for the different levels of respect.

In the early 1960s, I was asked to collect and analyze all tests of the previous six years—tests that involved media manipulations. It wasn't easy to do. There were more than eighty tests, and each one had been initiated by whichever brand manager had decided to test a way to increase his brand's sales. The P&G media department had watched over the execution of these tests with the sharp eye for detail which was its trademark. But it hadn't concerned itself with the test results; research results were the responsibility of the marketing research department. The media department had made sure that the executions were letter-perfect, but hadn't managed the results of these tests into any kind of coordinated learning experience from which broad media conclusions could be drawn. However, neither had anyone in the marketing research department, because their responsibility was to provide marketing insights for individual brands; it was not to draw broad media conclusions from the test markets of many brands.

A variety of media tests had been conducted during those six years. Often, a brand manager wanted to learn if his sales could be increased significantly, and profitably, by raising the level of its media exposures. Other brand managers wanted to learn if their sales could be increased by switching from daytime to nighttime TV. Some wanted to learn whether commercials running on network programs were more productive than the same commercials running in the breaks sold locally, on a spot basis.

Collecting these tests wasn't the most difficult part of my assignment. Our media department or the brand's advertising agency had a complete record of whatever media manipulations had been performed. But the results of these tests were quite another matter. The P&G media department had little information on test results. Brand managers were interested in how to increase their sales, not in learning anything profound about media effectiveness. Even a brand's advertising agency didn't always know the results of its own advertising test (or would not admit to knowing— presumably when the results had been negative rather than positive).

Some tests may have been intended to serve a purely political purpose. A brand manager who "did something" in an attempt to increase his brand's sales was thought of then, as he is now, as being "aggressive." Where job tenure was too short for a product manager to prove his long-term value to the brand's business, many activities were performed (as they are today, in many organizations) for their effect on those higher up in the management chain, rather than to increase business—testing included.

It was difficult to find test results that were not interpreted in the aggressive, highly positive tone which has always been associated with success in brand management. The media department had been told by many brand managers that their tests had been successful. Yet I discovered that the marketing researchers assigned to these brands had, after their analyses, labeled the results of these particular tests "statistically insignificant." Then as now, a brand manager had taken a numerically-higher test result, say an index of a hundred and three versus a control index of one hundred and had used the recurring (now classic) statement: "While not statistically significant, the test results were directionally indicative that the brand responds to increased advertising weight." (To have questioned how something nonexistent could be "directionally indicative" would have been to have challenged positive thinking itself.)

My sifting through six years of media tests uncovered a consistent pattern of findings—which would not be surprising today. These findings have been corroborated many times by other advertisers in the years since then. Extra-weight advertising was not the answer to brand management's eternal question of how to improve sales. While sales went up in a minority of the tests, they went down in an almost equal minority of cases, and they stayed the same in about half the cases. Neither did the media manipulations of day versus night, or network versus local, show the way to improve sales. It was easy to draw conclusions: either these brands had tested no media or weight variable that could affect their sales, or the technique used to measure the results of all this testing was not the right one to measure the effect of advertising variables.

My conclusions were greeted with something less than enthusiasm. In fact, I was asked to change these conclusions. When I said that I didn't know how I could do this, because all my support data pointed in the same direction, the report was given to someone else to write. The final report softened my negative findings, and said in effect, that we were not there yet, but that we'd keep trying. I pointed out that the testing base was so broad that it would take ten or fifteen years of reversed results to modify the findings of this large base of testing experience to a point where positive conclusions would be possible. My leaders should have seen that to keep trying to measure the same things, in the same way, would be no more productive than sitting by the fireplace all night, on Christmas Eve, waiting for Santa Claus to come down the chimney. But sit they did, for years and years and years.

After this experience, I quickly lost confidence in my media leaders, who obviously weren't leading me to the new levels of competence I needed to make me feel comfortable with my career development. I soon began to question everything in media's knowledge base before accepting it "on authority." I began forcing everything to prove itself, at least with logic or good sense, if not with numbers. Much of what I was being taught to do failed the test of logic. But the management of our media department displayed no interest in upsetting conventional media thinking. The focus of their energies was then, was a decade later, and may still be today, on how to spend media money more efficiently than their competitors.

Unlike Procter & Gamble's product-development department, the media department's theories were manfacturer-executional, not consumer-strategic. Media planning was very simple. The first buy for a brand was a daytime TV serial. Its second buy was another daytime serial, preferably on a different network. How did they arrive at this media-planning philosophy? Easy. Buying time on daytime TV serials, especially those produced by P&G, was the most efficient way to spend a brand's money. There was never any discussion of effective patterns of message exposure for consumers. Fifteen years after I left P&G, they still hadn't progressed to the stage of media thinking where they could discuss exposure to advertising from the consumer's viewpoint.

"Sir, How Does Advertising Work?"

While I was still at Procter & Gamble, one of the questions that bothered me most was: "How does advertising work?" I finally got the opportunity to pose this question to the smartest advertising person I could find in P&G's advertising management. It was an exciting moment for a young man in search of his career's real meaning. I asked him: "How does advertising work?" He was surprised by my question. "I guess I never thought about it before," he replied candidly.

Let's stop and think about this for a minute. The smartest advertising executive, working for the country's largest advertiser, had never thought about how advertising works! Now let's stop and think about something else for another minute. Twenty-seven years later, few, if any others, among advertising's top management

—whether advertiser or advertising agency—have given much serious thought to how advertising works!

In response to the question I asked my superior, "How does advertising work?", my long-awaited teacher continued: "I suppose, if you have a good TV commercial, and use enough daytime TV, and maybe some nighttime TV, your advertising is going to work for you." What could I say, other than "thank you?" I suppose I was too light-headed to think of anything else. It had been a long climb up the mountain to seek words of wisdom from the guru. Should I have asked more? But what could I have said to someone who obviously didn't understand that he hadn't even begun to answer my first question?

At this point in my career, I could have decided, easily, that I was wrong for this business of advertising. I knew I couldn't advance myself without learning how to be like those above me in the management chain. But I didn't want to do that. I knew I couldn't spend my business life in the parent-manager game of teaching others what I saw to be the unchallenged mythology of advertising. However, about this same time, I posed my favorite advertising question to someone who proved to be a source of inspiration for me, Larry Deckinger. Larry was working at the Biow Company, one of P&G's outstanding agencies during the 1960s.

I first met Larry while I was walking through the agency's narrow, wood-panelled hall. I glanced into an office and saw a pair of feet, with their shoes off, resting on top of a worktable. Propped on the legs attached to the shoeless feet was a Bible. Behind the Bible was the smiling face of Larry Deckinger. "Hi," he said. "You know, this is a very interesting book. A man could get some good advertising ideas from it."

It was a couple of years later, when I knew Larry better, that I asked him how he thought advertising works. "Like love," he replied. Then he continued to explain that when a beautiful young woman walks past a happily married man, she'll catch his attention. He'll follow her with his eyes until she turns the corner, and that'll be the end of it. But if the man no longer loves his wife, he'll follow the young woman around the corner, and get involved with her. He said that advertising probably works the same way.

A consumer has to fall out of love with the brand she's using before she can be seduced by another one.

Over the last quarter century, many advertising people have attempted to answer my question, but none has really bettered Larry's stimulating response to it. Actually, most advertising people avoid the question if they can. Few of them ask themselves, or anyone else, how advertising works. Even fewer can answer, with confidence, how it does work. Yet those who can't answer the question are convinced that they are qualified to work as well-paid professionals in the advertising business. I don't share their conviction. I wouldn't entrust a brand's advertising budget to anyone who isn't capable of offering a plausible theory of how advertising works for that brand.

Questions for a Disrespectful Doubter

An advertising agency can't write effective copy if it doesn't know what it's trying to do for a consumer, and how it's trying to do it. Is the copy trying to make a woman fall in love with its brand, without first making her fall out of love with the one she's currently using? How, then, will it work? More than one agency account executive has offered this reply: "Oh, women are regularly falling out of love with their current brand in this category. The problem addressed by this kind of product is never really solved to the satisfaction of consumers." Point accepted. Then the media plan probably needs to be structured so that its exposures coincide with enough of these "fallings-out-of-love" to make the copy cost-effective. But suppose the copy is trying to make women fall *out* of love with their current brand, and in love with the advertised one? How and when should exposures to this advertising be patterned to achieve the dual effect most efficiently?

There are dozens of questions, sometimes hundreds of them, that need to be asked and answered before agency people begin work on a media plan. Some are even more basic than how advertising works. For the last five years, I've used a questioning sequence that I myself developed. It contains twelve questions which have been sequenced to reflect the way I choose to think about how the process of advertising comes together to form a strategically responsible media plan. There's nothing magic about these twelve questions, nor about the sequence in which I ask them. However, they do have an interesting history of results, which may recommend them over a less structured approach to media planning.

The answers to these twelve questions have always led to media plans totally different from the plans developed prior to asking them. These changes in plans have occurred even when the answers to my questions were given by the same marketing and ad agency people who worked on the earlier plan. There was no change in the brand's marketing circumstances or advertising budget, and no conscious effort to change the previous plan. What this tells us is that the previous plan was not really what the agency and marketing people wanted for the brand. They simply hadn't asked themselves the questions that would get them to where they themselves had always wanted to be, but didn't know it.

Even more of a surprise to me was that, while using these questions, I found I was learning things about media planning that hadn't surfaced during my previous thirty years of working on media plans. New insights don't come easily to one who has worked on hundreds of media plans, who has worked as a client of the majority of the twenty largest advertising agencies in this country (and many smaller ones), and who has sought out and had access to many of the best media and research minds in this business. But I've learned something new about media planning, or advertising strategy, in the majority of meetings where my twelve questions have been used. Others, with fewer years in this business, have learned much more than I.

The twelve questions are important, but they're only the basic ones, those which start the strategic-thinking process. Follow-up questions must be asked of whoever answers the basic ones. Habit leads advertising people to answer most questions with an easy cliché, or even a verbal narcotic. To make the questioning process work, the pre-planning group must cross-examine every respondent until it has no more questions to ask. Then, and only then, can legitimate media planning begin.

Let's look at the twelve questions, the kind of answers they elicit, and how each of these answers plays a key role in the development of an effective media plan. The forum for this questioning is normally composed of (1) marketing and media people representing the advertiser, (2) account managers and media people from the advertising agency, and (3) sometimes research people from the advertiser, and, less frequently, a creative person from the agency. This is a pre-planning meeting, therefore it must precede any work on a media plan.

These questions were orignally composed to simplify, and make more logical, the thinking of people who contribute to the media-planning process. Thus, they came to be called S*I*M*P*L*E, which is an acronym for Sanity in Media Planning, Laboriously Extracted. I'm sure that the thought of "laboriously extracting sanity" from the process of media planning sounds like pure hyperbole to most people who have participated in the conventional ritual of media planning. After reading the next chapter, I doubt that they will think so. I'm positive that they will never think so, if they ever have the opportunity to participate in one of my S*I*M*P*L*E meetings.

6
Twelve S*I*M*P*L*E Questions

Question #1:
What Consumer Action Must Result
From Exposure to This Advertising?

In this question, the consumer is whoever the advertising is intended to influence. The consumer could be a retail customer in a drugstore, or in a supermarket; the consumer could be a third-party endorser, such as a pharmacist, or a nurse. The consumer could be someone in the retail trade, if the goal of the advertising is to lead members of the retail trade to take some kind of action. But to keep this sequence of questions manageable, the word *consumer* here will always mean the purchaser of package-goods products, at the retail level. However, I think you'll find that these twelve S*I*M*P*L*E questions can be used to develop media plans (and sometimes even copy) for almost any product or service.

Action, Not Awareness,
Is Advertising's Goal

All advertising ultimately must lead the consumer to action that wouldn't have taken place without the influence of this advertising. Advertising is a marketing expense, one that can be justified only if it leads to more sales than would have been made without it. Creating awareness isn't the ultimate goal of any advertising. Awareness may (or may not) be a necessary stage in the progression to an additional sale of the product. The measuring of this awareness may (or may not) be a way of measuring how well advertising moves a brand to this stage. But if consumers stop at the awareness stage, and never make a purchase, the advertising has justified neither its cost nor its existence.

There are many good reasons for not blaming advertising when consumers fail to go beyond awareness to the actual purchase of a brand. Reasons? The brand may not have been priced correctly. The brand may not have been in distribution when consumers, in response to the advertising, looked for it. A major competitor may have sampled or promoted heavily, thereby taking the brand's potential buyers out of the market until after the effect of its advertising had diminished to ineffectiveness.

But with or without reasons for blame, the advertising was unproductive, wasteful, and depressing on brand and corporate profitability. All nonadvertising factors—those that can prevent effective advertising from moving consumers to action—should have been addressed before the expense of advertising was committed. A dollar not spent on advertising goes directly to pre-tax profits. If advertising can't, for whatever reason, move consumers to action that otherwise wouldn't have occurred, this dollar should go directly to the bottom line—to pre-tax profits. Or it should be used to fund other marketing efforts which have the capability of producing incremental sales. It shouldn't be spent on unproductive advertising just because that's where it's always gone, or because the chairman, the marketing vice president, or some other power figure "believes" in advertising.

The Four Basic Consumer-Action Responses

Let's begin, here, to show how well we've learned to discipline our thinking. We can start by reordering our language to sharpen our focus on the consumer. We won't say that brand sales are the goal of our advertising. Instead, we'll say that the goal of our advertising is to get consumers to buy. This buying consumer can be classified, for strategic purposes, into at least four groups. Each of these four groups is different enough from the others to require different copy, or different media planning, or both. The buying consumer will be one of the following:

1. First-time triers of the brand.

2. Repeat purchasers of the same brand.

3. Switchers back to the brand after using another brand.

4. Users of the brand, who consume more volume because they have learned a new way to use it.

The answer to Question #1 probably will be selected from these action groups. The consumer action that will make a brand's advertising effective will be trial, repeat purchase, switchback from a competitive brand, or increased use of the brand after learning a new way to use it.

Many advertising people instinctively claim sweeping effectiveness for their advertising. They often want to set goals that span the first three action groups. These men and women seem to fear that modest goals will reflect badly on their capabilities. But the opposite is true. Under further questioning in a preplanning meeting, their sweeping claims usually show themselves to be unrealistic, and they themselves appear naive and unprofessional.

Selecting the Correct Action Response

Here's some logic to help focus on action goals. A consumer has tried our brand because of its advertising, but is now using a competitive brand. Why should she be motivated to return to our brand by the same advertising that led her to try it in the first place? She responded to our advertising, tried our brand, but didn't like it enough (for whatever reason) to continue buying it. She's now had experience with the advertising *and* with the product itself, yet her last purchase was a competitive brand. Why would she want to come back to a brand that gives her less information (only our advertising) than she had before (our advertising, followed by her experience with our brand)?

Consumers who switch back to a brand after leaving it probably do so because they've been given new information. This new information could be new advertising, changed pricing, new packaging, or from changes in the need structure of these consumers.

Or perhaps the competitive product has failed to live up to their expectations. But if consumers do switch back, will the motivating factor be a new exposure to the old advertising, or will it be the old exposure to the old advertising, plus their remembered experience with the product itself? Let's ask one more question, then we may have our answer: "Against what did the consumer measure the performance of her current brand and find it wanting?" If she comes back to our brand, it was probably our brand's performance, not its advertising, that supplied her with the higher standard.

In many pre-planning meetings, I've listened to advertising and marketing people claim that consumer action, in response to their advertising, will be both trial purchase and repeat purchase. Apparently, to many of these people it appears logical that the same advertising that leads a woman to try a brand will lead her to repeat her initial action ("trial again," or repeat purchase). Perhaps this seems logical. But what about the product experience she has had with this brand? Didn't the brand's performance have to come up to the expectations promised in its advertising? And if it did, and she buys the brand again, isn't it possible that the product, not the advertising, should get credit for it?

Ritualized Versus Impulse Products

But what kind of product are we talking about? Is this a product in ritualized use, such as detergents, cleaners, polishes, shampoos, shaving creams, deodorants, toilet paper, coffee, tea, and so on? These products feed information back to their users on a schedule established by their ritualized use in the home. When the packages are empty, this "tells" the consumer to repurchase the product category. But the incumbent brand is the one that communicates this repurchase message. The box of Tide is empty. The can of Pledge is empty. The roll of Charmin is used up. The jar of Taster's Choice is empty.

As they are being used, these brands have communicated powerful messages to their users. If advertising has led consumers to try them, their performance has confirmed, many times over, the promises made by the advertising. Or their performance has refuted the advertising. Either way, the brand in ritualized use doesn't always (or often, or ever) require reexposure to the advertising stimulus that led to its initial trial. Many long-term users of a ritualized brand rarely, or never, see or hear its advertising during years of ritualized use. However, not all products are in ritualized use. Let's examine what might happen to a packaged dessert or cake mix. The dessert or cake is made on Saturday afternoon, the package is discarded before the finished product is consumed, and the product itself is gone and forgotten within twenty-four hours. What stimulates a consumer to purchase the dessert or cake mix again? Does she remember which *brand* she purchased the last time?

If she's a fairly regular user of this product category, and also of this specific brand, she'll probably remember. But here's the catch for advertising people. If she's a regular user of this brand, she may have ritualized her use of the product. If she has, she probably doesn't need reexposure to the advertising that originally introduced her to the brand. If she's not a regular user of the product category, the advertising may be helpful, even essential, in getting her to repurchase. But infrequent purchase means that she is a light user, one of those many who contribute, proportionately, so little to a brand's total sales volume.

Trial: A Good Reason, but a Bad Excuse

There's no disputing the importance of advertising in getting consumers to try a brand for the first time. Women who have never tried our brand receive little communication from it, other than its advertising. However, this doesn't mean that we must accept first-time trial as the consumer action that always justifies and directs the planning of our advertising.

If a brand has been marketed for a decade or longer, and is saying nothing new in its current advertising, why should consumers, who have chosen not to try the brand for so long, suddenly change their mind? Most of them shouldn't. Circumstances may have changed for a few of them. These few are now new consumers for the brand, indistinguishable from the category entrants who increase the ranks of many product categories each year. But usually there are so few of these new prospects for old brands in the marketplace, that they're more often an *excuse* for advertising, rather than a good reason.

New Uses for Old Products

Conversely, to show consumers a new use for our old brand puts us on the side of the angels. Who can argue with this advertising goal, especially when we can cite how much Arm & Hammer baking soda we've used to deodorize our refrigerators or freshen our bathroom drains? Of course, these ideas for increasing product usage don't always work. Consumers were shown how to add floor polish to a bucket of wash water, and refresh the shine every time they damp-mopped their floor. Some did, but many didn't. Those who did may have polished less often, because the shine was refreshed each time they cleaned their floors.

For decades, Ben-Gay has been well-known as a pain reliever for sore muscles. But new-use advertising for Ben-Gay encouraged athletes to use it to warm muscles before exercising, to prevent the pain of strained muscles. I don't know how successful it was, but the idea was a logical marketing move. We applaud these legitimate attempts to show consumers how to use more of our products for their own benefit, as well as ours. They may not succeed often, but neither does advertising of any kind (other than price advertising—which is another subject).

I can summarize in eight words what I've said about answers to a media planner's basic Question #1: Don't accept these answers without asking more questions. You'll find, as you ask more questions, that the original answers often will be changed, sometimes by those who gave you the initial answer. Most easy answers don't hold up under cross-examination. Make sure you persevere with your questioning until you get the hard answer, the right answer. The wrong one will make you double back later on, in order to change key answers, after you've discovered inconsistencies caused by the pre-planning group's answers to the eleven remaining questions.

Question #2:
Who Is the Consumer
Who Will Take This Action?

Unless we've accurately defined the consumer action that justifies our advertising's existence, we can't accurately answer this second basic question. When the desired consumer action is trial of our brand, its advertising won't be directed at current or past users. When repurchase of our brand is the desired action, current users will be the only target of its commercials or ads, as they will be for new uses of the brand. Users of competitive brands will be the exclusive target of advertising specifically designed to switch former users back to a brand they've abandoned.

Many advertised products have a small base of current users, some only a few percent of the population. But on many occasions, I've heard advertising people discuss plans to communicate, via the mass medium of network television, to the users of one of these brands. They ignore the waste that results when only a few percent of an advertising audience are prospects for what one of their brands wants to tell its users. When our plan must take into account this situation, we ask the product manager, or whoever else is responsible, how much it will cost to include an advertising message in, or on, the brand's packaging. The package itself is the one advertising medium that offers 100 percent coverage of its product users, with virtually no wasted audience. Where the incidence of product usage is low, a brand's packaging may well be the most efficient way to advertise to its users.

Perhaps advertising agencies are discouraged from offering insight into this efficient advertising medium because its costs are normally charged back to manufacturing. This makes them non-commissionable to the agency. You can see how the commission system can put agencies in the absurd position of being asked to work gratis, by giving up commission revenue, in return for showing an advertiser how to advertise more efficiently. It's no surprise that these agencies almost never suggest this efficient alternative to commissionable media, nor that they greet its suggested use—from another source—with something less than enthusiasm.

Nonusers of a product category are often identified as the target of a new brand that is looking for first-time triers. When this occurs, we should ask: "Why haven't these nonusers ever bought a brand in this product category? Perhaps they've had a good reason for not buying. Does our new brand offer something that eliminates their good reason for not having bought a brand in this category before?"

Marketing research can identify potential triers in demographic terms, but many more potential non-triers will have the same demographic profile. A consumer's interest in a brand may be the only characteristic that distinguishes her from the disinterested consumers who share common demographics. The challenge then becomes, how to match media with consumer interest in a brand? Psychographics attempts this, but users of psychographics, like all others who work in advertising, offer the use of their data, rather than measured business results, as proof that they have successfully matched media with consumer interest in a brand.

Sometimes a target audience can be defined situationally. For example, a shaving cream might want to "talk" to its users while they shave. An objective for coinciding advertising with use of shaving cream might be to cue users to observe and appreciate a sensory benefit they would otherwise ignore, or fail to appreciate, while they use the product. Drivers of cars with a dirty or dull hood might be a situational target audience for a car wax. I have participated in a planning session where it was decided to communicate with air-freshener users while they were experiencing bathroom malodors. To try to coincide our media exposures with a consumer's bowel movements isn't easy, but it should qualify us as creative users of media.

In general, target audiences are selected with more than enough care by those who have accurately defined the consumer action that must result from their advertising. This is especially true when mass television is the only medium being used by the brand being advertised. Most prime-time TV programs don't survive long enough for us to measure their audiences in fine detail, and then use this information. Before we can do this, the programs are either moved to a different demographic environment, have different competing programs, or have been taken off the air.

A target-audience trap to watch for is the "enthusiastic" consumer, who, by virtue of this enthusiasm, becomes a truly sophisticated consumer. For example, products that are expected to appeal to health-conscious consumers may be unappealing to these consumers if they contain questionable additives. The enthusiastic consumer is likely to benefit educationally from his or her enthusiasm over time. Advertisers must not only define their brand's targets correctly; they also need to understand the mind-set that these targets bring to their encounters with advertising.

Question #3:
What "Something Positive" Must Take Place in the Consumer's Mind to Lead Her to the Designated Action?

Simple logic has already allowed us to conclude that effective advertising—the only kind of advertising that can be justified economically—makes something happen that otherwise wouldn't have happened. The consumer wouldn't have tried Orville Redenbacher's popping corn for the first time if she had not seen its advertising. The infrequent user of Chun King chop suey wouldn't have thought of buying it last week if she hadn't been reminded by a commercial on TV. The user of Arm & Hammer baking soda in the refrigerator wouldn't have discovered this way to use more of it, had an ad not shown her a new way to satisfy one of her legitimate needs.

For a consumer to have taken action that wouldn't have occurred without exposure to advertising, means that something positive must have taken place in the consumer's mind. Her hand did something different from what her mind had signaled it to do the last time she reached the same supermarket shelf. Why? Something changed her thinking process, something positive for one brand, and either negative or neutral for other brands.

How Crest Gave More Consumers
a Positive Experience

When Crest toothpaste was introduced in the mid-fifties, a three-page ad in *Life* magazine announced a "triumph over tooth decay."

Many consumers experienced something positive when they discovered what they believed to be the first toothpaste effective in the prevention of cavities. Millions of them bought Crest. But many others, who also wanted a toothpaste effective against cavities, failed to experience that "something positive" which had led other millions to buy Crest. Why not? They all saw the same advertising. Ah, but the majority of them simply didn't believe it.

This conclusion was proved emphatically six years later, when the American Dental Association endorsed Crest as the first and only toothpaste to have proved itself effective in the prevention of cavities. Crest's market share tripled within a year of this endorsement. The benefit claimed for the brand in its advertising was unchanged. The advertising itself was actually more low-key, less creative. But authorities in the field of dental hygiene, those whose words were accepted as believable, said that the advertising was honest, that its claim was true; then something positive happened in the minds of many more consumers.

Two Key Words: "Discover" and "Intrigue"

Certain words are notable for their frequent occurrence in the discussions that take place during our pre-planning meetings. When trying to answer Question #3, we often use the word *discover*. Discovery of something that better serves the self-interest of consumers is assumed to be a positive mental experience for these consumers. Discovery implies absence of prior knowledge. As such, the word fits well with our advertising jargon, which says of a brand, that it is "bringing news" to consumers. Thus, the positive something is usually expected to have a news-like quality. For example, in 1988 many consumers discovered new and more appetizing ways to obtain the dietary benefits of oat bran. This was the year when major cereal manufacturers introduced many new oat cereals, as they tried to take advantage of medical publicity on the health value of oat bran.

But advertising people initially bring into these meetings words that betray belief in their own powerful achievements. The word *convince* is one of their favorites. For something positive, they're likely to say that their advertising will "convince" consumers that their client's insect repellent is more effective in keeping away mosquitoes than the brand he currently uses. However, advertising's power to convince has not fared well in the discussions that have spanned five years of media planning for a dozen or more product categories. We invariably conclude that the consumer reaches a state of conviction only after trying the brand, only after she has satisfied herself that the advertising is true.

On the other hand, we generally agree that advertising can intrigue a consumer with the benefit that it offers for using a brand. We might even agree that advertising can persuade the consumer to give the brand a chance to prove that what it offers her is true. Note, however, that this is a more conditional meaning than is usually associated with *persuasion*.

It's probably accurate to say that something positive happened when a consumer became intrigued with the idea of using a product in her clothes dryer to soften her family's clothes, eliminate their static cling, and give them a clean, fresh smell. Many of these intrigued consumers decided to give Bounce fabric softener a try. If Bounce worked as well as they were told by the commercial, their laundry task would be made easier, and their laundry would feel soft and smell good.

When the product itself performed as well as the product in the advertising, consumers became convinced that Bounce really performed as well as its advertising said it would. But all that Bounce's advertising actually did, all that it could do, was to intrigue consumers enough to try it, to give it a chance to prove itself. I don't mean to denigrate this advertising when I say "all it did." Most advertising doesn't do as much. Only good advertising can accomplish as much as Bounce's did. When the product is as good as its advertising says it is, when the price is right, and the distribution adequate to meet demand, an enormous new business can result.

The Self-Serving Bias of the Teaching Theory

During the first two or three years of trying to answer Question #3, we often used the phrase "the consumer learned that . . . " The idea of learning seemed consistent with the consumer's taking in new information, and retaining it long enough to convert this information into delayed action in the store. I suspect we may have liked "learning" as much for placing us in the implied power role of teachers as we did for what appeared to be its initial logic.

If we believe that consumers respond only to advertising that successfully appeals to their self-interest, we must always challenge anyone who argues for a teaching process. Who can argue, at least with any logic, that we need to be taught something that we recognize as having already appealed to our self-interest? Is it logical that we must be taught to want something we already want?

Advertising agencies instinctively betray their own self-interest by adopting the teaching-learning process as their reflex-action response to Question #3. This process gives them support for recommending more advertising exposures (to teach), rather than fewer exposures (to intrigue). The need for more exposures ensures that the advertiser will spend enough money to prejudice success for his advertising campaign (if not for its profitability). This need for more exposures also assures more revenue for the advertising agency—thanks to the inverted logic of the commission system of compensation.

The Flawed Logic of "Reassurance"

The advertising agency's economic self-interest also has been made evident by another word, which was frequently offered by someone in the group during our early efforts to answer this question. The word is *reassure*. The strength of its attraction for advertising agencies is evident: it is, predictably, the suggestion made by agency people (new to this questioning process) when they are given their first opportunity to participate in one of our pre-planning sessions. The thinking behind an advertiser's need to reassure users of his brand with advertising seems to go something like this: consumers using a mature brand, which has nothing new in its advertising, experience something positive when this brand's advertising does nothing more than communicate that it is still a quality product. A consumer's reassurance-driven thought process supposedly keeps her from switching to a competitive brand, which she has discovered, and which has intrigued her with something in its advertising (or other form of communication).

There's a notable absence of logic in this thinking. For a consumer to discover something of interest in the advertising of a brand she isn't using, she, presumably, does not believe she already receives the benefit of this "something" from the brand she currently uses. (How, otherwise, could she discover this benefit as "something new" elsewhere?). If she doesn't believe she already receives the benefit from use of her current brand, how can its advertising reassure her that she does?

Logic is absent from this reassurance, even if we assume that the consumer believes she already receives the said benefit from use of her current brand. For instance, if she believes she already gets "waxed beauty without build-up" when using her current furniture polish, why would she be *intrigued* with another furniture polish whose advertising offers her "waxed beauty without build-up?" Have you ever seen a new product succeed by offering consumers, in its advertising, nothing more than what they believe they already have in hand, at the same price as they're paying for it now? I haven't.

But perhaps the benefit offered in the advertising of a new brand isn't obvious. Perhaps this benefit is the "protection" offered in the advertising of so many products, a quality visible only on the rare occasion when the product fails to protect. Perhaps the benefit is the "ingredient" story, which advertisers have used in an attempt to intrigue consumers for products as different as toothpaste, pain killers, and motor oil. Perhaps the benefit is nothing more than a clever demonstration, which can be done using a mature brand as well as the new one, but which the advertiser of the mature brand never thought of doing.

Can the advertising of a mature brand reassure its users that it, too, can demonstrate superiority over another brand, or that it, too, has the magic ingredient that guarantees results? Can the advertising of a mature brand reassure its users that it provides the invisible benefit of protection over a long period of time? It can try. But once it has lost its incumbency position to a new brand, a mature brand may find it difficult to regain this position with what many consumers will regard as a claim of parity, not superiority. The advertising of a new brand attracts the consumer's attention by intriguing her with what she sees as a different benefit. If she takes action to try the new brand, it will be because she likes this different benefit. Why should she believe the advertising of her current brand, when it tries to reassure her with this new claim, one she has never heard it make before, one she has never experienced while actually using the product?

Reassurance sounds easy. It appears to leverage consumer inertia. Isn't it easier to hold something in place than to move it? It certainly is. But we've been discussing a consumer who is already mentally in motion. She has discovered, and been intrigued by, the advertising of another brand. Her mind is no longer inert. It has begun its movement toward another brand. It may be too late to reassure. The task of reassurance is never as easy as it sounds. It's likely to be very difficult. It may be impossible.

Question #4:
What Creative Stimulus Will Trigger
Something Positive in the Consumer?

The instinctive answer to this question seems to be: "We have a great 30-second TV commercial, and a good full-page magazine ad." Perhaps most advertising people think that this is all the information a media person needs to know about a brand's creative output to construct an effective media plan. Or perhaps they assume that a media person has no right to question what it is in the advertising that will intrigue consumers about the brand. I've heard them say more than once: "This is really a copy question, not a media question, isn't it?"

Perhaps it is a question of copy. So what? For a media person to understand what he's doing while crafting the media plan, he ought to understand how and why the advertising is supposed to work. A media person also deserves the reassurance that others have done their work thoroughly before he commits time and energy to crafting a media plan. (This assumes that the media plan wanted for a brand is something more than fifty-two boxes, filled with numbers, on a flowchart. It assumes, perhaps too charitably, that brand management doesn't want someone's formula media plan pulled out of a drawer.)

But there are sins of commission as well as sins of omission. Some advertising people will answer Question #4 with such enthusiasm that they seem to be trying to build the skeletal media plan themselves, on the spot, and save media people the time, energy, and creativity needed to do their job. "Music is the most critical element in our creative executions. Young people will identify with the contemporary music surrounding our message, because it's their kind of music. So we can only use TV and radio." Thanks for writing my media plan for me! What about in-store sound systems, where you can also play your commercial's music? What about creating a mall event, or college campus events? How about running sound trucks through college towns, and through Ft. Lauderdale during the spring break? How about . . . ?

Like the other questions in this sequence, Question #4 should be answered, must be answered, in a way that stimulates and enlightens the entire group. Contrary to conventional advertising wisdom, the development of an effective media plan is a very difficult task. So many unknowns exist, including how the advertising itself works, that the group responsible for answers to these questions must help each other discover the best probabilities for success. This alone would be a remarkable accomplishment.

Sometimes the pre-planning group concludes that the creative stimulus which has already been approved (and sometimes even made into finished advertising) isn't the right one. Questions #1, #2, #3 either had never been asked, or hadn't been answered carefully before the advertising was created. We may even find that the creative strategy has been written in a way that doesn't allow the advertising (if carefully created according to this strategy) to make something positive happen in the consumer. More than one media pre-planning meeting has given new, clearer direction to the development of a brand's advertising copy.

Some Examples of a Creative Stimulus

Let's look at a few examples of what I call the "creative stimulus." Masterlock TV advertising has demonstrated the dependability of its locks for many years by firing a bullet into and through one of them. The locking mechanism remains intact after the lock has been all but destroyed by the bullet. Sears has demonstrated the dependability of its Die Hard battery in winter weather, simply by having it start five cars with dead batteries, all at the same time. The advertising of both Masterlock and Die Hard have left something positive in my mind, and in the minds of millions of other TV viewers.

Crest toothpaste, when it was endorsed by the American Dental Association (ADA) as having been proved effective against cavities, simply showed the ADA statement, in quotes, in its TV and print advertising. The statement was a powerful creative stimulus, because it came from the most authoritative source of information on dental care. The source was also an objective third party. It's statement was seen almost as a news release, rather than as a piece of advertising.

The creative stimulus used in the advertising for Crest was totally different in character from the creative stimuli used for Masterlock and Die Hard. The individual character of each creative stimulus can lead to different kinds of media usage. The commercials made for Masterlock and Die Hard are outstanding examples of *demonstration*; it's difficult to image this communication being done as effectively anywhere other than on television. The Crest example is *endorsement* by an undisputed authority. Crest was able to use the print media as effectively, if not more effectively, than television. The same seal of approval that appeared on its package was displayed for consumers to read, and absorb at their own pace, in print media.

Packaging as the Creative Stimulus

Many years ago, the Procter & Gamble Co. purchased a regional food company, which put them in the business of selling prepared baking mixes. As soon as P&G learned enough about this new business, they began testing a new Duncan Hines Deluxe Cake Mix, in areas of the country where the older Duncan Hines products weren't in distribution. At that time, other cake mixes, such as Betty Crocker and Pillsbury, weren't called "deluxe." In fact, cake-mix manufacturers were working to take costs down so that they could minimize the premium that consumers had to pay for the convenience of prepared mixes. P&G's test-market product instantly upgraded the visual quality of cake mixes at the supermarket shelf. The Duncan Hines Deluxe package was superior to existing products: the paper used to wrap the cardboard box was of excellent quality, and the graphics on the packaging paper were beautiful.

Something positive happened to consumers in the Albany test market. And it happened in the store, even before the advertising began. The creative stimulus (the dramatically better packaging) so intrigued regular cake-mix users that their purchases made Duncan Hines the number one brand in the basic cake-mix category, even before its first ad appeared. Television and print advertising quickly expanded this same communication to women who hadn't yet discovered Duncan Hines Deluxe Cake Mixes via the in-store communication from its packaging.

Later, when other mixes upgraded their packaging to be competitive with Duncan Hines, P&G continued to make something positive happen in the mind of cake-mix users, this time with a clever creative stimulus in its TV commercials. P&G had discovered how to fork a bite-size piece from a slice of cake without cutting through the icing. When the fork lifted the piece of cake, it pulled the icing, allowing it to stretch, break, and curve seductively from the fork. Even those of us in the P&G advertising department, who were screening a Duncan Hines commercial in a conference room, couldn't watch it without salivating.

Pricing as the Creative Stimulus

When Glade made its late entry into the solid-air-freshener business, our company pre-priced the product at thirty-nine cents, which was dramatically lower than the fifty-nine cent pricing for other brands in the marketplace. When it came time to start the introductory advertising, I was told to delay it. The brand was selling so fast that orders couldn't be filled. Glade Solid was by far the number one brand in the solid air-freshener category before its first commercial appeared on TV. Its price was all the creative stimulus needed to move the consumer to action.

In the years since Glade Solid's introduction, I've often told people, only half in jest, that I wish we had used nothing but skywriting (or matchbook covers, or portable sandwich boards) to advertise this brand. Had we done so, I could have "proved" that the most effective way to launch a new air-freshener was by using skywriting (or matchbook covers, or portable sandwich boards). My case history would have been a dramatic one, an effective one. I could have fooled just about everybody. Others are already doing it—with less convincing evidence.

A Verbalized Idea as Creative Stimulus

The creative stimulus may be nothing more than a verbalized idea, especially when delivered at the right time. Visualize a single parent—a working mother, tired at the end of a full day's work. She's not looking forward to cooking, cleaning up, doing laundry, and helping with her daughter's homework. Driving home, she hears a commercial on her car radio: she deserves a break today, and she nods her head in agreement. The words tell her to stop and let someone else take care of dinner for her and the kids. If she does stop, it will be because something positive has happened in her mind. The advertising will have done its job. The medium of radio was mandated by the creative stimulus. For this ad, other media might have been suggested: bus or subway cards, perhaps mall posters. But control of the critical timing of the stimulus would have been lost if one of these other media alternatives had been chosen.

Advertising Often Lacks a Creative Stimulus

Question #4 sounds basic, and easy to answer. It should be easy to answer. Anything important enough to make something positive happen in consumers (especially when communicated briefly in a torrent or other stimuli; especially when it deals with things as unimportant as the products they use in their daily/weekly/monthly routines) must be very obvious to its creators, mustn't it? No, it isn't always obvious. And it isn't always easy to answer. That's why so much ineffective advertising is wasting brand and corporate marketing funds. That's why the consumer's leisure-time environment is so polluted with unproductive interruptions in television and radio entertainment.

Too often a manufacturer has nothing more than another "good" product to offer consumers, who already have a choice of dozens of good brands of the same product. When this happens, the search for a creative stimulus that can make something positive happen in the minds of these satisfied and uninterested consumers is long, frustrating, and often futile. We're likely to see brands try to relate, inferentially, to the life-style of specific consumers, saying, in effect: "If you're this kind of person, you'll like this brand." Do intelligent advertising people really believe that our primitive herding instinct can be exploited for the benefit of any and every kind of civilized product?

We're likely to see or hear advertising with no meaningful content, ads that try to imply superiority by using wonderfully legal weasel words. "No detergent cleans better than _____." "No other antiperspirant keeps you drier than _____." "No polish shines brighter than _____." Or they will use this variation: "_____ is unsurpassed in its ability to relieve headache pain." Legally, these brands are saying nothing more than that they perform as well as an unspecified number of other brands. Not better. Just as well. Then why buy them? Can something positive take place in the mind of a consumer when she discovers that another brand performs only as well as the one she's now using? (Will she even discover it?) Why switch to a brand that can't say it's better than all others, or even most others, or at least better than the specific one she's now using?

What do these "as-good-as" brands hope to achieve with their advertising? Could it be that they expect consumers to misinterpret their claim to be not that of *parity* but that of *superiority*? This kind of misinterpretation would certainly be an effective creative stimulus. It would make something positive happen in the consumer's mind. It would also be *deceptive* advertising, no matter how "legal" it was.

In 1985, a new air freshener raised advertising understatement to a level that may never again be equalled. To appreciate this brand's effectiveness claim, you need to know that the consumer doesn't give solid air fresheners high marks for the duration of their effectiveness. These products are highly fragranced when first opened, but their scent diminishes over time. The experienced user of solid air fresheners doesn't expect a brand to perform very well after the first two or three weeks of continuous use. Thus, any solid air freshener that could claim to be as effective after being used thirty days as it was when first opened, would get the interested attention of consumers.

The new brand, which enjoyed such spectacular success in 1985, met the challenge of lasting fragrance with this remarkable understatement of effectiveness in its TV commercial: "It works for over a month, and is as effective day one as day thirty." You may want to reread this claim, to make sure you understand it as they wrote it. They are telling you that their new brand's initial performance is as effective as it will be thirty days later, a time when consumer expectations of freshening performance is very low, not high. Your current brand of solid air freshener works much better on day one than on day thirty. So day one isn't your problem. Day thirty is. If you understand the new brand's claim as written, why would you be interested in buying it? But then, perhaps you didn't read the claim as they wrote it. You may have understood it backwards. If you did, don't be embarrassed. You're not alone.

Another classic substitute for developing a better product is to claim, in advertising, that your brand does something that every other brand already does (the product form itself does it), but that no other brand has yet thought to claim. For example, hair conditioners are attracted to human hair by a minute electrical charge; hair is negatively charged, and conditioners carry a positive charge. Hair that has conditioner on it already has been neutralized, and won't attract additional conditioner. Thus, the advertising for a new conditioner can say that it has been formulated to condition hair "only where it needs conditioning." One new conditioner found a profitable place for itself in the market by using this very claim. All hair-conditioner users were already receiving the same benefit from their current brand. But they didn't know it, because nobody ever told them.

Yet another substitute for genuine product superiority is the "effective ingredient" stimulus, which is usually much more apparent in the advertising than in consumers' use of these brands. What is ignored by advertisers is that consumers have been well educated by their exposure to hundreds of thousands of advertising contacts over the last few decades. They're increasingly hard to fool. And almost as hard to stimulate.

Question #5:
What Is the Relative Value of Each Medium's Creative Executions for This Campaign?

Advertising people rarely seem to believe they can create with equal effectiveness in two or more media. A TV commercial is usually judged to be their most effective piece of creative work. They frequently ascribe great power to the medium of television, because of its combination of sight, sound, and motion. If they've happened upon a musical theme that excites them and their client, they may elevate radio to a position of parity with television, despite radio's lack of sight and motion. They may devalue their best print creative work to half of TV's value, or they may even claim that they can't communicate the brand's message effectively in print. (Some see nothing strange in denying all value to print ads for a brand that was created only after consumers responded positively to its concept test, which was executed exclusively in the form of a crude print ad.)

Assigning Communication Values
to TV Commercials

The strategic selection of media alternatives always deals with cost/value relationships. Even if a brand's message for its consumers can be communicated in only one medium, say television, advertising strategists must confront decisions on the relative value of different lengths of a creative execution. Does a 30-second TV commercial contain maximum creative value for the brand? If so, then this 30-second commercial is given a full communication value of 100. This decision simultaneously establishes that commercials of 45, 60, 90, and 120 seconds must also be given a value of 100. It further establishes, de facto, that there is no economic sense in using a commercial longer than 30 seconds in length. But the strategists must still decide on the relative value of a 15-second commercial. Is it precisely as effective as the 30-second commercial in communicating the brand's message (and making something positive happen, which will lead to consumer action that otherwise would not have taken place)? If the shorter commercial is precisely as effective as its longer version, it too receives a value of 100, which means that the 30-second version will be consigned to storage, and will not be used.

But let's assume that the 15-second commercial is less effective than its longer version. How much less effective is it? We must put a number on it. The words "less effective" are useless verbiage. If by less effective we mean an index of 25, we will never use the 15-second length. If we mean an index of 50, we may use the two lengths interchangeably. If we mean an index of 75, we may never use the 30-second length.

Assigning Multimedia Creative Execution Values

By bringing a second medium into the discussion of strategy, we liven things up immeasurably. Let's imagine a discussion in which the TV executions (30s/15s) were assigned values of 100/50. A value of 70 was assigned to a full-page magazine ad, and 50 for a half-page ad. Unless we tack qualifications onto these values, the full-page ad will never be used; the half-page ad, and the 30- and 15-second commercials, are interchangeable whenever media costs combine with the weighting of response functions to bring them into parity.

What usually happens next in this sort of session that is a review will be needed regarding the decisions that gave each creative execution the preceding values. Why? Because nobody will like the media plan that has been dictated by these decisions. The agency will want to use its 30-second commercial, exclusively, to begin the campaign. They also will want to use their full-page print ad. But wait. Weren't their creative weightings also what they wanted? At the time they made them, they thought the decisions were correct. But now that they see where these decisions are leading them, they "know" their decisions were wrong.

But hold on for a moment! How do they know their decisions were wrong? Well, the plan doesn't look like they think it should look. But how can they know how the total plan should look when they're unsure of the value of simple, individual components of this plan? The answer is that they can't. But they have preconceived notions of how a media plan should look, based on their years of "experience" in advertising. They have no preconceived notions of how the components should look, because they have little or no experience in evaluating components of their media plans. They want media plans to come out looking like they've always looked. Although they can't make logical decisions to achieve those plans this is rarely a deterrent. They would prefer to compromise their individual judgments rather than give up their vision of what a media plan should look like.

Creative Weightings Encourage Reasoned Thinking

Creative weightings, when arrived at honestly, prove to be an easy way to get rid of much of advertising's intellectual rubbish. When someone champions the use of two-page spreads in magazines because of their *impact*, ask this person to put a numerical value on impact. Simply ask this person to relate the spread to a single page with a pair of numbers. Can a full-page ad deliver the brand's message to its full potential of making something positive happen? If it can, the page gets 100, and "impact" gets laughed out of the room. If the full-page ad is given a value of only 80, our judgment has room to give a spread 25 percent more value (100 points). But a spread costs about twice as much as a page. So, no spread, no impact. In this case, impact would be a creative self-indulgence, with no responsibility to cost/value relationships.

Without question, it's difficult for us to assign defensible communication weights to all the creative components available to us. But the alternative is to assign creative weightings that can't be defended. Every media plan, by no device other than its own existence as a media plan, gives weightings to the components it uses, as well as to those it doesn't. A planner can't choose to run pages instead of half pages without having decided, explicitly or otherwise, that the page communicates sufficiently more to the same audience, or communicates the same substance to sufficiently more audience, to justify its higher cost. However, this decision is too often made arbitrarily, without having reached individual, reasoned decisions on the components of the plan.

Creative Weightings Don't Limit Media Creativity

Many people involved in the advertising process consider creative weightings to be an overly confining process. They see the plan as too mechanical, once they've provided numerical values for the creative product. But a media plan is ultimately "mechanical" anyway, whether they provide reasoned numbers or impulsive hunches for use in a final grinding of the numbers. Actually, creative weightings can be surprisingly creative in themselves, and at the same time adhere to the discipline of logical media planning.

For example, I've seen a magazine page given a creative weighting of zero, when exposure to the ad *preceded* exposure to the brand's television commercial, but a value of 85 when exposure to the ad *followed* exposure to this commercial. The assumption was that the ad thoroughly explained something that would have been of no interest to the consumer who had not seen the creative device used in the TV commercial. The consumer, therefore, would not have bothered to read the ad prior to exposure to the commercial. This is an extreme example; and perhaps the zero weighting was lower than it should have been. But it did ensure that a television exposure preceded—to the maximum extent possible—exposure of consumers to the print ad.

Variable weightings are often used within the confines of a medium itself. For example, a 15-second commercial is often given a low value when it's the first exposure seen by consumers. Its value is increased, in the planning process, for consumers previously exposed to the 30-second version. However, variable weighting confirms a dependency relationship between exposures in the pattern. If a 15-second commercial changes value for a consumer after that consumer has seen the brand's 30-second commercial, the two commercials operate as a related sequence, and they must be patterned as such in the media planning. We again confront a critical-interval problem: how long after exposure to the 30-second length can the 15-second version be delayed and still take from it what it needs to be effective?

We can search among our own experiences for clues that will help us answer this and other communication questions. For example, the first three notes of a well-learned melody will often evoke from our memory the whole song, even though we haven't heard the song for many years. On the negative side, we can forget the name of someone we once worked with casually for several years. The degree of interest in what we try to evoke seems to be important. Where there is a high level of interest or relevence, it seems easy to evoke, and vice versa. But what does this mean for your advertising? What your advertising says is very important and relevant to *you*, but is it for the consumer?

How to Weight Creative Executions That Evoke

Advertising exposures, when asked to evoke, have a totally different task than that of the basic creative stimuli. Instead of making something positive happen for the first time, these exposures evoke, or bring the memory of that experience to the surface of the consumer's mind, where it can become a staging point for the action that was not previously taken (purchasing the brand). A coupon can serve to evoke something positive for a brand that already has made this happen with its TV commercial or its magazine ad. An in-store media exposure can function in the same way. But so can a full-length commercial or ad.

Much, if not most, effective advertising works by evoking. Once something positive has happened inside a consumer's mind, as the result of an advertising exposure, all subsequent exposures (at least in the near term) evoke this consumer's experience. Read carefully through Herbert Krugman's famous paper[1] on how three exposures are enough, and you may conclude, as I have, that the third exposure is the one that evokes the consumer's original response, but at a time when action is, finally, possible. In Krugman's theory, the third exposure is a symbolic number, and can be the twenty-third actual exposure received. The number of the exposure is not really important, but its timing is.

Weightings for creative executions in media that serve to evoke have their own numerical scale; these numbers relate in no way to those for the basic creative stimuli. Weightings for creative executions that evoke are simple: they are either 100 or 0. An exposure can either evoke (100), or it can't (0). If in-store shelf cards can evoke the something positive which took place in the consumer's mind, they receive the same value as a 30-second TV commercial. Their selling value may be 0, compared with 100 for the TV commercial, but they are equal as evokers. A 7-second promotional announcement on a TV game show may be able to evoke the consumer's earlier response to a commercial or ad. If it can, this brief message can be given the same value as a 30-second TV commercial, but only for evoking, on the same show. It can be given the same value as a full page ad in *Good Housekeeping* magazine.

Advertising people who disdain the idea of using anything short of full-length commercials or full-page ads, will point out that their full-length creative execution performs the dual function of evoking that something positive where it exists, but also of stimulating this response where it has yet to occur. They are correct. And full-length creative executions should be used wherever the advertising task needs it.

This dual function may be required where consumers respond in small numbers to the full creative execution at any point in time, and when they tend to take immediate external action in response to this advertising. In this situation, there are few delayed consumer responses to evoke at an appropriate time for them to be carried through to a purchase. Full-length creative executions are needed here. But if large numbers of consumers have responded internally with something positive, and have not yet taken store-level action, there is little immediate need for more "selling." There is, however, substantial need to evoke those earlier responses.

The advertiser who buys a 30-second commercial on a TV game show simply to evoke an earlier response, is not using his money wisely; he could buy a 7-second promotional spot on the same show for less than 10 percent of the cost of this 30-second commercial. Media that can do no more than evoke are priced so low that they are ideal for their function, that of making contact with large numbers of "sold" consumers at the right time, in order to evoke an internal decision made many days or weeks before. To use expensive conventional media forms to do nothing more than evoke the results of a job already done reduces the number of evokers to a small percentage of what they could be. However, if you follow the discipline of assigning the proper creative weights to all media alternatives, simple media math will prevent you from making this expensive mistake.

Question #6:
How Is the Advertising for This
Brand Supposed to Work?

This question will stop most advertising people faster than an elephant gun at twenty paces. Some will stagger on, and answer, "But nobody knows how advertising works. You just know that it works. You've got to believe in it." Others will give you a practiced and polished statement to the effect that "Advertising builds awareness, and awareness generates trial and repurchase." Neither answer is satisfactory. Let us examine why they are not.

"But Nobody Knows How Advertising Works"

Perhaps nobody does know how advertising works. But then, how can a media planner structure a sequence of advertising exposures in a way that makes it work? The planner who doesn't know, but who is committed to developing a plan, must obviously guess how it works. Even the symmetrical filling of boxes on a fiscal calendar is a guess as to how it works. Boxes are chosen to be filled. Boxes are chosen to be left empty. The number of boxes filled, and the number that are left empty, are dictated by a guess at how much is needed in the boxes that are filled. And the number of boxes that are unfilled are dictated by a guess at the rate of decay in the effect of the advertising that was scheduled in each of those filled boxes.

Granted, the media plan will probably be discussed only in terms of how well it spends the advertising budget, rather than in terms of how effective it is in making the advertising work. But the physical plan—the piece of paper with numbers in boxes, along with words of media wisdom to defend them—is an implied statement of how the media planner guesses that the advertising will work. This implied statement, when examined critically, is usually discovered to be something as vague as "This advertising works by spending the budget efficiently, in some kind of symmetrical pattern during the budget year."

This isn't meant to be an indictment of the media planner. The planner was probably the lowest-paid member of the group attending the media pre-planning meeting. Account and brand management people were there. Media management people were there. These are the well-paid decisionmakers. Why did they plead ignorance about how advertising works, and ask the poor media planner to decide for them? This act of delegation is the biggest buck-passing in the advertising industry.

There's no pleading ignorance for anyone who wants to be part of the media pre-planning process. Anyone can say, "I don't know." But this statement must be followed by, "This is the way I think it works." Anyone who can't even think, or guess, how advertising works for the brand in his or her charge doesn't belong in the room, or anywhere in the planning process (or even in this business, if the decision were mine to make). Assumptions (guesses) must be made as to how the advertising works, or the media plan becomes nothing more than a piece of paper at which a group of people have thrown someone else's money.

Effective Advertising Does More Than Build Awareness

To return to the second answer we often hear to Question #6 ("Advertising builds awareness. . . . "), we see that our question wasn't answered with any information that could help media planners. Our original question needs to be rephrased: "How does advertising work to build awareness for our brand?" And additionally, didn't we give a more specific answer than "awareness" when we defined, in response to Question #3, the "something positive" that must happen in the mind of our consumer? We certainly did. We went beyond simple awareness to intrigue, which we said resulted from discovery of something with a news-like quality. Most brands are tried by far fewer consumers than are aware of them. Most likely these are consumers who have gone past the stage of awareness to what we have labeled "intrigue," for lack of a better word.

We hope our pre-planning group will now stop being evasive, and will confront their responsibility for coming up with a theory of how advertising should work for *this* brand, in *this* product category, at *this* point in time. The use of specifics (*this* brand, and so on) can't be given enough emphasis. Advertising probably doesn't work in the same way for a toilet-bowl cleaner as it does for a diamond ring, or for a trip to Hawaii. It can't be expected to work the same way for the tenth, or twentieth, or thirtieth brand in a category as it did for the brand that created the category. It can't be expected to work in the same way for a brand purchased weekly, or monthly, as it does for a brand purchased annually, or only once in a lifetime. "Advertising works by building awareness" is, at best, just another verbal narcotic. At worst, the simplistic claim belongs with the weaseled claims of brand parity, which hope to be misunderstood to mean more than they can legally support.

Let's explore the line of reasoning mentioned earlier. I said that the only justifiable advertising is advertising that makes something happen, something that would otherwise not have happened. To make something happen, advertising must deflect the consumer's action from where it otherwise would have taken her, to where the advertising wants her to go.

How Advertising Works for a New Brand

If our brand is a new one in an established category, its advertising will try to influence her to substitute our brand for her usual brand the next time she goes to the store to buy this kind of product. If our new brand has found a "niche" in which it outperforms the consumer's usual brand, effective communication of this superiority, at the correct time, will presumably work to intrigue the consumer with the idea of getting better results from our brand for the product's intended purpose. But what is "effective communication?" And what is the "correct timing?"

Effective communication is probably nothing more than establishing, in the mind of the consumer, the believable possibility that our brand is better, in some way, than the one she currently uses. However, we should be realistic in our appraisal of how difficult it will be to establish this superiority. Is the consumer overtly dissatisfied with her current brand? Is she waiting eagerly for a new brand to come along? Or is she reasonably satisfied with the brand she now uses? Will the advertising have to make her "fall out of love" with her current brand before she accepts the promises of our new brand? Is she really aware of the "problem" addressed by our brand in its advertising, or must she use her current brand after exposure to our brand's advertising in order to recognize the problem?

Advertising for a new floor cleaner, Clean 'n Clear, told consumers that it dissolved "clear" in the bucket, to leave the floor, after it dried, looking cleaner than other brands did. To support this claim visually, Clean 'n Clear advertising showed that other cleaners made their wash water "cloudy." However, few users of floor cleaners would have thought of their wash water as being cloudy, even though it was. But after seeing Clean 'n Clear advertising, women were expected to notice, the next time they cleaned their floors, that their wash water was indeed cloudy. This made a product-usage occasion part of the working of the brand's advertising.

Clean 'n Clear's side-by-side demonstration was irrelevant to those who had never observed that their wash water was cloudy. These consumers had no reason to be intrigued by a new brand whose advertising offered to solve their problem, because this problem didn't yet exist for them. But after seeing Clean 'n Clear advertising, and having been cued to the "cloudiness" of their current brand when they next cleaned their kitchen floor, consumers needed again to see this advertising to learn the name of the brand that had alerted them to the problem, and could solve it for them. Thus, the media plan was constructed in a way that would provide consumers with an exposure immediately before and after a usage occasion—a media "sandwich," with a product-use occasion in the middle.

The Bounce Story: A Study in Effective Advertising

Contrast this working of advertising with how advertising presumably worked during Procter & Gamble's introduction of Bounce fabric softener. At the time of Bounce's introduction, women were adding liquid softener to the rinse cycle of their washing-machine's sequence. Some machines had an automatic dispenser for fabric softener. But most women were required to time the rinse cycle so that they could manually add softener at the right time for it to coat, smoothe, and soften the fibers roughened by the cleaning process. In other words, they had a real problem. Advertising didn't have to create one, or even cue women to its existence. They knew they had it.

A year or two before the appearance of Bounce, we had attempted to capitalize on this opportunity to solve a real consumer problem (having to run back to the washing machine precisely at the rinse cycle, stop it, and add fabric softener). We introduced Rain Barrel, a liquid fabric softener which could be added with the laundry water at the beginning of the wash, and which "worked" in the wash cycle. Rain Barrel quickly tapped the interest of consumers who wanted to avoid an extra trip back to every washload just to add fabric softener. The brand achieved an early market share in the 10 to 15 percent range, respectable for a category dominated by P&G's Downy.

However, the use of Rain Barrel required consumers to change from their habitual sequence of loading the washing machine to one required for the proper functioning of this product (first water, then fabric softener, detergent, clothes). Also, the cost per usage of Rain Barrel was about double that for Downy. Both factors limited and discouraged use of Rain Barrel to solve the problem of getting fabric softener into the consumer's washer at the right time.

But then came Bounce. Bounce's advertising task was both clear and difficult: make consumers understand that their dryer, not their washer, was now the place to soften clothes. And perhaps even more difficult, Bounce advertising had to explain to them that what looked like a small paper towel could effectively soften a dryer load of clothes. The makers of Bounce had neither the need, nor the desire, to create dissatisfaction with the consumer's current brand of fabric softener, which for most users was P&G's own profitable Downy.

Many women were waiting to try a new fabric softener that would eliminate their rinse-cycle problem. They showed, in their response to Rain Barrel, that P&G could also expect Bounce's ease of use to attract new users, and make the fabric-softener market itself grow. And there was yet another factor working for Bounce. Fragrance ("smells so clean and fresh") is an important benefit offered by fabric softeners. Heat increases the amount of fragrance released by perfume. Thus, a fabric softener used in the dryer "communicates" its fragrance benefit at a higher level than a softener used in the washing machine.

Bounce's advertising task was to intrigue women with how easy it would be to use their dryer to soften the wash, but another task was to assure them that something resembling a small paper towel could provide all the softening benefits they received from a washing machine filled with liquid. P&G decided to demonstrate how the Bounce sheet touched all the clothes in the dryer: they photographed the process. The TV viewer was shown a Bounce sheet weaving its way over and around the tumbling clothes, as though it were determined not to miss touching any of them. For benefit assurance, P&G chose to use the testimony of ordinary, unbeautiful people.

The Bounce commercial sounds like classic formula P&G advertising, and perhaps it was. But this introductory commercial, in its sixty seconds, attempted—and probably accomplished—more selling than any commercial that has ever won an award from industry insiders for its creativity. The commercial's format was deceptively simple: on camera is Roy's mother, who has discovered Bounce, a convenient new fabric softener that works in the dryer. (As she talks, she casually tears off a Bounce sheet and throws it in the dryer.) She explains that, as Bounce touches Roy's polo shirt, it makes it really soft. (As she talks, we see, as though inside the dryer ourselves, a Bounce sheet weaving its way around the tumbling clothes.) The commercial then cuts to Roy and his father; the father repeats the benefit "Hey, Laura. Roy's polo shirt is really soft!" The same sequence of visuals is repeated twice for these benefits: "controls static cling," and "smells clean and fresh."

Laura than tells us that Roy's teacher used a liquid fabric softener, so she told the teacher about Bounce. Roy's teacher then comes on, and goes through the identical sequence of claims, during which the tumbling-clothes demo is repeated, for her daughter Ann. In this segment of the commercial, benefit repetition is provided by Ann herself ("My cotton shirt is really soft, my tights don't cling, things really smell fresh"). Thus, the three basic fabric-softener benefits are each stated/supported four times. The visual that shows Bounce weaving its way through tumbling clothes is on screen six times. "Convenient/easy-to-use" are mentioned twice, and are demonstrated twice, for a total of four support points.

Most theorists would say that Bounce needed frequency of exposure to explain how this unique product worked, and perhaps to overcome consumer scepticism about its ability to provide all the benefits of a liquid, in-wash fabric softener. I'd change "frequency of exposure" to read "repetition," because I think the theorists are looking for a teaching effect. I don't think they're looking for opportunities to coincide with sporadic occasions in the life of the consumer when she can be sold a new product. If repetition is what was needed for the advertising to have been effective, Bounce certainly seems to have had all the repetition it needed in a single, 60-second commercial. After only one exposure, most consumers could probably have taken a quiz on Bounce, and have answered any question that a potential buyer might have asked. The media planner working on the Bounce account should have been directed, by this kind of thinking, to build a plan that reached as many women, as infrequently as possible, at any limited point in time.

Bounce's media-planning issue was not that of how many exposures of its commercial were needed to communicate effectively with the target audience, but (1) how long the effective communication from a single exposure (of its repeated copy points) would last before it decayed, (2) when the next exposure should be scheduled for consumers, and (3) what reminder stimuli could be used to assure that the consumer would execute her mental decision to give Bounce a try the next time she needed a fabric softener, or perhaps the next time she shopped for staples. The Bounce commercial was, in its packed sixty seconds, an "introductory flight" in itself. Anyone who said that Bounce needed frequency of exposure didn't appreciate the functioning of the repetition that was packed into these introductory sixty seconds.

P&G could have split Bounce's sixty seconds into two, self-standing 30-second commercials. For the same budget, it could have doubled the frequency with which consumers saw one of its Bounce commercials. But would it have taught any better by putting dozens, or hundreds, of other people's commercials between the repeated communication elements? Why do so many advertising people claim that they need frequency in a short time span of days or weeks, yet react with horror at the idea that they control this repetition (which they carelessly call "frequency") by putting it into a single, longer message?

The Misconception of "Sustaining" Advertising

Planning media for new brands is relatively easy, even though the advertising of these brands works in ways different from that which we usually hear in the superficial discussion of most media plans. But established brands are undeniably difficult to plan for. They certainly are if you hold fast to the principle that advertising can only be judged to be effective when it makes something happen that otherwise would not have happened had the advertising not taken place.

How, for example, is "sustaining advertising" supposed to work? If the product is an impulse item, that is, one that's not in routine or ritualized use (such as detergents, toilet paper, ground coffee, and so on), perhaps no purchase would have been made of the product category had the consumer not seen its advertising. Let's say it's for an infrequently eaten Chinese food, or a prepared dessert mix. The advertising may truly sustain a consumer's interest in using or buying the product category, as well as the brand. But use of the word *sustain* for ritualized products is another case of inappropriate language. Dirty laundry, not advertising, sustains the sale of detergents. Marketers of ritualized products use "sustaining" in a manufacturer-oriented sense, without thought of consumers. The consumer will buy detergents, whether or not she sees advertising for them. A manufacturer may assume that his brand of detergent needs advertising to keep consumers buying it. But does he? How does the advertising work to make this happen?

If Cheer detergent has done a fine job of cleaning my wash for the past four years, what will make me change brands? A bad performance by Cheer on new fabrics, or a change in my living situation? A price deal on Fab, which I used before Cheer? A new detergent which has found an esoteric niche for itself? Whatever the reason, how will Cheer advertising, with nothing to say that I don't already know about the product, address these other situations in a way that will prevent me from deserting the brand?

If Cheer advertising has news, it won't sustain my interest in the brand, but will modify this interest, will elevate it. The effect on Cheer sales may be to sustain them in their totality, but the advertising won't be sustaining in its effect. It will be introductory, both in its character and in its effect on users of detergents. This "news" advertising will only sustain Cheer sales if these sales are in the process of declining; the increment contributed by the new advertising will offset what's being lost somewhere else. Without an offsetting decline taking place, the news from Cheer should make the brand grow, not sustain it. On the other hand, if Cheer's advertising leaves me with nothing more than I knew or felt about the brand before being exposed to the advertising, I won't be resistant, or impervious, to competitive advertising.

Sustaining advertising often means "preemptive" advertising, and should be called such when it is. Advertising that deflects a consumer's interest from switching to another brand is really preemptive. A consumer who is susceptible to being switched often can be given the switching stimulus first by the advertising of her current brand, and thereby be discouraged from switching to the other brand. When a new brand comes along with a "magic ingredient," other brands in the category are likely to add the same ingredient if they can, and as quickly as they can, in order to preempt interest in the ingredient by their users, thereby sustaining sales to those users.

In conventional media planning, sustaining advertising always follows introductory advertising. Implied in this practice is the belief that a product's performance can't, by itself, lead to repurchase; can't sustain continued purchase by the consumer. We should always challenge self-serving, but unsupported, beliefs of this kind. Often, that which has been labeled "sustaining" advertising serves only to sustain the revenue of the advertising agency, as the brand continues to communicate redundantly to its users, long after its legitimate advertising task has been fully accomplished by the copy and media plan created for this purpose.

In summary, use of the word *sustaining*, like the use of other verbal narcotics, allows the planners of media, and the creators of copy, to stop short of strategic thinking, and rest on their imaginary accomplishments. Manufacturers who accept this level of performance from advertising and marketing people, deserve what they get in return. Usually nothing.

Question #7:
What Pattern of Exposures Best Executes
This Theory of How Advertising Works?

You can see, from this question, why the pre-planning group needed to reach agreement on a theory of how advertising works. Obviously, one can't select a pattern of advertising exposures (the skeleton of the media plan) to execute a theory that doesn't yet exist. Of course, it's done on paper every day. But it only happens on paper.

One of the instinctive responses to the question of how advertising works is that it "teaches" consumers. Teaching is believed to require repetition, which becomes *frequency* in advertising jargon. A teaching pattern of three media exposures is easy to visualize, as in figure 6–1.

Searching for the Effective Time Interval

What isn't easy, when you try to understand the communication process, is choosing the time interval between these exposures.

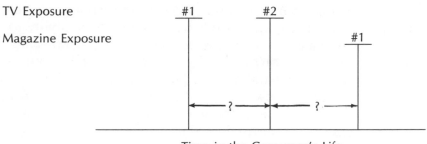

TV Exposure

Magazine Exposure

Time in the Consumer's Life

Figure 6–1. *A Teaching Pattern of Three Exposures*

During our early pre-planning meetings, participants betrayed how thoroughly their reflex responses were tied to the calendar. Unanimously, they wanted to schedule exposures in weekly boxes. They first chose exposure intervals of one or two weeks. But two weeks between exposures often created "hiatus anxiety." A compromise interval of ten days was chosen next, even though it created another kind of anxiety by not fitting between the vertical lines of a calendar (or a flowchart, as we know it in media terms).

But even greater anxiety was created by using common sense to cross-examine the respondents. The teaching sequence had three exposures, placed, at best, one week apart. This meant that the 60 percent of women who account for 85 percent of total television viewing would see an average of about 750 other TV commercials between each commercial in the brand's teaching sequence. Can a consumer's thought process flow, in any kind of cohesive sequence, from a brand's first commercial to its next one, with 750 other TV commercials sandwiched between them? And don't the multitude of other media exposures during the week (radio, magazines, newspapers, outdoor, in-store, and so on) also make it unlikely that what is not taught by exposure number one, or number two, will not be taught by number three?

When we considered advertising to be a teaching process, one that required three exposures to teach, we effectively devalued to zero the first two exposures. Nothing was expected to happen until consumers were exposed to commercial number three, or until they were "taught." This created yet another anxiety. We debated the idea of moving the three exposures closer together. If consumer learning from our teaching depends on the consumer's ability to make a mental link between exposures one and two, and then between two and three, won't this linkage be easier if the commercials are closer together rather than farther apart?

To bring exposures close together, however, creates still another anxiety. A calendar contains fifty-two weeks. A budget year spans fifty-two weeks. Few advertised products can afford to contact a mass market fifty-two times a year. Thus, if three exposures are scheduled for the consumer in one of the fifty-two weeks, other weeks will be empty. Hiatus anxiety returns.

But the pressure of logic prevails. We really don't want to put hundreds of exposures for other brands between the three in our teaching sequence. How close together must ours be? Our discussion then shifts from the use of weeks to the use of days. And then, once we have committed our three exposures to the same week, once we have learned to endure the stress of hiatus anxiety, we can swashbuckle into a discussion of having only *hours* between exposures. And before we're even aware of the danger, we find ourselves discussing exposure intervals of minutes!

Now we find ourselves beginning to talk about putting more than one exposure on the same television program. At first, we gingerly offer to schedule two commercials on a program. Then someone will point out that this won't allow us to complete a three-exposure teaching sequence. A reflex response will be to schedule a third commercial later the same evening. But an astute media person will probably volunteer that audience turnover, from program to program, will prevent many viewers from seeing the critical third exposure.

Then a very sharp media planner will point out that program viewers leave the set in large numbers, from time to time during the show, usually during commercials. If one-third leave the room during the average commercial break, only two-thirds will see the first commercial; only two-thirds of these will also see the second; and even if the third commercial is on the same program, only two-thirds of the viewers of commercials one and two will also see the third. Multiplied, only 30 percent of the women watching the program will see all three commercials. If we schedule three commercials in the same break, we increase the coverage of our teaching sequence from 30 to 67 percent of women watching the program.

Isn't this a ridiculous way to schedule our television commercials? Certainly it is. Yet this is where the logic of the teaching sequence leads us. If we really need to teach the consumer by using repetition, and with material that won't fit into a 30-second commercial, we should learn from the Bounce example. We should ask our creative people to give us a longer commercial, with enough internal repetition to teach within the controlled timing of a single exposure.

However, long commercials create hiatus anxiety. They reduce the number of boxes that can be filled on the flowchart. Even worse, long commercials reduce the number of GRPs in the media plan. And this means that they raise the overall cost per thousand of the target audience reached by the media plan. What do they offer in return for all these negatives, negatives that threaten to put the account in jeopardy? Nothing more than sound theory, defensible logic, and probable effectiveness. These values obviously have no place in advertising—or so it seems to someone who has looked for them in this industry for the last thirty-seven years.

How Advertising Might Work at All Exposure Levels

Does all this criticism mean that the teaching sequence of exposures must be discarded in favor of another theory of advertising? Not necessarily, according to its supporters. The teaching sequence, they say, can be modified to allow it to work at all levels of exposure. The assumption is made that some consumers are quicker to learn than others, because of their higher level of attentiveness, their superior communication skills, their greater need for the product being advertised, or their being more familiar with the brand itself. Thus, some consumers are assumed to be taught, and to respond after the first exposure, others after the second, still others after the third, and so on.

Advocates of the S-Curve-response to advertising were the first to volunteer a set of exposure values. But in their theory of consumer response, little is expected to happen after the first exposure, say 10 percent or less. Little more can be expected from the effect of the second exposure without losing its *S*-shape. Thus, these people offered no solution to the problem posed by the need for three exposures in close proximity. Advocates of the *S*-Curve really were aggravating the problem rather than solving it.

However, proponents of the geometric, or convex, response curve arrived on the scene in time to save the day. The geometric curve is nothing more than a diminishing-returns curve. Advertising that works on a geometric curve stimulates more response by its first exposure than by its second, more by its second than by its third, and so on. A tabular version of geometric response to advertising exposures might have numbers similar to those in table 6–1.

If this is the way our advertising works, planners don't have to force multiple exposures into a short period of time. Where exposures one and two were thought to have no value, independent of being made effective by a third exposure, a planner was encouraged, by logic, to buy multiples of three exposures on the most efficient TV shows. The first two had no value without the third. They each had 33 percent value after the purchase of one more commercial. The value mathematics were unassailable.

A geometric response curve reverses the buying strategy. Each successive commercial purchased on a TV program has less value than its predecessor. Two commercials might be an efficient buy, but if the consumer encounters a third (and possibly fourth) exposure a few days later (on another program), a third on the same program would render these later exposures redundant and therefore financially wasteful. The geometric response also seems to take some of the pressure off putting commercials in close proximity. If one exposure can effectively commuciate with a large

Table 6–1

Exposure	Percent Responding	Cumulative Response
1X	40%	40%
2X	30	70
3X	20	90
4X	10	100

segment of a brand's target audience, perhaps we can theorize that consumers who need more than one are close (psychologically) to effective communication after the first exposure. The residual effect of each commercial may be stronger, and longer lasting, than was assumed in the dogmatic theory that "nothing happens until the third exposure." (If you find flaws in our early theorizing, feel justifiably proud of yourself, and remember that the industry has given us little to build on.)

But How Much Time Can Be Allowed to Elapse Between Exposures?

Still to be addressed is the need to place a finite dimension on the interval between commercials, so long as any relationship between them is assumed. To receive a second exposure, a consumer must have received, and retained, a first exposure, or at least some critical elements of it, if the second exposure is to access and build upon it. If the effect of the first exposure has totally decayed, the second exposure is not really a "second" one. It is, in reality, a repeated first exposure, ready and waiting to be accessed or built upon by another exposure, which arrives in time to work with this second "first" one.

It is impossible to argue logically in support of an indefinite interval between exposures that have any kind of dependent relationship. It is difficult for anyone to defend a well-defined *long* interval between interrelated exposures. You can prove it for yourself by using the technique of offering expanding and contracting alternatives. Ask: "Will the effect of exposure number one be accessible for number two to build on after a year?" The answer will be, "Of course not." Ask next, "Six months?" "Certainly not." "Three months?" "No." "How about one month?" At this point, the negative response will probably come after a thoughtful pause. If a brand is using monthly media, such as magazines, a negative response to an interval of one month between exposures begins to put the squeeze on magazine selection and scheduling. But you still can expect a negative response. So keep asking your contracting questions. "Three weeks? Two weeks? One week?" Somewhere after one month, and before or by one week, you will probably reach agreement on an (assumed) effective interval between exposures that have a dependency relationship between them.

You will also have achieved—after going through this kind of exercise—a new level of awareness and understanding of how many different decisions can be made by a brand trying to communicate with consumers. You will also achieve the sophistication of assuming variable intervals between exposures in their sequence. For example, you may decide that the third exposure can have two weeks between it and the second, while the first and second can't be more than a week apart without losing some of the first exposure's effect, through memory decay.

Multimedia, Multiexecution Response Patterns

You'll need to have reached a modest level of sophistication before you can address the issue of how alternative creative executions (TV commercial versus magazine ad, 30-second versus 15-second commercial, full-page versus half-page ads) fit into the pattern of exposures to which you've finally assigned a time dimension.

To be able to choose, and to defend, an effective pattern of message exposure for one of your consumers, you must have answered, with some degree of understanding, two of the earlier questions. For example, suppose you've said that your television commercial dramatizes a problem that the consumer doesn't know she has, but that a full-page magazine ad is necessary to document the way in which your brand is able to solve the problem. Using this assumption about how your advertising works, you can give variable values to your television commercial and your magazine ad. The ad can be given full value (100) for every consumer who has previously seen your TV commercial, but only small value (say 25) for those who haven't yet been sensitized to the problem by your commercial. Similarly, the TV commercial, when not followed by the magazine ad, can be given only partial value (say 50).

In response to earlier questions, you could have decided that once a consumer has seen (first) a 30-second TV commercial, and (second) a full-page magazine ad, all further communication is evocative, and can be achieved by exposure to a shortened stimulus.

Fifteen-second TV commercials and half-page magazine ads are the shorter stimuli you've been able to create. You may have decided that these "evokers" have the ability to tap into the consumer's memory bank as much as a month after your full creative executions make closure between the consumer's problem and the solution offered in the advertising of your brand. Suppose you also have decided that two weeks' time is the ideal "evoking" interval. Figure 6–2 shows what your exposure pattern might look like in chart form.

When to Stop Evoking and Start Selling Again

Figure 6–2 is a snapshot of a single pattern of exposures. It doesn't address the issue of for how long the original closure can be evoked. Certainly, the process of evoking has a finite dimension, because it too has a dependency relationship between exposure to the full and to the abbreviated creative elements. Let's assume that consumer response to this full-length creative execution can be evoked

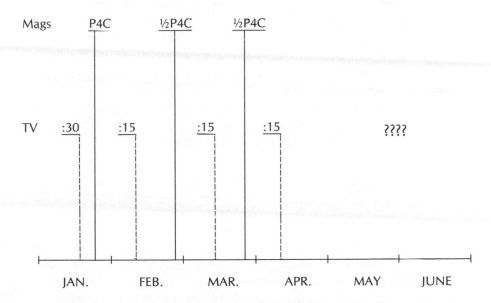

Figure 6–2. *Selling, Followed by Evoking*

for three months after it has made closure in the mind of the consumer. Three months have passed. The full-length creative execution should now be repeated in its original pattern, shouldn't it? Perhaps, but not necessarily. If consumers haven't responded to your full-sell message and exposure to three or more months of evokers, you have to ask yourself: "Why haven't they responded?" Perhaps these consumers weren't sufficiently stimulated by your television commercial. If they weren't stimulated the last time you made effective contact with them, maybe most of them, possibly all of them, won't be stimulated this time either.

In a similar turn of logic, if the interest of these consumers was stimulated by your television commercial, but they weren't given adequate substantiation for purchase by your magazine ad, exposure to the same ad will probably leave them unsold again. To justify repeating the original full-creative cycle, one of three things must change: the TV commercial, the magazine ad, or the consumer. Mixing the same chemicals that failed to give you an explosion the first time will give you no bang the second time, either.

What should be apparent by now is that you can't continue to advertise effectively without knowing how and why the consumer is responding, or not responding, to your patterns of exposure. The number and variety of media exposure patterns are close to being infinite. We can't choose accurately from among them without learning when and how the consumer responds to the patterns with which we (and others) have tried to stimulate her. Prior to acquiring this feedback from consumers, we have no choice but to wrack our brains mercilessly for what seems, to our results-impoverished minds, the most logical choice.

Relating Ad Exposures
to Nonadvertising Stimuli

Advertising exposures don't have to relate to each other in order to create effective patterns of communication. Certainly, there must be a relationship of some kind to create an effective pattern, but not necessarily between advertising exposures themselves. We've just examined an imaginary triangle of consumer, TV commercial, and magazine ad. We can as easily envision a triangle of consumer,

TV commercial (or magazine ad), and the consumer's purchase occasion. The purchase occasion can be split into the need to purchase the product category, or a price incentive that transforms an otherwise wasted exposure into an effective one.

Some advertising people see their promotional pricing as a tiebreaker for the consumer who has received advertising of equal effectiveness from two brands. But we can see how an advertising exposure could function as the tie-breaker for a consumer who has been offered promotional pricing of equal value for two brands. Figure 6–3 shows how this kind of advertising would be scheduled.

The Essential Communication Prototype

Whichever pattern we select as the one most likely to be effective, it becomes the prototype for the multimillions we will massproduce in the components of the recommended media plan. If the pattern is wrong, it will be mass-produced wrongly by the

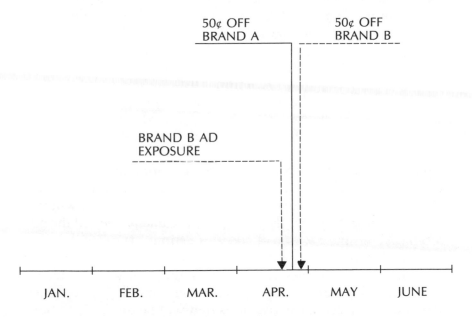

Figure 6–3. *Advertising Exposure Scheduled to Function As a Tie-Breaker*

millions. If the pattern is ineffective, the best media buying won't make it effective. Extra spending tests won't make it effective. The exposure pattern must be reasonably correct if it is to work at all. To work at full efficiency, it must be precise. When we plan with as little knowledge as we have about the effectiveness of alternative patterns of message exposure, we shouldn't be surprised that there is so little effective and efficient advertising in the United States today.

Engineers build working prototypes. Prototypes are tested to see if they function according to their theoretical specifications. For engines, automobiles, aircraft, and missiles, a working model is always made and tested, refined, and retested before quantity production is authorized. But a communication pattern goes into advertising's mass production without ever having been tested. Even worse, the communication pattern is rarely subjected to any theoretical analysis before it is thrown together and approved for mass-production, in the form of a media plan. If automobiles were built to the standard of media plans, they couldn't be driven off the assembly line. No, that's too charitable. They couldn't even be assembled from the parts provided.

Question #8:
Are There Differences Among
Targeted Consumers That Might
Affect the Media Plan?

Up to now, we've been examining how to communicate effectively with a single consumer. If we've done our work diligently and honestly, we have (1) correctly identified the action that will take place in response to our advertising; (2) accurately selected the pro-totypical consumer who will take this action; (3) precisely stated what must happen in the mind of this consumer to stimulate the identified action; (4) described in detail the creative stimulus that will make this happen in the consumer's mind; (5) accurately weighted the specific creative units that will be used; (6) thought through, logically, a theory of how our advertising is expected to work for this consumer; and (7) carefully outlined the pattern in which the creative executions will be used to make the advertising work as effectively and efficiently as possible.

It hasn't been an easy job, even for those of us who have done it dozens of times over a span of more than five years. But we've found it possible to do because we've simplified the process. We've dealt with a single, prototypical consumer. But what if there are different kinds of consumers, different in ways that could significantly affect our media planning? And there may be. To make the point as clearly as possible, let's look at an exaggerated example.

Ethnic Variations on a
Target-Audience Prototype

My target audience is women between the ages of twenty-five and fifty-four. But my target is *all* women in this age group, including Hispanic women. Immediately, you can see my problem: I have a potential language barrier. My 30-second commercial was given a value of 100. But that index value assumed that the commercial was trying to communicate with an Anglo consumer. In fact, I tested this commercial using a research audience with no Hispanics in it. The Anglos understood it, exactly as I had hoped they would.

But the symbols I used in this commercial were as American as the classic car commercial that sang out "baseball, hot dogs, apple pie, and Chevrolet," in their loose, idiomatic approach to communication. Most Hispanics will "receive" them like a joke without the punch line—even those who have learned to speak the English language. I have a problem. My strategic answers were to questions that ignored the issue of advertising to Hispanic consumers.

But the solution to my problem may not be all that difficult. I need Hispanic creative executions, and I need to give them a series of creative weightings similar to those I developed for my Anglo creative execution. I may also need to adjust my pattern of advertising exposures for the Hispanic market. If their consumption is paced differently from the Anglo segment of this market, and if my exposures were patterned to triangulate with purchase occasions, Hispanics will require a modified pattern. Or, perhaps these Hispanics are not as aware of the problem my brand solves as are their Anglo counterparts. If they're not, my creative executions will have to address this issue. My exposure pattern for this Hispanic creative may also be different.

Need Variations on a Target-Audience Prototype

Now let's examine some of the more subtle differences among consumer needs. If my product solves a dry-skin problem, consumers most sensitive to a dry-skin condition are likely to respond more quickly than the rest of the market, or not at all. They're either waiting eagerly to find a product to solve an acute problem, or they've already made enough effort to solve it. The latter are likely to be satisfied with, or resigned to, what they're now using.

The "evoking" period for this special consumer group will be shorter than for the market as a whole. The intensity of their need should make them less likely to postpone store action after they've made a decision to try a brand of skin lotion. The experienced users among them may need a sequential variety of creative stimuli before responding to the solution my product offers. This need could modify my media scheduling: nurses' magazines might receive different selling ads, and fewer or no "evoking" ads, than general women's magazines. Nurses wash their hands more often and therefore would be more prone to dry skin.

Geographic Variations on a Target-Audience Prototype

Geographic differences among consumers are commonly used in media planning, but often only in a crude, manufacturer-oriented way. Decisions can be as primitive as to spend more money in an area where category or brand sales are generally higher. But to be able to plan effective media, based on geographic differences, we need to know why sales are higher. If more consumers are using the category, but no more frequently than elsewhere, we know that the path to higher volume is through reaching more consumers at a specific point in their purchase pattern.

On the other hand, if consumers are using and purchasing the brands in this category more often, we won't need to reach as many of them to build our sales volume. And more purchase occasions are there for our advertising to intercept. However, a little thinking reminds us that a consumer who uses more of any product than other consumers is getting an accelerated education in product satisfaction. This more sophisticated consumer is less likely than the average user to be won over by advertising that is mostly style, and with little substance for a more critical viewer, reader, or listener.

How the Consumer's Age Disrupts Audience Targeting

Consumer sophistication isn't limited to the frequent user of a product category. Given enough time, the average user of most product categories ultimately becomes a sophisticated user. In general, older people are wiser than younger people, not because they're more intelligent than younger people, but because they've had more opportunities to make mistakes and learn from them. Product usage probably works in the same way.

An average user, at the age of forty-five, has had twenty more years of making product mistakes than a comparable user at the age of twenty-five. Whether you need to experiment with five brands or ten brands to settle on one that satisfies you, you're more likely to be at the point of satisfaction at the age of forty-five than you were at the age of twenty-five. This is why products can target their advertising to an older age group (a heavy-user demographic, for example), yet find that their highest rate of trial occurs among younger age groups.

I worked on the media plan that was used to introduce a hand and body lotion several years ago. Because women thirty-five and older are the most frequent users of hand and body lotion, the media plan was targeted to this age group. The copy also was written to appeal to this target. But after the introduction was completed, marketing research discovered that the highest rate of trial was among women eighteen to thirty-four. The same thing happened to a new hair conditioner for "overworked hair," which was presumed to appeal to women thirty-five and older, who had the highest incidence of "overworked" hair. After the brand's introduction, its trial also was found to be highest among women eighteen to thirty-four. That doesn't seem to make sense, but it really does.

In general, the easiest consumer to influence with advertising—which is no more than a symbolic, or substitute experience with a product—is the consumer who has the least *real* experience with which to counter the claims of the advertised brand. This novice consumer is also less likely to have sampled a sufficient variety of brands to be confident in her choice of which brands to use. The category entrant is truly a "soft touch" for the hustler of new business, in any category. Think of the adolescent female, who tomorrow will discover the need for a feminine hygiene product. Think of the adolescent male, who tomorrow will face himself in the mirror with razor in hand for the first time in his life. These are fish in a barrel, to be shot by the advertiser who wants less sport and more fish.

But now think of these adolescents fifteen years hence. The adolescent female has become an experienced user of many feminine hygiene products. The adolescent male has shaved three to four thousand times, with several different brands of shaving cream. The advertising that was so salient for these consumers fifteen years ago will have disappeared into the wallpaper pattern that unimportant advertising becomes for mature consumers. By now, they're both reasonably satisfied consumers. It's going to take advertising of substance, for a brand or product of substance, to get them to try a brand they haven't already used.

Question #9:
What Is the Timing
of the Advertising's Effect?

Since much of what is done in the name of advertising is planned and executed in a way that it should not be done, it's not surprising that the subject of timing also is usually looked at from the wrong end. When advertising people discuss how to time a campaign in broadcast or print media, they inevitably worry about when to start the first commercial or ad. They try to link the start of their advertising process with an event, for example, a promotion, or the achievement of adequate distribution by a new brand, or the first surge of seasonal sales in the spring or fall.

They may have said, previously, that nothing happens until the consumer has been exposed to three exposures, yet they will fail to plan to deliver that third exposure when distribution is right, or when sales begin their seasonal surge, or prior to the biggest week of the promotion. Instead, they will plan to *start* the advertising at the very time that the completed effects (of their three desired exposures) are needed to make the advertising fully effective—by their *own* definition of effectiveness.

We really must pay more attention to the date by which advertising's effects need to be completed, when advertising should *stop*, rather than to when the advertising should start. If in doubt, a brand should err in being too early rather than too late. If the effective exposure reaches a consumer after she has already made her one annual purchase of insect repellent, no action will take place at the retail level this year. If the exposure occurs a week, or two weeks, earlier than the strategically ideal time, there is still a possibility that it will influence a consumer purchase. The consumer's memory for low-interest product advertising may be short, but to be late is to fail even to challenge that memory.

Good media planning synchronizes the effect of advertising with the effects of interdependent marketing activities; it then plans backwards from this intersection, and schedules exposures needed to achieve the completed advertising effect on the consumer by the time this intersection is reached. Let's say that a new brand wants to send consumers into stores looking for it when its all-commodity distribution reaches 60 percent. Advertising people must determine how soon before 60 percent distribution is reached they need to begin delivering exposures, in order for a significant number of consumers to have been brought to the point of action by that time.

The Power of Accurately Timed Advertising

We so often hear of the importance of timing in advertising that we begin to think of the phrase as a cliché. But it isn't. Timing may be the single most important word we need to understand in this business of advertising. To be the second good brand in a new product category may be to have failed, while the first brand has prospered. To have delivered a solution to the consumer before she knows she has the problem, while a competitor delivers his solution right after she discovers she has a problem is to have done everything else right and still fail. To "evoke" for too long is to have lost the ability to evoke effectively; to "evoke" too briefly is to spend marketing funds wastefully. Few if any brands have such enormous advertising budgets that they can spew out a continuous stream of exposures for consumers. It must be decided, for virtually all of them, when an exposure should be delivered, and when large time gaps should be left between these occasional exposures. Well-conceived timing strategies must direct where these exposures are placed in the life of the consumer if they are to be effective.

In a 1987 planning meeting, I first thought of asking the following question regarding a brand that was targeting users of a leading competitor for its advertising: "Can your advertising exposures be made more or less effective by their coinciding with, or by their avoiding, the advertising or promotional activity of your competitor? In other words, will your exposure be more effective when your competitor is not advertising, or when he is not promoting, than when he is?" The answer was yes, it would be more effective, especially when the competitive brand was not promoting. Price promotions were judged to be very effective for the competitor. An advertising exposure for our brand was judged to be much less effective, or even ineffective, when its competitor was feature-priced. Our brand's media plan was then structured to time its limited number of exposures to reach consumers when the targeted competitor was not promoted, was at full price, and would be more vulnerable to the influence of our brands' advertising.

It takes a lot of hard thinking, logical thinking, even creative thinking, to ferret out strategic timing issues. But the effort must be made. Accurate decisions in this part of the planning process often are the key to success or failure of the media plan itself. Later in this book, a separate chapter will provide examples that highlight the critical importance of timing.

Question #10:
What Is the Media Budget?

This is a simple question. But its answer isn't always simple. Often there are qualifications. "If our re-stage copy is successful, we'll have another million dollars to put behind the re-stage." So the budget can be larger than a simple answer would indicate. And it can be smaller. "We can't commit our last five hundred thousand dollars, because we may need them for profit protection. You can put them in the plan. Just don't commit the money." But suppose Plan A depends for its success on that five hundred thousand dollars. And suppose Plan B's more modest goals can be achieved without this money. Which plan should the agency recommend?

The answer to a simple budget question is rarely simple; if a simple answer is given, it is frequently inaccurate. An unqualified statement of budget often is discovered to have been overstated, after the agency has invested many hours of work in the development of a media plan. Or the budget is discovered to have been understated by a product manager who has been keeping money in a reserve fund, in order to protect his profit goal, and didn't share this information with the agency. The revised media plan may look more like a camel than a race horse.

If any restraints have been placed on committing the media budget, this understanding should be made clear at the inception of media planning. It can make a difference in the kind of plan the agency offers as the best one for its client's money. Alternative plans are best evaluated before a media plan has been approved and is partway through its execution. Revised media plans are little different from doing the job twice, or three times, or more. A business doesn't move forward efficiently by doing the same task over and over again. The right budget questions can help eliminate some of this wasteful backtracking.

Question #11:
Is the Media Budget More Than Needed,
or Is It Less Than Optimum?

This question will put a sarcastic smile on the face of many advertising agency account managers. We're likely to be told that there's never enough money to do the job that needs to be done. We're cautioned to remember how high inflation has driven the price of the advertising we use, especially TV. Nor should we forget how *cluttered* media has become, and how much it takes to break through this clutter. We're told how much other brands are spending, and how little our *share-of-voice* really is.

"No," we're told by these advertising people (who generally receive a percentage of what is spent in advertising media), "we certainly don't have more to spend than we need." We shouldn't even ask if any of these media dollars could be spent more productively in a public relations campaign, or in a consumer promotion. We shouldn't even ask if any of the money would be more effective if spent in media the following year (by horse trading across fiscal barriers with another brand). Every media budget is either "just right," or, more likely, "less than needed" for whatever advertising task is at hand.

But if the budget is truly less than needed to accomplish the task at hand, does this mean that the money will be wasted if spent. Whoa! Of course not! That's not what they meant to say. What they meant is, "The task will merely have to be reduced in scope. We'll do an effective job, but our advertising will influence fewer consumers than it would if we had more to spend."

Not necessarily true. I don't think this conclusion need be accepted yet. All we've agreed to is that the budget is not more than can be well spent in media, and that it is, in fact, less than optimum for achieving some kind of measurable business response from consumers. This is where the advertiser must begin to play a game of mental chess with his advertising agency.

Use and Avoidance of Leverage in Advertising

Have we explored all possible ways of achieving *leverage* in the communication process? Are we planning to "sell" at points in time where it is still possible to evoke the effects of earlier selling exposures? Are we planning to use our 15-second TV commercial to do no more than evoke these earlier effects when we could use promotional spots on TV game shows to perform the same function at a fraction of the cost? Have we arbitrarily decided on a full-page magazine ad when equal communication can be achieved by using two-thirds of a page, or when we can communicate effectively at a lower level, but more efficiently, in half-page ads?

You'd think that advertising people would be dedicated to the pursuit of leverage for their clients who have media budgets that are less than optimum. But they're usually not. Another conflict of interest, in addition to the destructive commission system of compensation, works against agency productivity. The kind of creative execution used for leveraged media is not "beautiful." It certainly isn't the kind of execution with which an agency would try to impress a prospective client.

A game-show card would look foolish, and out of place, in an advertising agency's new-business presentation. But this modest card may be the best way to leverage part of a brand's media budget. By playing its modest role of evoker, it may lead to more client sales than the same money spent on TV commercials, of any length. But what does it do for the agency?

In-store advertising may efficiently provide the critical last exposure which makes the whole campaign work, the exposure that stimulates the consumer action without which none of the advertising could have been justified. But what does it do for the agency? It will never be part of a new business presentation. What advertiser would be impressed by a dinky little card that shows nothing more than one picture and eight short words? And to rub it in, some short-sighted clients are likely to classify in-store advertising as a form of promotion, with the intention of denying their agency a media commission on this form of advertising, even when the in-store creative piece is a shortened form of the agency's current campaign.

Full-page ads look more impressive to people inside the business than do fractional pages. Two-page spreads look even more impressive to them. Thirty-second commercials look better than fifteens on an agency's presentation reel. And life-style 60-second commercials look even better. But what looks good on an agency's presentation reel is almost guaranteed not to be a leveraged creative execution. For the agency, perhaps it is, but not for the advertiser.

An advertiser will almost always have to ask for leverage in his media plan, or he won't get it. The other way is easier, and of more value to the agency in ways which don't necessarily serve the needs of the advertiser. And, perhaps most compelling of all, the other way is safer. Whether or not a brand's business is affected significantly by its advertising, the advertising will probably be blamed when something goes wrong with the business. The agency that has used large, conventional creative executions for a brand with business problems is better able to defend itself than an agency that has departed from convention to leverage a brand's inadequate budget.

Depressing, isn't it? Other words that come to mind are *destructive*, and *unproductive*. But this is how it has been in the advertising business. And this is the way it will continue to be until there is real and honest accountability in the function of advertising. But accountability requires consistent and accurate measurements of advertising results, and we don't have them. What's worse, we don't see any interest in obtaining these measurements. But that's why we have Question 12!

Question #12:
How and When Will the Working of the Advertising Be Measured?

We've already established that nobody knows how advertising works. But we also concluded that no media plan or creative campaign can be constructed without some assumptions as to how this specific advertising should work. If our assumptions are structured from a logical sequence of reasoned conclusions, we can call this our theory of how advertising works, or at least how it should work for this brand, at this point in time.

But after the media plan has been executed, when the advertising budget has been fully spent, did it really work? How will we know unless we measure it? If we don't know how advertising works, every campaign we execute will be a test of the theory on which the media plan was built. Do we run tests without measuring the results? The question sounds absurd, but it isn't, because this is what we do—tens of thousands of times a year. Virtually every advertising campaign is an *unaudited test market*.

Think about it for a moment. No manager of advertising would authorize five hundred thousand dollars for a test-market campaign if no research were budgeted to measure the results of the test. But the same manager will approve a media plan costing five million dollars, even though there is not one cent budgeted for research to measure its results. He will trust his judgment, or experience, to evaluate how well or badly the advertising has performed. Yet this same manager will know no more how advertising works, or how it actually has worked for this brand, than anyone else in this business. He may know the jargon of advertising evaluation well enough to sound qualified to judge the effect of the advertising. But we could grant him the same capability for evaluating test markets, if we were to use this logic.

Hundreds of thousands of advertising campaigns have taken place during the years I've worked in this business. If 10 percent of them had been measured with any degree of accuracy, by now we'd know precisely how advertising works. If even 1 percent of them had been measured with any accuracy, we'd be infinitely more knowledgeable about how it works than we are now. But during these last thirty-seven years, advertisers have skillfully avoided learning anything important from these hundreds of thousands of advertising "tests."

The Art of Not Measuring Advertising Results

Much managerial skill is used to justify *not* measuring how well a brand's advertising has performed its function. "We can't afford any research. We need all our budget for media. We're already being outspent by competition." These words are from a manager who thinks he's being careful not to "waste" advertising dollars on unproductive, nonmedia expenditures.

Or we're told, "There are too many variables that influence the success or failure of an advertising campaign for us to measure the contribution of the advertising itself." It's remarkable how these many variables prevent any measurement of how well the advertising has performed; but these variables do not prevent the manager of the advertising function from using his judgment or

experience to perform a definitive measurement of this same advertising's performance.

Then there's the manager who rejects measuring the results of
his or her advertising on these grounds: "The information will be
inactionable by the time it becomes available," because yet another
campaign will already be in the works. The short-term manager
never seems to worry about his or her successor. I guess the feeling
is that having to work under the handicap of advertising ignorance
is something that should be passed from one manager to another
(and let the brand fend for itself in the process).

On the other hand, it might be that most of these managers are
skillfully avoiding an objective evaluation of how well or how badly
they've done their job of putting together an advertising campaign.
Their skill in avoiding this report card for their advertising on such a
broad-scale basis may be serving them very well. If most results would
have been judged to have been bad, the managers have avoided blame
and criticism. They've obviously furthered their careers by suppress-
ing the learning process. But if results had been judged good, these
results would have served to enhance the career of these managers.

The overwhelming vote not to measure results suggests an overwhelming belief that the measurements would have been negative
rather than positive. Well! The managers of advertising have been
surveyed, in a manner of speaking, and they have voted overwhelm-
ingly against the probability of success for their advertising! If you
don't like this reason for their refusal to measure the results of their
advertising, choose one of the other lame, unprofessional excuses.

The Consequences of Not Measuring
Advertising Results

If we don't measure how well our advertising has done what we
have so laboriously determined it had to do, we'll repeat our efforts during the next budget year, with no more knowledge than
we have now. And will next year's media plan succeed? It may, if
this year's plan has been a success. Ah, but we don't know whether
it has been a success or a failure! Which means we won't know
whether next year's plan should be constructed in the same way
or in a totally different way.

It should be obvious that without feedback from the results of our advertising efforts, there's no way to verify success or failure, and no way to learn more than we know now, and no way to improve upon what we've done in the past. It should also be obvious that an industry that keeps itself in this condition of perpetual ignorance, of perpetual amateurism, is an industry that can't contribute constructively to an economy that is under pressure from global competition. How long can we tolerate it? Will you tolerate it through yet another media plan?

**The Questions That Must Be Answered
Before Work Begins
on a Media Plan[a]**

1. What consumer action must result from exposure to this advertising?

2. Who is the consumer who will take this action?

3. What "something positive" must take place in the consumer's mind to lead her or him to the designated action?

4. What creative stimulus will trigger something positive in the consumer's mind?

5. What is the relative value of each medium's creative execution for this campaign?

6. How is the advertising for this brand supposed to work?

7. What pattern of exposures best executes this theory of how advertising works?

8. Are there differences among targeted consumers that might affect the media plan?

9. What is the timing of the advertising's effects?

[a]As mentioned earlier, these dozen questions summarize the thinking process of one career media person. A more advanced media theoretician will be able to refine them, or reorder them, or add to them, or whatever. Think of them as being a minimum effort, and build on them from there, in whatever way you can.

10. What is the media budget?

11. Is the media budget more than needed, or is it less than optimal?

12. How and when will the working of the advertising be measured?

7

The Development and Approval of Media Plans

Y ou can expect, from what you've just read, that a meeting
dedicated to answering the twelve S*I*M*P*L*E questions
would be neither perfunctory nor short. It should last at least two
to three hours, no matter how experienced the participants, or how
well prepared they are to answer the questions. For advertising
agencies new to this questioning discipline, initial meetings have
lasted about twice as long, or four to six hours. A few marketing
and advertising people complain that we spend too much time "trying to answer theoretical questions for which no answers are
known." But these same people will demand that others spend
ten times this number of hours to revise media plans that haven't
been preceded by a thorough session of pre-planning. Worse yet,
when these complainers are allowed to circumvent the discipline
of a good pre-planning meeting, their final media plans are usually
little more than overrevised nonsense.

I mentioned earlier that there's nothing magic in my twelve
questions. If any magic exists, it's in what happens when responsible marketing and advertising people ask themselves enough difficult questions about how their advertising works. As you've seen,
all my questions are easy to understand. Their answers are fundamental to the process of effective and efficient media planning.
There's no way that an advertising agency can recommend an effective, efficient media plan without having been given accurate
answers to these twelve questions, or their equivalent.

Yet, until the last few years, these questions were never asked
in a serious, structured way. Even today, they aren't asked outside

the leading-edge media groups working in the Chicago offices of Foote, Cone & Belding Communications and the J. Walter Thompson Co. Stranger yet, these agencies can't use their superior planning skills for all their clients. Why not? Because an advertiser gets what he wants. If better planning produces media plans that look too different from the advertiser's preconceived notions, the agency probably won't be allowed to use its improved planning. Sometimes a pre-planning meeting is intentionally avoided, with predictable results. Here's an example that predates the development of my S*I*M*P*L*E discipline.

The Media Plan That Never Was

Over the last quarter of a century, the Benton & Bowles advertising agency (in today's merger land, it is known as D'Arcy Masius Benton & Bowles (DMB&B) has earned and kept the reputation for having an outstanding media department. Some years ago, Benton & Bowles worked on our furniture-care and air-freshener brands. One winter morning, they arrived in Racine with an armload of large manila envelopes. I was surprised to learn that these envelopes contained a media plan they were about to recommend for one of our furniture-care brands. Why was I surprised? Well, we hadn't met to discuss advertising strategy and whatever else we routinely covered in our crude pre-planning meetings. Apparently, time was growing short, and someone had made the decision to write a media plan based on the assumptions provided by the agency's account management.

They were about to open the envelopes, as we met with the marketing group, when I asked if they would first brief me on what the media plan was expected to accomplish for the brand. I also asked the brand manager for his thoughts on what was being said during the briefing, so that I'd have an agency-brand consensus with which to evaluate the media plan. We worked our way through about thirty minutes of questions and answers, at the end of which I said, "Thank you, I think I now understand well enough what we're trying to do. Let's look at your media plan."

The media planner, who was standing at the end of the conference table, with the manila envelopes in front of him, looked around the table at the people from his agency. He looked down at the unopened envelopes. Then he looked up and said, "I don't think I want to show you these plans." The marketing people didn't understand what was happening. They looked toward their account manager for answers.

The account manager cleared his throat, then spoke "Based on what we just discussed in this room, I don't think our media plan is exactly what you want. I think we have to go back to New York and rework it." And so they did. We never saw what was in those envelopes. There was good reason for us not to see it. The media recommendation, put together by an outstanding media department, had not been given the direction needed for it to be the right plan for a brand with the advertising objectives we had just discussed. That was the only time in the twenty-five years I worked as a client of Benton & Bowles that I saw their media department embarrassed by the work they had done. I liked and admired these people, and I hadn't enjoyed embarrassing them. But I knew I'd had to. They never skipped a pre-planning meeting again.

How a Pre-Planning Meeting Becomes a Good Media Plan

Not having a pre-planning meeting may guarantee our getting a bad media plan, but having a meeting doesn't guarantee us a good one. We have to ask the right questions. We have to ask the difficult questions. And when these questions are answered, the media plan often begins to evolve right there in the pre-planning meeting. An experienced media manager can't avoid allowing his thoughts to leap ahead, and begin to visualize the shape of a media plan, as he participates in the discussion of how the brand's advertising is supposed to work, of the brand's effective exposure pattern, of the relative values of each medium for the brand's copy, and so on.

I've always found it easy to evaluate a media plan that has evolved out of a good pre-planning meeting. The reason is simple. I've left the meeting with a media plan already partially written in my mind. If the agency brings back a recommendation that improves on this plan, I receive it with enthusiasm. If the media recommendation matches the plan in my head, I accept it with token questions that try to communicate: "Isn't there any way you could make this just a little bit better?" If the media recommendation appears inferior to the plan in my head, I look for the differences, and ask questions about them.

If it's easy for me to evaluate a media recommendation that has been pre-planned thoroughly, it's equally easy for the agency's media group to construct this media recommendation. They have no unanswered questions on advertising goals, or media strategy, or copy values. Every question has been asked and answered in the pre-planning meeting. All nonmedia input needed for the plan has been extracted from the client's marketing people, and from the agency's nonmedia people attending the meeting. Professional media people are ready to do what they have been thoroughly trained to do: construct a media plan from a set of clear, complete, strategic instructions.

This is what *should* happen. It would be in the brand's best interest for it to happen. It would be in the brand manager's best interest for it to happen. But too often the brand manager (or, more likely, someone higher in the chain of marketing management) doesn't allow it to happen. Here's an example (from my personal experience) of the self-destructive manipulation of a media plan.

Destructive Manipulation of a Media Plan

In response to Question #5 (the relative value of each creative execution), one brand marketing manager gave his magazine ad a value of only 70, versus 100 for his 30-second TV commercial. He also decided that his brand's communication worked without the need for multiple exposures at any point in the consumer's purchase pattern. The recommended media plan, quite rightly, included a substantial amount of magazine advertising. Magazines, even when discounted by 30 percent for being less effective than TV for a specific campaign, are an efficient way to extend the reach of a modest television schedule.

The frequent viewer of prime-time TV is also likely to be a daytime TV viewer. A plan that extends the reach of daytime TV by adding a prime-time TV schedule keeps piling messages on top of these same frequent viewers. Because this brand didn't require (or benefit from) multiple exposures at any point in time, prime TV literally discounted itself enough to be a less efficient way than magazines to extend the short-term reach of the plan. The media experts at the agency understood this. Their recommendation was a logical and responsible execution of this understanding. But the brand marketing manager didn't want this much magazine advertising in his media plan! And he wanted prime-time TV! In his infinite managerial wisdom, he had constructed his own mental media plan. And it didn't look like the one the agency presented to him.

Ah, but the agency was able to defend its recommendation, using the brand marketing manager's own decisions, which had been reached in the pre-plan meeting and confirmed later in a jointly signed conference report. The agency's defense was brilliant. But it was also a waste of time.

The brand marketing manager simply reconsidered the way in which he had weighted his creative elements. He dropped the value of his magazine creative execution from an index of 70 to an index of 50. The agency people went home and did their job all over again, using the "new and improved" set of assumptions. A week later, they returned with a new media recommendation. But this one had more magazines in it than the first plan!

The brand marketing manager was beside himself. Initially, he thought that the new plan was a joke, something to break the tension of the meeting. When he discovered that his agency was serious, he became angry. "I told you I had revised my thinking on the value of our print ad, and took it down, not up." Yes, boss, you took it down. And so did they. And because they did, the plan quite logically calls for more print, not less. Here's how it works:

Your optimum pattern of exposures, as determined by your own strategic input, is accomplished with a combination of 100 TV GRPs and 50 magazine GRPs. The initial plan presented this combination to you. Then you discounted magazines, lowering them to an index of 50 from an index of 70, or by about 29 percent of their GRP value. The media group had to add more magazine insertions to get those GRPs back into the plan. You see, even at an index of 50, magazines are a more efficient way of extending the reach of daytime television than prime-time TV would be.

The meeting continued in a polite and subdued manner. Questions were asked. Questions were answered. The brand marketing manager confessed that the plan and its implications left him a little unsure of his judgments. He concluded by thanking the agency for its extra effort in reworking the plan, and by asking their indulgence while he "thought about it some more" before giving them a final decision.

The next morning I received a call, asking if I could meet with the brand marketing manager. I appeared in his office later that morning. He went straight to the point. "What do I have to do to get rid of magazines in my media plan, or at least get them down to some reasonable number? I just can't see having that much print in my media plan."

I realized that he understood that he was short-circuiting his own planning process, and that it would be a waste of his time and mine to lecture him about why this was a dumb thing to do. So I was candid with him. "If you want to get magazines out of the plan, you have to give your ad an index value of 25 or less."

A pained look came over his face. "I can't do that. The ad isn't a great one, but it's better than that. Tell me, what kind of an index number will get them to reduce the amount of magazines below where they had them in the first plan?"

I couldn't keep from smiling. Here was a manager who was trying to shoot himself in the foot, and asking me to help him aim the gun so he wouldn't miss. But I went along with him. "To reduce the number of magazine insertions from what was recommended in the first plan, you have to *raise* the creative index for your magazine ad from 70 to a higher number. For example, if you raise the index from 70 to 85, you raise the GRPs delivered by that schedule of magazines by about 20 percent, which means the number of insertions will be decreased proportionately, to keep them at the optimum level (100 TV/50 magazines GRPs). If you raise the creative index from 70 to 100, making it the same as TV, you'll give the magazine GRPs full value, or an increase of almost 43 percent over what was in the agency's original plan. This higher index value will require the fewest number of insertions to get to your goal of 50 magazine GRPs."

He finally understood how to manipulate the media plan to get the combination he wanted in the first place. He understood, but he thought there was something basically wrong with buying more of a medium after you gave it a lower value, and with buying less of a medium after giving it a higher value. I tried to explain that the lower value was relative to its own prior value, and that it didn't change magazine's ranking value relative to primetime TV. I also tried to explain that raising the value of a print ad was the same as raising the GRPs of all the magazines that carried the ad, and that this would enable him to reach his 50 GRPs with fewer total insertions.

Whether he understood the media logic or not was irrelevant. He now understood how to manipulate the plan, and that was all that he needed. He got the plan that he wanted, not the plan that should have evolved out of his own answers to the questions asked in the pre-planning meeting. The meeting had been rendered worthless for his brand. The media plan this brand received was the best hunch of its marketing manager, not the professional execution of his sound, strategic decisions.

How would you label this outcome? Ignorant? Arrogant? Irresponsible? Nonmanagerial? Any of these labels might seem appropriate to us. But not to many of the marketing men and women who practice this kind of advertising management. In many cases, it may be viewed as being not bad management but good politics. Up the line of marketing managements, there lurk many preconceived notions and managerial hunches as to what a good media plan should look like. Good politics may require that the lower manager bring in a media plan tailored to his boss's preconceptions. I've seen it happen many times.

Yes, the best pre-planning meeting can still lead to a very bad media plan. Good media people—not political, ignorant, arrogant, or irresponsible marketing people—must develop the media plan. Marketing people can, and should, give the media plan its strategic direction. If they answer my twelve questions carefully and honestly, they will have given their media plan the strongest, most confining direction it can be given. Intelligent as they are, they should have no difficulty understanding this. Yet they often do.

Destructive Manipulation of Media Plan #2

Here's another example from our sophisticated world of marketing. A high-level manager decided that his brand's advertising worked by coinciding with the problem it solved. He concluded that the advertising wouldn't work if an exposure preceded occurrence of the problem by any significant interval of time. This meant that the effect of the advertising was assumed to decay rapidly if it didn't encounter a consumer who was, at that specific point in time, experiencing a problem.

This brand happened to have a large share of market. In the opinion of this manager, this meant that his brand needed to reach a large percentage of the consumers who made up this market; it also meant that his brand needed to use prime-time TV. Daytime TV, he knew, could reach only a minority of consumers, and he was convinced that his brand needed to reach the majority of consumers.

The media people took his strategic direction seriously—and literally. His brand needed the maximum reach it could afford, but the brand needed this reach as often as possible. The effect of the advertising that reached its target audience during the first week was assumed to have decayed to ineffectiveness (in the manager's judgment, and in his confirmed direction) by the second week, or shortly thereafter. The building of high reach would require prime-time TV. But prime-time TV was so much more expensive than daytime television that it would, in reality, reach fewer targeted consumers, on a regular basis, than would daytime TV.

Quite logically, the agency recommended a media plan that included not one commercial in prime time. The client's response was brutal. How could they recommend such low reach of the brand's market? This was the leading brand. It needed leadership advertising, which meant, among other things, that the brand needed "leadership reach." The agency demonstrated, with hard numbers, that the brand would reach more sales prospects by having many low reaches rather than one or two high reaches. What good would it do, they asked, to reach the majority of the market once or twice, when only a few percent of category sales could be influenced by the effective duration of that high reach? Pure logic. Logic driven by the manager's own decisions. But acceptable logic? Of course not.

Frequent low reaches were not acceptable. The leader brand was given a media plan that gave it the leadership reach that was demanded, even though the effect of this high reach was not expected to influence more than 10 percent of annual sales. The high-reach number was shown as a "plan reach," although an objective critic would be likely to label it an *antiplan reach*, since it did more to violate the planning process than to flow from it, strategically.

You might legitimately question why a leading brand would be subject to decisions supported only by management hunches. Leading brands do research on the effects of something as important as their advertising, don't they? Well, not always. But this one actually did. However, the findings ran contrary to the hunches of the manager. For example, one of his line extensions had its advertising effects measured during and after its introduction. Months after advertising stopped, this new line extension had lost only 30 percent of the peak effect achieved during the early months of its launch period.

Other line extensions fed back similar information, and established a generality that contradicted the manager's belief in the instant decay of his advertising effects. What does he do in a situation like this? Simple. He stops approving budgets for advertising research. "It's getting too expensive. We've got better things to do with our advertising funds." And so ends the conflict between advertising research and managerial decisions.

When situations like this occur, I usually recommend that a professional pre-planning meeting should *not* be held. It would only serve to authenticate a nonexistent process, that of good media planning. It seems blatantly unfair to ask capable media people to author and sign a document that was dictated to them by someone empowered to make others accept his ignorance as wisdom. Let them, instead, label the document for what it really is: the client's best media hunch.

What Clients Must Do to
Ensure Good Media Plans

A brand or marketing manager who sincerely wants a good media plan has to do his or her job well. Components of a job well done are few, but important:

1. He or she must answer the pre-planning questions as thoroughly and as honestly as possible and be willing to search diligently for the best answer that can fill a factual void.

2. After he or she has answered all the questions asked by the media people, they must be allowed to construct the best media plan possible. He or she must insist that nonmedia people scrupulously avoid interfering with the planning process.

3. When the recommended media plan is presented, he or she must ask the media people to show how their plan evolved from his or her answers to their pre-planning questions.

4. He or she must identify unknowns that can have an important effect on the working of the media plan, and insist that, wherever possible, they be researched to find answers that will assure a greater probability for the success of subsequent advertising campaigns.

Media people always work under an awesome handicap when they construct a media plan. They simply don't know what an effective media plan really is. They have no way of assuring you, or even themselves, that their work is what it should be. How can they? There is no effective-plan benchmark against which to measure it. They've been taught how others plan, or have planned, media in the past. But their teachers have planned under the same handicap. In media, as in all advertising, the blind with experience have always led the inexperienced blind. They do their best, but they still give us as many descriptions of what an elephant looks like as the elephant has parts.

Pre-Planning, the Key Stage in Media Planning

The media pre-planning process has become, here in a small midwestern community, an advanced course in media planning for agency media people. These people have learned, in our meetings, how to plan media far better than they ever could before. They have been helped to new levels of understanding of their own profession by the dialogue that evolves from the incisive questioning process of the twelve S*I*M*P*L*E questions. For these people, pre-planning meetings have been, and will continue to be, seminars in the advanced theory of media planning.

In a sense, then, the media pre-planning meeting with the advertising agency and its client is not really "pre" at all; it's a vital part of media planning itself. Client marketing people who answer the twelve questions are a key part of the planning process. So are the agency account managers. So are any research or creative people who attend. They all help the media department develop the situational capabilities needed to create the best media plan that their combined intellectual talents can produce. The cumulative result of these enhanced situational capabilities is a more highly skilled media planner. The client manager who does his job well in the media planning process is doing more than getting a better media plan; he's getting better media planners. He's training better media planners for the future benefit of the brand being advertised.

The agency media department goes home with enhanced skills, after one of these pre-planning meetings. They will better evaluate major media components, they will crunch more relevant numbers though their computers, and they will discuss unexpected alternatives in a newly professional way. Answers to S*I*M*P*L*E have helped them become more professional. Answers to these twelve questions have virtually forced them to become more professional.

Comparing Disciplined and Undisciplined Agencies

They no longer think, for example, like the media department of a major advertising agency that worked on a brand we acquired a few years ago. I was shown, and asked to comment on, the annual media recommendation for this newly acquired brand. In support of the flighted media plan was a rationale that went something like this: "We subscribe to the industry-held belief that three exposures in a four-week period are necessary for the advertising to be effective."

Our media planners would shake their heads in disbelief at the naïveté of this statement. Their pre-planning meetings have taught them that there is no universal pattern of message exposure that can be used by all brands, at all times, for all purposes. They have learned that whenever a sequence of three is mentioned, the interval between these exposures is critical, and must be addressed. They have learned that four weeks is nothing more than a calendar cop-out. They have learned that only those consumers exposed to a brand's advertising can be used in media planning, never those exposed only to the media vehicle carrying this advertising, as was the case in this new agency's recommendation.

When our media planners go to work on a new media plan, they don't look at last year's plan. They don't look at plans they've done for other brands with the same advertising budget and the same target audience. They don't visualize a "known effective" pattern of advertising exposures that can always be used in one form or another. They look instead at what was discussed and agreed to in the pre-planning meeting—for this brand and its unique marketing situation.

They look at how its advertising is expected to work. They look at the number and pattern of exposures, and at the intervals between them, those that best express the theory they agreed to. They look at the relative value of each kind of creative execution and of each length of each type of creative execution. They look at the consumer's communication prototype, which they helped to construct during the pre-planning meeting, and at its subsequent confirmation. Then they take their first step into the unknown: they begin to create a unique media plan that will address this unique communication challenge.

Dealing with Patterns
of Overlapping Exposures

They know, for example, that media often scatter their consumer exposures over a broad expanse of time. Monthly magazines are usually shown on a media chart by entering a large X in the calendar month during which they appear on newstand. Or, to be precise, their X covers mid-month to mid-month, the period between the appearance of issues of the magazine. But different percentages of the magazine's total audience are "contacted" each of these weeks. And some of an issue's total audience contacts are made after the next issue has appeared on newstands. Our media people deal with patterns of exposures that need weekly data. They can't plan with monthly Xs. They can't combine a number of television GRPs with the letter X for magazines. They must work with magazine audience numbers, by the week, to construct their effective communication patterns.

They know that media exposures almost always overlap each other to some degree. A brand's next TV exposure will reach some consumers exposed to the last one. A magazine exposure will overlap consumers exposed to one in its last issue, or in another magazine, or exposed to a TV commercial. Conventional media planning can lump these overlaps together and call them "frequency" or "duplication." Our sophisticated media planners must be able to visualize these overlaps as different patterns of communication, each of which has a specific value. Plan A and Plan B may have the same average frequency, or even the same distribution of frequency, but the patterns within their overlaps may strongly favor those of Plan A.

Deflating Inaccurate Advertising Audiences

Consumer exposure to commercials or ads has never been measured. Media audience measurements, at the time of this writing, have been precisely that: audience measurements of the

media carrying the commercial or ad. Conventional media planning has always used, and still uses, these media vehicle audiences.
But none of them is accurate. They are all inflated. The use of
inflated audience numbers influences the kind of media plan an
agency develops. An agency will recommend a different media plan,
using media vehicle audiences, than it will using estimated audiences for its commercials and ads carried by those same media
vehicles.

For example, if a brand's optimum pattern of advertising exposures requires that its agency buy 100 TV GRPs before it buys
the brand's first magazine ad, the agency will think that the brand
has reached this optimum level after buying 100 TV *media* GRPs.
But the brand hasn't. To provide a level of 100 TV *commercial*
GRPs, the agency has to buy more than 100 media GRPs. The
agency must discount media exposures by some factor in order
to estimate the brand's (unmeasured) commercial exposure. Thus,
to have stopped buying TV at 100 media GRPs is to have started
buying magazines before the agency really wanted to. The same
would be true if the optimum pattern of advertising exposures
began with 100 magazine GRPs before buying TV. This would
be equally true if the optimum pattern called for 100 GRPs in
daytime TV before buying nighttime TV, or vice versa. The use
of media exposure will always overstate what a media plan is doing in its first media choice, and will lead the agency to put a brand
into its second media choice before it should be there.

These examples are the simplest to understand. The consequences of overstating a brand's communication achievements in
any and all media are numerous and complex. Conventional media
planning ignores these consequences, uses inflated audience
numbers, and provides clients with bad media plans. The excuse
usually is that there are no accurate measurements of exposure to
advertising. This isn't universally true. But even if it were, everything
else in this business of advertising is far from being accurately
measured. People in this business feel quite comfortable in
estimating just about everything but the audiences of their commercials or ads. Why not them, too?

This is exactly what our media planners are asked to do. And
they do it. We're absolutely certain that women who are reported

as watching TV for an average of ten hours per day (the heaviest-viewing quintile) don't sit for ten hours without leaving the room. We're equally certain that women who watch TV an average of seven hours per day (the quintile second in their amount of viewing) don't sit for seven hours without leaving the room. We're quite certain that women who watch TV for almost five hours per day (the middle-viewing quintile) don't sit through all the programs they supposedly watch fully, or in part.

These three quintiles account for more than 85 percent of total TV viewing. In other words, these are the women an advertiser reaches when he buys TV, and where 85 percent of his TV money is going, whether he needs it or not, whether he likes it or not. And these are the women who certainly don't watch the TV they are said to watch. Therefore, it isn't a question of whether or not media audience measurements overstate the size of commercial audiences. It's only a question of how much these media-audience measurements overstate the number of women who see a TV commercial.

No responsible advertiser can allow its advertising agency to use numbers that are known to be inflated, just because their inflated size is accurately measured. No responsible advertising agency can ask its client's permission to use these inflated numbers. To the contrary, agencies should be asking permission to use their best estimate of the size of advertising audiences. Advertisers should be delighted to throw away the inflated "real" numbers, in return for a more accurate estimated number. Their media plans will be more accurate if they do. Jules Fine, of Ogilvy & Mather Worldwide, has said it most succinctly and memorably: "It's better to be roughly right than precisely wrong."

Foote, Cone & Belding estimates the real audience of every piece of advertising in their media plans. A full-page ad will have a greater probability of exposure than a half page in the same magazine. The full page will have a greater probability of exposure in Magazine A than in Magazine B, depending on the product and its particular copy. A TV commercial will have a greater probability of exposure in one day-part than in another. And no media vehicle is given full exposure value for the advertising it carries.

Many people are intimidated by the quantity of numbers generated during the FCB exposure-weighting process. It can't be denied that this agency has carried the weighting process to an extreme that makes its gray areas more difficult to defend than a simple series of black and white adjustments. But by going further than solid information can support their data, the agency throws down the gauntlet to others: "Challenge our data! Show us something better, and we'll use it." Is there a better way to goad a lazy industry into making a small effort to find the numbers they should have been using for a decade or longer?

We have encouraged FCB to use their audience adjustments for as long as they've had them. Since the early seventies, we have asked all our advertising agencies to face up to the reality that no numbers representing the size of a media audience can be used at face value without distorting the media plan that uses them. We hope the industry will also begin to face the reality of smaller advertising audiences when advanced "people meters" can read movement in and out of a room during TV commercials, and when electronic sensors (worn by magazine readers) can measure exposure, and duration of exposure, to magazine ads.

Until then, good agencies will estimate advertising audiences for good clients. And if these agencies have obtained good answers to questions that are the equivalent of my S*I*M*P*L*E ones, they'll bring back good media recommendations for their good clients to approve. But how will these clients recognize a good media plan when they see it? There's no pat answer. No formula exists for guaranteeing a good media plan. But there are ways of improving the odds of getting one.

How to Recognize a Good Media Plan

I've already said that a good manager gives his agency all the answers needed to develop a good media plan. And I've said that he should ask the agency to demonstrate how its media recommendations evolved from these answers. If the agency can do this without resorting to head-spinning industry jargon, or verbal narcotics, the media plan is likely to be far superior to its predecessor. It's also likely to be far superior to most media plans, which are being paid for by billions of dollars that are spent in mass media today.

If the agency can defend its media recommendation without resorting to vacuous support words such as *balanced schedule, synergy, continuity, intrusive, competitive presence, impact,* or any of the other verbal excuses for not thinking, its recommendation is almost certain to be better than any media plan that needs these meaningless words to support it. A good media plan doesn't need verbal narcotics to recommend it. A good media plan has internal logic and common sense, which give us a feeling of confidence in its ability to succeed.

A good media plan demonstrates that it understands consumers to be real, flesh-and-blood people; and it is structured to encounter these real people at times designated to make something positive happen in them, something that wouldn't otherwise have happened. A good plan explains, in simple language that nontechnical people can understand, how each of its parts functions. Where needed, it shows how alternative media components would not have been as functional, or would not have functioned as efficiently, in order to perform the task outlined in the pre-planning meeting. A good media plan considers where it has been before, and where it is likely to be in the future. It can even reverse what was done for its brand the preceding year, and make everyone involved feel comfortable with both decisions.

A good media plan is the logical extension of the clear thinking that goes into a disciplined pre-planning meeting. But clear thinking must be permitted in these meetings, and some media departments aren't allowed to think clearly. Clients or account managers often ride roughshod over them. I've been in meetings where I could see anguish in the eyes of media people as they said things they themselves didn't believe in, things they knew were wrong for the brand. But they were taking an "agency position," meaning that they were doing what they were told to do by someone who knew little about media, but who had the power to impose his ignorance on those who were knowledgeable.

Lee Rich's Contribution to Media Planning

I mentioned earlier that the former Benton & Bowles agency has been known for its outstanding media department for more than a quarter of a century. It is less well-known that this reputation was given its original impetus by Lee Rich, well-known for his talent as executive producer of "The Waltons," "Dallas," and successful feature films; originally, Lee Rich was a media man. Lee was in charge of media and programming at Benton & Bowles during the early sixties.

Lee knew how good his media people were. He also knew that a lot of good thinking and hard work went into their media recommendations, and that they always supported these recommendations with persuasive facts and figures. He saw, on the other hand, that account managers, with no understanding of media, would sometimes ask the media department to change their recommendations to bend the way political winds were blowing.

One day, Lee did something that set a positive course for Benton & Bowles media during these last two and a half decades. One of the agency's account groups had just asked the media department to change its recommendation to fit their own idea of what would be best received by the client. Lee stalked into the account manager's office with the attitude of an enraged bull elephant. "Listen," he said, "We're not changing this media plan. It's a _____ing good plan. In fact, it's the only _____ing plan that makes sense for this brand. If you don't like it, go write your own _____ing plan. Subject closed."

Something wonderful happened to the Benton & Bowles media department after that day: it got respect, the respect it deserved. It built on that respect by attracting and holding some of the best media people in the business. And, in a real sense, helped to dignify the media function for all of advertising—thanks to Lee Rich. Agency media departments everywhere should celebrate a Lee Rich Day (by reenacting his blow for media dignity at an appropriate time), in return for what he did for them. He's earned it.

Why Most Media Plans Aren't Good Ones

Good pre-planning helps prevent the short-circuiting of good media planning through the exercise of management prerogative. A media plan created and recommended using a dialogue of verbal narcotics is easier to bend than one that has been tailored to address the specific answers to our twelve questions. A client can still misdirect the plan if he wants to, simply by giving answers that he knows will lead to the plan he wants. We can't prevent him from shooting himself in the foot. It's his gun. But if he answers the twelve S*I*M*P*L*E questions as honestly as he can, in the best interest of his brand, it will make nonmedia people work harder to interfere successfully with the development of a good media plan for his brand.

Perhaps I write too optimistically about the possibility of getting good media plans. Even when media professionals are allowed to do what they want to do, they face other obstacles in their efforts to produce a good media plan. The absence of known business results is perhaps the worst obstacle. It makes trial and error an exercise in futility. We can't correct our errors if we don't know when they occur. Ask any advertising agency what percentage of its media plans succeeded last year, and what percentage failed. They may look at you very strangely, as though this were a silly question to ask. What else can they do? They could explain to you how difficult it is to measure results. Or they could tell you how well most of their brands are doing in the marketplace. But these aren't answers to your question, are they?

They simply don't have an answer. They don't even look for an answer. Why not? Because nobody ever asked them this question before! Do you find this difficult to believe? You won't if you understand advertising. But if you do understand the thinking of advertising, you should also understand that a media department can't think clearly when trying to achieve an advertising goal if its people have no idea how that goal can be achieved. They need a set of precedents. What has worked before, with any consistency? Isn't there any information available? "Sorry, sir, nothing is available."

Media people are, in general, resourceful, persistent, and willing to work hard to prove their professionalism. But they are denied feedback on the performance of their plans; they are misled by their teachers; they are informed, selectively, by the sellers of media (who have provided, directly or indirectly, through their financial support, most of the industry's knowledge); and they are biased in their thought processes by ramifications of the commission system of compensation.

Perhaps the best way to illustrate this point is by showing some examples of how the same information can lead media people, with similar intellectual capacity, to draw entirely different conclusions from their data. The only real variable will be the learning, or the thinking bias, of the people looking at this information.

8
Discovering Mislabeled Media Values

R eal values can be distorted, or hidden from us, by the subjective values we ourselves place on them. This is true both
in our business and personal lives. Often our own prejudices and
preferences spill over into our work. Advertising suffers from a
similar spillover. Examples in media planning are easy to find.

Those Uncouth Weekly Tabloid Magazines

Major weekly tabloid magazines, such as the *National Enquirer*
and the *Star*, are read with great interest by millions of consumers.
These publications are priced low to advertisers, relative to their
audience size, making them an efficient way for many package-
goods brands to reach consumers. Yet they are conspicuously absent from the magazine schedules of most of these brands. Why?
Sometimes a good reason is given: the *Star* duplicates more with
TV than the magazines recommended by the agency, and
magazines are being used to extend the reach of TV. (But the *Star*
is probably a more efficient extender of the brand's TV audience
than some of the magazines on its schedule, even if the agency
had discounted all its excessive duplication with TV.)

Another good reason for not using the tabloids is because they
can't always reproduce a certain kind of ad at the level of quality
required for its success. (Sometimes a quality magazine on this
brand's schedule will also fail to reproduce the ad well enough,
on its cost-cutting paper stock. The tabloids, on the other hand,

will often test-print an ad where its reproduction is an issue, and will guarantee its quality if they accept an order after testing.)

A *bad* reason for not using the tabloids is that the advertiser has a quality product, and that these publications are not a quality environment in which to advertise it. What snobbery! See how it spills over from the personal life of these marketing and media people? They don't eat in fast-food restaurants, so McDonald's isn't a quality place to eat. They don't shop in the cheap mass-merchandisers, so K-Mart isn't a quality place to shop. They don't read romance books, so Janet Dailey novels aren't quality books to read.

But millions of consumers define quality in a way that differs from theirs. And often these are the consumers who buy the quality product of a snobbish advertiser. These are the consumers who determine what quality is or isn't, for everything they buy, including this advertiser's product. In marketing, quality isn't determined by PhD's in the laboratory. Susan O'Grady and other untitled consumers make the final decision on how good or how bad the product is. Often the two parties agree, but many times they don't. Researchers have been told by consumers, time after time, that a product that "proved" to be superior in their laboratory was really inferior to the consumer's current brand.

Consumers also make the final decision on the definition of quality in their media environments. If they like a tabloid, it has all the quality it needs to get them to part with their hard-earned money to buy it. What advertiser would refuse to sell his product to consumers who disagreed with him on what constitutes a quality media environment? None who hope to survive in the marketplace. Then why does an advertiser bring a country-club mentality to his place of business, and refuse to offer his product to consumers in their own environment, just because they aren't members of his imaginary country club? It doesn't make good business sense. But it happens every day.

Many media departments give the tabloids a misleading label because of their own prejudices. Others are forced to mislabel the tabloids by their account managers, or by marketing people who make demands from the client side of their business. But good media departments don't mislabel them. Good account managers don't ask for them to be mislabeled. Good clients contribute marketing expertise to the advertising process, and don't use their power to impose media mistakes on others who are capable of good media judgments.

Who Made "Syndication" a Dirty Word?

Syndicated television has become quasi-respectable during the last few years, but ten or more years ago it was definitely a dirty word. "Why is he buying all that syndication garbage?" I heard these words many times, usually through a third party. Most advertising agencies wouldn't put syndicated television in their media plans. Many wouldn't allow syndication to be an option for any of their network budgets. Some of them had a good reason for not wanting to replace network commercials with commercials on nationally syndicated programs.

Network coverage was national, and syndicated programs may have covered only 60 or 70 percent of TV households. These media people rarely, if ever, checked to find out if their national ratings were lower in the 60 to 70 percent area covered by the syndicated programs. Had they done so, they might have wanted to use syndicated programs to even out their audience levels. Subsequently, they have done this, with enthusiasm—on cable TV, once it grew to adequate size. Ironically, cable TV, at 40 percent national coverage, was accepted without qualification, whereas syndication was rejected, with disdain, by the same media people, at 60 percent national coverage!

Like the tabloids, syndicated TV programs were tarred with the back of the "quality" brush. "Low-rated junk programming," said one media planner. The same planner was observed a few years later looking for low-rated magazines to include in his media plan. He wanted to use some magazines that targeted specific audiences by virtue of their specialized, and limited, editorial content. He couldn't see how most magazine readers considered the specialized editorial of small magazines "junk" in terms of their own interests. Thus, syndicated programs were avoided because of their limited interest, but specialized magazines were sought out because of theirs. He passed up bargain pricing on syndicated TV programs, and paid premium pricing for the specialized magazines.

Low ratings justified avoiding syndicated programs for many years. "But it only gets a three or a four household rating." So spoke an indignant media planner, ten years ago. Today, the same planner packs his media recommendations with cable budgets for programs that will average little better than a one national rating. Now, he justifies the low coverage and low ratings of cable TV by labeling them "compensation for low network ratings in cable TV households." He's oblivious to the fact that his brand's magazine schedule delivers more of its audience in cable homes than in noncable homes, thereby compensating for his TV problem in these homes. He also neglected to find out, ten years earlier, if he needed similar compensation in the markets where the viewing of syndicated programs had reduced network ratings to below where he wanted them to be.

Some media people denied syndication respectability, on the grounds that these programs carried more commercials than network programs, which was true. Why, then, were some of these same media people the first to shoehorn more commercials into network shows, as soon as their acceptance of 15-second commercials made it possible? There has been no consistency, across the years, in what many media people have done, or believed in, or argued against. Yes, they were working under the handicap of being given inadequate information on the results of their work. Yes, they were given too much irresponsible direction, in the form of pressure and direct orders from account managers and clients. But good media departments were allowed to recommend syndication. Some were even encouraged to recommend it, but they gave it a different label, first in their own minds, then in their media documents.

TV Game-Show Promotional Spots

Everyone is familiar with the brief announcements that identify brands that have contributed prizes for participants on TV game shows. These 7-second spots allow a brand to appear on a TV

program for 10 to 20 percent of the cost of a 15-second commercial, the shortest standard unit of time that networks sell to
advertisers. You can say these spots are "the most efficient use
of TV available," or you can say they are "a virtually worthless
use of TV, which does little more than contribute to television's
increasing clutter." Which is correct? Which agency media department is more skilled, the one that considers game-show spots to
be "garbage," or the one that includes them in their media plans?

Actually, it was originally the advertisers, not advertising agencies, who became interested in these game-show spots. Agencies
were usually ordered to use them, or the advertiser himself con-
tracted for them directly with a game-show broker. The advertiser who had little to say, and not a lot of money to say it, assumed that he could at least establish his trademark, and perhaps
even some kind of consumer-benefit link with this trademark, if
he bought the many brief exposures he could afford on game
shows. Turtle Wax devoted most of its advertising budget to game-
show spots during the years it established its name with
consumers.

Other advertisers used game-show spots as "smoke" to cover
the fact that they were not advertising in conventional (expensive)
media. They could promise the retail trade that their brand was
"advertising regularly on TV," and still not be lying. They could
even add up the GRPs of the game-show spots, and give the trade
an impressive number. Or they could add the game show GRPs
to their regular advertising, and make it look larger than it really
was. They had little or no respect for the selling effectiveness of
these spots, even though they were an important strategic element
in their brand's marketing program.

Their advertising agencies obviously took no pride in this part
of a brand's advertising campaign. They didn't believe in it. They
hadn't recommended it. They sometimes didn't even participate
in creating the material used by their brands on these programs.
Under the circumstances, it's not surprising that they often labeled
game-show spots "garbage." On occasion, they may even have been
correct. But overall, they were wrong. Game-show spots, when correctly labeled for what they are, and for what they can do, are
the most efficient way to perform specific communication tasks.

For example, let's try switching labels on these spots. An agency has labeled them "ineffective, watered-down TV." This agency finds the strength of TV in its unique combination of sight, sound, and motion. Game-show spots have only sight and sound, and they're very short—only about seven seconds long. Ah, but this same agency recommends radio in its media plans, and radio has only sound, no sight or motion. This agency also recommends magazines, which have sight, but neither sound nor motion.

Suppose we take one of this agency's magazine ads, one with a simple illustration and relatively short text, and make a game-show card from it. (The TV camera uses this card in place of a commercial; the picture is held still, in front of the viewer, for about seven seconds.) We now have the agency's prized magazine ad shown full-screen on the consumer's TV set for a full seven seconds. The viewer can't turn the page, because we've taken control away from him by putting it on the TV screen. And instead of depending on him to read the text, we've engaged an announcer to speak our words directly to him. What I'm now describing is not "watered-down TV." Let's call it what it really is, a form of *energized print advertising*.

We've taken an approved print ad, one that was successfully tested (or should have been), and added an element of aggressiveness to it by having the text read to the consumer. Why shouldn't it be at least as effective as when it was shown passively in magazines? "Hold on," you reply. "The ad was shown for only seven seconds on that game show." My answer is an obvious question: "How much time does the average reader spend with your ad when he sees it in a magazine?"

Remember that we said we were going to use an ad with a simple illustration, and a relatively short text. Does the average magazine reader spend more than seven seconds with this kind of ad? One of the research companies that tests magazine ads exposes the test ad, on two separated pages, in a portfolio of other ads and editorial material. The combined time of the two exposures has been measured to be an average of 8.2 seconds. And this is for the typical ad tested, not for ads that are composed only of a simple illustration and a relatively short text.

So perhaps we should change the label on game-show spots from "watered-down TV" to "energized print ads." Suddenly they become the most efficient way to advertise—not "ineffective garbage." They won't always be strategically correct, but many times they will be. If, for example, magazines are recommended to extend the audience of daytime television, which they do well, daytime TV game shows would be strategically wrong. But prime-access game shows, such as "Wheel of Fortune," or "Jeopardy," effectively extend the reach of a brand's advertising beyond the daytime audience.

Game shows are an opportunity to *time* the exposure of the simple illustration and brief text better than can be done by a brand using ads in magazines. Consumers read magazines whenever they feel like it, which at times can be a desired strength for magazines. But if exposure of this advertising can benefit from being timed after dinner (during prime-access game shows), or on a specific morning or afternoon (daytime game shows), exposing it on game shows can be an executional improvement.

Game shows can also be an efficient way to evoke communication that has previously taken place between a brand and its consumers. If the role of the magazine ad was to evoke, the game-show spot can certainly perform the function more efficiently. If 15-second TV commercials are being used only to evoke, a game show spot can often perform the same function at a much lower cost.

Those who label these spots in a negative way will usually challenge their ability to communicate anything to viewers of the shows carrying them: "Viewers leave the room, instead of watching these spots." Viewers also leave the room during commercials. "These spots are run back-to-back, in clusters." So are the TV commercials you buy in network programs. "They just don't work the way TV advertising is supposed to." Many viewers confuse these spots with commercials. They tell us they saw one of our commercials on a game show last night. But it wasn't one of our commercials, it was a promotional spot.

Here's a recent example. This brand was preparing advertising for a re-stage of its improved product. The media plan called for 30-second television commercials and full-page print ads to announce the improvement. Promotional spots on TV game shows, using the magazine ad for their visual presentation, were scheduled to follow the initial run of the TV commercials and magazine ads. But the TV commercial ran into production problems. Not enough time had been allowed for its use of new high-tech elements. It wasn't ready to use until after running the promotional spots, which had been scheduled to evoke prior reaction to the commercial and/or ad.

Sales managers around the country regularly send reports of general information to the home office. One of these came from San Francisco, a few weeks after running promotional spots for the re-stage that failed to get its TV commercial on the air. The sales manager had just called on one of his important buyers. The buyer remarked to him that he had recently seen the re-staged brand's commercial on TV, and thought it was a really good one!

Buyers for the retail trade apparently don't watch much TV. They are notorious for belittling the TV campaigns of the products they buy. They often claim that they never see commercials for the brand represented by the salesman sitting by their desk. For one of them to have volunteered that he had seen your commercial, and then actually praise this commercial, is as rare as a pearl in your restaurant oyster. Yet such an event was made possible by a buyer's encounter with a single exposure of the brand's 7-second promotional spot on a prime-access game show. Admittedly, the creative execution was very good. The simple illustration was effective as a magazine ad, and it was used, almost literally, for the promotional spot.

The creative executions used in most game-show spots fail to take advantage of this opportunity for mass communication at a relatively low cost. This failure stems from game-show spots being mislabeled "inexpensive throwaways" by the advertising agency. No creative time or energy is ever put into throwaways. But once an agency "reads" the new "label," and sees these spots as incredibly efficient "energized print advertising," their entire attitude changes. They become interested in creating for this medium. They work hard to translate their magazine ads into effective game-show cards. They become a more effective advertising agency, simply by taking off one label and putting on a more accurate one.

Cocktails and High Ratings

Hors d'oeuvres are usually served with cocktails, but high ratings are equally appropriate. High ratings are something an advertiser can talk about with pride at a cocktail party, assuming his TV programs are blessed with high ratings. He won't volunteer any conversation about his low-rated TV programs at one of these parties. It's pleasant, and in keeping with the cheer of an alcoholic environment, to talk about how many of his TV programs are in the "top twenty." But he certainly wouldn't start a conversation by saying that all his commercials are on shows that are about to be canceled. He would quickly become the proverbial party-pooper.

I use the cocktail-party setting advisedly; it's an appropriate environment for this kind of thinking because it doesn't belong in an office, where people are working hard in a competitive situation to advance their company's business. The executive who brags about his top-twenty TV shows probably has paid 50 percent more to reach his consumers than he would have paid to reach the same consumers while they watched shows that were about to be canceled because of low ratings. Is this something to brag about? Would the same executive brag about paying 50 percent more than necessary for his factory's raw materials? How did he come to label his TV buying a success rather than a failure? Simple: he designed the label himself, ignored the advice of professional media people, and approved putting the label on his buying.

Executives, good and bad, are capable of making quick decisions. The good one knows how to use the intellectual talents of others, instead of becoming expert in all the areas of his business on which he draws when making his decisions. The bad executive saves time by short-circuiting the thinking process. Though inexperienced in a given area, he disdains help from those who are, and makes a decision without thinking. He has good eyesight, and can read labels as well as anyone. If the label says "top twenty TV programs," that's all the information he needs in order to reach a decision. Why not? His decisions are consistently reinforced by the reaction of others at the cocktail party.

Let's try our label-switching game again. To begin, we'll reduce high-rated and low-rated programs to the smallest proportionate sample we can use. Our assumption will be that the high-rated program has 50 percent more viewers than the low-rated one. If we give the low-rated program (A) two viewers, Carol and Eleanor, and add one additional viewer, Pauline, we have a high-rated program (B). We'll assume that Carol and Eleanor are happily watching program A, and that they continue watching when program B comes on. But now Pauline turns on her set, and also watches program B, giving it a 50 percent larger audience than program A.

The network executives responsible for keeping shows on the air, or canceling them, have labeled program B one of their "winners," and program A a "loser." They've listed program A among those to be dropped at midseason. From their point of view, considering their job responsibilities, the labels are accurate ones. Networks have a fixed number of hours to program. The more audience they can capture in these hours, the more they have to sell, and the more money they make. If they can replace a low-rated program with a high-rated program, they make more money. Simple. Logical.

But the advertiser isn't in the network business. He doesn't care how the networks "trade" the viewing audience back and forth amongst themselves: that's their problem. His customers are Carol, Eleanor, and Pauline. Reaching them with an advertising message is his problem. And the cost of reaching them with these messages is a critical part of his problem. The more expensive his cost of reaching these three women, the fewer the opportunities to make contact with them at the right time for him to make a sale.

Program B has 50 percent more viewers than program A, so its commercials will cost more. But program B is also a winner, which means that its commercials can't be bought for only 50 percent more than program A's. A premium will be tacked on to its cost. Why? Because the selling of TV time for commercials is governed by the law of supply and demand. More people want winners than want losers. The higher demand for winners pushes up their price; the lower demand for the losers pushes theirs down. So a commercial on program B may cost double what it will cost on program A.

Carol and Eleanor are common to both shows. They're worth no more, or no less, while viewing program *B* than they are while viewing program *A*. The fact that Pauline joins them as a viewer can't change their value as consumers for the advertiser. Pauline is worth the same to him as Carol and Eleanor. But a commercial on the show that all three watch will cost twice what it costs when only two are watching. Sounds like program *B* is a bad buy. It is. But it makes great cocktail conversation.

Perhaps I treat this serious subject too lightly. Isn't it possible that a high-rated TV program does something to make its commercials more effective, person by person, than a low-rated program? Yes, it is possible. We don't know that Carol and Eleanor aren't more receptive to a commercial on program *B* than they are for one on program *A*. But we can't think of one good reason why they should be. And according to whatever research there is, all of it indicates that a commercial on program *A* is equally as effective, person by person, as a commercial on program *B*.

Attentiveness research has shown the same level of claimed attentiveness to programs of all rating levels. Analysis of day-after-recall scores from the testing of TV commercials has found that commercials are recalled as well on low-rated shows as on their high-rated counterparts. Both findings are logical. Why should Carol pay more attention to program *B* just because Pauline is also watching it? Why should Eleanor remember a commercial shown on program *B* but not on program *A*, just because Pauline is also watching program *B*?

When network salespeople come calling with their new programs to sell each year, our cocktail-party-goer will ask to see their winners. Price is not the object. Value is not the object. *Ownership* is what he's looking for, something that goes well with his dark-blue suit, white shirt, and bold red tie the next time he goes to a cocktail party.

Good media people will ask the same network salespeople to show them their *losers*. Good media people want to be able to identify and evaluate the programs that the networks know they will have trouble selling because of their lower ratings. The law of supply and demand ensures that commercials on these programs will cost less (to reach Carol and Eleanor) than commercials on the network winners. Good buyers won't bother looking at these winners. Winners usually are an indulgence, not a good media buy. You can spot these good media buyers at a cocktail party. They're the quiet ones. They stand around and smile at each other while they listen to someone else brag about high-rated TV shows.

Cable TV Specs Need Not Be Written on the Head of a Pin

Earlier, I used cable TV's low ratings to demonstrate how some media people wrongly valued syndicated television programs. In this comparison, my intention was not to discredit cable TV. To assure cable people that it was not, I will now show how some media people fail to give cable its full value because they mislabel it, too.

Cable TV has been recommended primarily for two major benefits: first, for its ability to supplement the lower network ratings in cable homes, caused by the competition of cable programming itself; second, for its ability to "narrowcast," or to focus its commercials on a narrower, more specific, audience than the broadcasting of the three major networks. These two benefits have led many media people to think of cable in terms of "small," or specifically targeted. But cable TV has a very productive function as a mass, nonfocused medium. All we have to do is give it a new label.

We're going to call cable TV of all kinds (prime, fringe, daytime) our *fourth daytime network*. (How about that for an intellectual curve!) But is it really? Let's think about it for a minute. If an advertiser has a mass-market product for female heads of household, a television commercial, and a modest advertising budget, he's likely to use daytime network television. He understands that this medium provides uneven coverage of its audience: its ratings are low on the West Coast, high in the South, low among working women, high among blacks, and so on. But the low cost of this daytime television provides his brand with more total advertising to its target audience than any alternative. He'd like to reach more women if he could afford it, but he really doesn't care where he reaches them. A customer is a customer, as far as he's concerned. He's a business man, not an artist looking to make his advertising coverage symmetrical.

A good media department will point out to him that cable TV can be bought about as efficiently as network daytime TV on ABC, CBS, and NBC. If he buys a group of cable networks, he can aggregate a target-audience rating that equals or exceeds the best of the three mass-audience networks. The coverage of this multi-cable network will not be "national," as are the three major networks; therefore it will provide uneven coverage of his target. But so does each of the major networks! And we've already established that this brand is happy to increase its low advertising base in any way that it can afford to.

Let's proceed to the subject of negotiating time. Whenever one of the three networks is sold out, and an advertiser has only two parties to deal with, the price is likely to be higher—sometimes much higher. The converse is also true. When more network inventory is on the table, the price is likely to be lower. Isn't that nice? We have just increased the daytime network inventory *by creating our own fourth network*! Now our brand can negotiate with ABC, CBS, NBC, and MCN (our Multi-Cable Network).

Our brand can buy all four networks, thereby increasing its reach of the target audience available to only three. Or it can negotiate a better price on two or three networks, thereby obtaining more total advertising messages for its modest budget. By changing nothing more than the way it labeled cable TV, a good media department has created new value for one of its brands, value that is easy to demonstrate with its buying numbers, value that will show itself in brand sales if the advertising itself is really effective.

Magazines' Secret Recipe for Success

As I did with cable TV, earlier in this book I used magazines in a negative sense, to make a favorable point for game-show spots. I didn't intend to put a label of "less effective" on magazines. First of all, too many people already commit this error. Secondly, I believe that magazines can be the *most effective* advertising medium for the specific task of a specific brand. Yes, more effective even than TV, the gold standard of advertising effectiveness.

Magazines have one enormous advantage over TV, and it's one that most media people never talk about. It's one that few creative people take advantage of. No, it isn't the better audience of magazines: the women who are younger, better educated, more affluent than the audiences that most commercials access via television. Neither is it because a brand can reach a target audience better in magazines, with less waste than in TV. Nor is it for any of the other reasons that media plans direct us to use magazines instead of television, or at least instead of *more* television.

The real advantage that magazines have over television can be read clearly on our new label: More *dwell time*. Dwell time? New advertising jargon to learn? No, not really. Just a good description of the major difference between the consumer's encounter with a TV commercial and that same consumer's encounter with a magazine ad. Think of what hapens at the end of a brand's beautifully produced, dynamic 30-second commercial. The viewer is confronted with another brand's beautifully produced, dynamic commercial. Or maybe even worse, the viewer is whisked back to the dynamic, beautifully produced TV program, the viewing of which was the reason she turned on her set in the first place.

Can this consumer sit there and dwell on what the brand tried to communicate in its commercial? Does she have time to become personally involved with this advertising? Does she have the time to relate this advertising to her own needs or desires? Probably not. To dwell on commercial #1, she must be able to ignore commercial #2. Advertised brands are randomly commercial #1 or #2, so they either cancel the dwell time of another brand, or have their own dwell time canceled by another brand's commercial. And the last brand in this daisy chain has its dwell time canceled by the return of the program that the set was turned on to in the first place. Whatever consumer response failed to occur during those fifteen or thirty seconds of the brand's commercial, probably failed to occur.

Magazines are different. The dwell time for a magazine ad is as long as the copywriter can make it. The reader isn't pushed into the next ad, or back into the editorial. The reader *chooses* when to leave an ad. The reader chooses how long she dwells on the content of the ad, and on its implication for her if she responds to its communication. An ad that does its work well is the one the reader is encouraged to dwell on. Recipe advertising is all the proof we need in order to establish this as fact. Most print ads are glanced at, and left, in seconds. But some recipe ads have a life of *hours* with consumers!

Recipe ads prove dwell time for magazine ads. They prove the ability of magazines to involve consumers in their content. They prove the ability of magazines to *move consumers to action*. The only commercials that can document dwell time, and involvement comparable to recipe ads, are the 120-second direct-response commercials for records, gadgets, and an assortment of other bargains. These commercials are usually not followed by another commercial, and the programs that carry them are not the kind we would expect consumers to turn the set on for. In fact, a famous buyer of media for direct-response advertising was, a few years ago, quoted as saying that he bought the "dullest shows possible," because his clients obtained the highest rate of response from them. This thinking nicely fits the theory I have just outlined.

Not every brand can take advantage of the dwell time offered by magazine advertising, but many who can aren't. Most, if not all of these brands who can, haven't put the right label on magazine advertising. They haven't asked their agency to use dwell time to their brand's advantage. Most creative people haven't tried to create to a strategy of extending dwell time, increasing the probability of involvement, and getting more response from consumers in the marketplace. They should talk to their friends in the copy department, those who have worked on recipe advertising. Their friends have the secret recipe for using magazines more effectively than television. Maybe they'll share it.

9

Please Touch
My Media Plan!

F inished media plans tend to be sacrosanct. Delivery of the plan
to an agency's media buyers is usually accompanied by these
unspoken words: "Don't you dare touch my media plan. Execute
it exactly as it reads. Everything is there for a good reason." The
last statement is only half right. Everything in a media plan is there
for a reason. But the reason isn't always a good one.

Prime-time TV may be in the plan because account managers
know that they can't get client approval without bending to an
irrational demand for "quality." Less efficient magazines may be
in the plan because the agency doesn't like to see its creative execution in the weekly tabloids. A medium may be grossly overused,
to conform to an illogical need to "dominate one medium before
using a second one."

A Media Plan Is a Means, Not an End

But even when a good reason exists for something to be in the
media plan, there is nothing wrong with replacing it with something better. A media plan is not an end in itself. A media plan
is a means to accomplish the most effective pattern of communication from a brand to its consumers. The most effective pattern
of communication is sacrosanct, but the media plan that gets us
there isn't.

Prime-time TV may be in a media plan to reach more of a certain kind of consumers than planners believed could be reached

without it. But planners came to this conclusion by using specific assumptions on the cost of prime-time TV and its alternatives. Most media plans are written at a time when actual costs can't be used. Planners almost always use estimated costs. Frequently, the media marketplace offers the buyer a different set of media costs when it's time to execute the plan. Let's suppose that the relative cost of prime-time and late-night TV have changed enough to increase the reach of the plan by switching some of the budget from prime time to late night. To which does the buyer remain faithful, the media plan, or the objective of the media plan?

The Need for Mutual Agreement on Executional Latitude

An informed, thinking buyer will never go ahead and execute the plan as written, when given this choice. But neither will the buyer execute a revised plan without telling the planners that the media marketplace has changed the assumptions they made when writing the plan. Good planners give their buyers a thorough briefing on the intent of their media plans. They then discuss the buying strategy with the buyers. They examine alternate pricing scenarios which could change their media plans. They give buyers the executional latitude to modify the plan as they buy, in order to achieve what the original plan was written to achieve.

Executional latitude is a key element in a media plan that takes its communication goals seriously. When an agency or a client insists on executing a media plan exactly as it exists on paper, no matter what changes occur in the media marketplace, you'll know that those in charge are more concerned with appearance than with effect. "Don't touch my media plan" is their cry. For them, the media plan itelf is thought to be the product of their work. They fail to understand that *the effect of their media plan on consumers* is the product of their work.

The best media planners aren't afraid to say, "Go ahead and touch my media plan. In its execution, improve it. Take advantage of every opportunity to make it better for the brand." These enlightened media planners also educate their buyers in relative media values, so the buyers can make real improvements. For example, if prime time is believed, for good reason, to be better than late fringe time for this particular brand, a pair of relative numbers are given to buyers. The buyer then qualifies the marketplace numbers by the assigned values. If, after qualification, fringe time gives the brand more of what the media plan is looking for, he or she buys fringe time instead of prime time.

Substitution for elements of a media plan occurs most often in TV, where prices gyrate in response to the changing pressures of supply and demand. A campaign planned for local TV, but covering a large percent of the U.S., can sometimes be switched into network TV when high network inventories combine with few network budgets to drive the price of network low enough. Few local campaigns are planned with the intention of denying advertising to other areas of the country. The brands for which these local campaigns are planned simply can't afford to do what they think they need to do in the local areas, and still be able to afford to advertise elsewhere. When low network pricing gives one of these brands the level of advertising called for by its media plan in important local areas, and gives this brand the rest of the country "free," the plan is rewritten by its own execution.

Planned magazine schedules have been less susceptible to improvements in their execution, at least until recently. Magazine costs have been more predictable, over the years, than TV costs have been. But recent cost-cutting by some magazines has stimulated executional changes in media plans. A magazine that doesn't make a brand's list because its unduplicated audience doesn't justify its cost, can leapfrog its way onto the list by offering the brand a special price.

Flexible Timing Improves the Efficiency of TV Buying

Media substitution isn't the only way to improve a plan at the execution phase. When TV is in the plan, timing flexibility can almost always make a good media plan better. TV schedules start on a specified date and end on a specified later date. Even when timing is treated rather casually, as it is in the loose planning of today's media planning, TV schedules are confined within the weekly boundaries of a standard flowchart. But usually there is no strategic reason to force all a brand's commercials between these calendar boundaries.

For example, let's look at a prime-time flight that begins on a Monday and ends two weeks later, on a Sunday. Assume we have talked to the product manager, and have been told that these commercials haven't been scheduled to work in conjunction with a promotional event, or with anything else timed in or around these two weeks. The inventory of commercials, which constitutes the supply side of our supply/demand equation, is limited to what falls into those fourteen days. By extending the artificial barriers two days on one side and only one on the other, we will have increased our supply by more than 20 percent. The increase almost always improves the efficiency of a buy. There can be bigger improvements when networks have inventory they're desperate to sell during these three additional days. When one of them comes to us with "an offer we can't refuse," should we reject it in order to preserve the symmetrical appearance of the media plan?

Let's now change one of our assumptions. There's a newspaper coupon scheduled at the end of the two-week flight of TV. In fact, the plan specifically indicates that all commercials must run before the final Sunday. This restriction will limit our executional flexibility, but only at the *end* of the schedule. We're still able to advance the starting date of the schedule, provided that the commercial is available, and provided, also, that nobody has decided that a commercial must be seen within thirteen days of the coupon date in order for it to be effective. We can still expand the supply of commercials available to us. We can still allow a network to make us an offer we can't refuse.

Flexibility of timing is equally important to the most efficient execution of a local TV campaign. If an agency can allow stations to preempt some of its spots and run them a week later, the agency will pay a lower rate than it would if the stations were denied this flexibility. Sometimes there will be good reason for not allowing TV spots to be preempted. An advertiser can't run spots announcing a sale price after the sale is over. He can't run spots before the merchandise is available. But many of the product managers who ask that their schedules be executed to the letter of the media plan are paying a higher price for their TV spots than they should, without good reason for doing so.

In summary, I always told my skilled buyers: "Go ahead. Touch my media plan. Show me how to make it better. Whatever you do, don't execute a plan that you know can be made better. I'm not proud of my media plan. I'm proud of what I expect it to accomplish."

10
Facing Up to Media Planning's Biggest Mistake

W hat would you guess to be the biggest mistake the men and women of advertising make in the way they think about media planning? Admittedly, in this business, where so few results are known, perhaps it's impossible for us to identify mistakes with any degree of certainty. We can only talk of mistakes in terms of probabilities, as we must always do when we discuss advertising. I think the biggest mistake (and I've been guilty of this one, too) is the unending search for the answer to the question of how much advertising is enough.

How Much Advertising Is Enough?

Thousands of people have joined this search during my many years in media, yet none of us has come up with a satisfactory answer. We have been applauded for our diligence in pursuing this elusive goal. We have been encouraged to continue. "Keep trying," they say. "We need to be sure that we're doing enough for our advertising to be effective." How foolish they are. How foolish we all are to have spent decades digging through facts, figures, and hypotheses. We weren't even asking the right question! We were looking at the whole business of advertising *backwards*! The question isn't How much advertising is enough? The question is, and always should have been How much advertising is *too much*?

Are the two questions really different? Aren't they really trying to arrive at the same answer? You might think they are. But one question orients your business life toward trying to prove you need *more* advertising; the other leads you to spend your business years trying to prove you need *less*. Because of its long-term dependency on the commission system for survival, the advertising business has dedicated itself, en masse, to the question of how much advertising is enough. The idea of having too much advertising is generally dismissed as absurd, as something laughable. Almost all tests of media-weight levels have probed for the value of more media weight, not less.

The Origin of Advertising's Threshold Theory

The threshold theory of advertising has evolved from the question of how much is enough. This theory is one answer to the question, and a good answer, from an advertising agency's economic point of view. The threshold theory is that a message needs sufficient repetition before anything happens at the consumer end of the process. Isn't that nice? It means that a brand must spend enough to cluster multiple exposures, if it wants to make sure that its advertising is effective. This level of media spending guarantees more commission revenue for advertising agencies than would a lower spending level (one dictated by another theory of advertising).

The threshold theory of advertising can be shown graphically (see figure 10–1). Its graphic representation is sometimes known as the "Step Curve." For some people, the name is confusing because it's not a curve at all. Its perpendicular straight lines are actually the denial of a curve and are more accurately described as the Step Response Function. The threshold theory, as graphed in the Step Response Function, proclaims that all consumers need the same amount of information, the same number of advertising exposures, before they respond. It says that the product-category background of all consumers is identical, or that this background is irrelevant in the working of advertising. It says that consumers respond in relationship to a universal theory of communication that applies to all people, at all times.

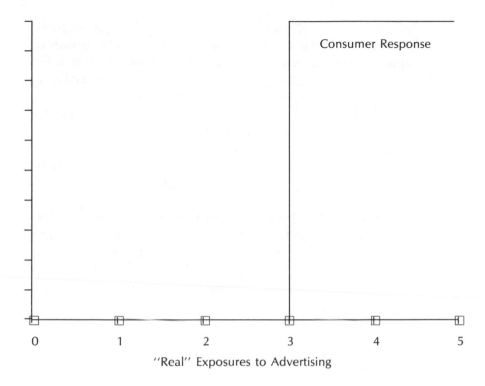

Consumer Response

"Real" Exposures to Advertising

Figure 10 1. *The Step Response Function*

The Step Response Function brings to mind a frustrated parent trying to teach his child. We can almost hear an annoyed father saying, "I'm telling you for the *third* and *last* time. Put your bike in the garage when you've finished riding it!" Or maybe you can hear a mother saying, "*How many times* do I have to tell you? No dessert until you clean your plate!" Perhaps these memories of teaching parents are what gave birth to the Step Response Function. If they didn't, I don't know what could have. There is absolutely nothing to substantiate the existence of a Step Response Function, or of its threshold theory of advertising.

Enter the Seductive S-Curve

Intelligent advertising research people, even those benefiting from the commission implications of the Step Response Function, long ago dismissed it as implausible. However, what they substituted for it was little more than a less extreme, more salable version of advertising's threshold theory. It retained the implication that little (rather than nothing) happens during a consumer's initial one, two, or few exposures to a brand's advertising. Then, as occurs in the hypothetical Step Response Function, there is rapid escalation of consumer response, which tapers off as sharply as it begins. Unlike the Step Response Function, this response theory has a seductively curving shape, rather than the other's hard, perpendicular lines. Appropriately, it has been labeled the S-Curve. (See figure 10–2.)

The S-Curve implies that consumers have different communication needs. As shown in figure 10–2, many consumers respond to the third exposure, but many of them need a fourth. However, it is believed that only a token few are able to respond to the first or second exposure, which suggests that consumers are more alike

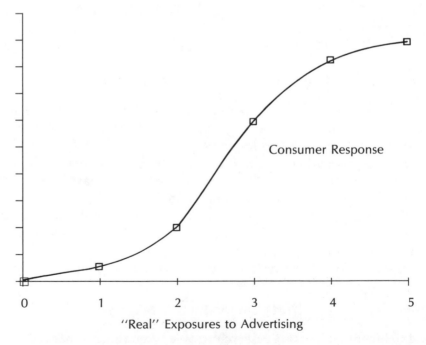

Figure 10–2. *The S-Curve*

than different in their ability to respond to communication in advertising. This S-Curve promotes the theory that most consumers need a base of two exposures on which to build a third before any response occurs, and that a large number need even more.

The S-Curve is a logical product of those who ask themselves: "How much advertising is enough?" It's a logical product of minds that are working in the biased environment of a commission compensation system. "More" is a safe reaction to "How much is enough?" "More" is an economically sound reaction in a compensation system where more advertising provides more revenue for the employer of the theorist. Is the bias intentionally self-serving? I would argue that it is not, as least not universally. I've known some very honest researchers, of the highest intelligence, who believed they were seeking the truth when trying to prove the theory of the S-Curve.

The commission system of compensation creates an obvious conflict of interest in the area of advertising theory. "How much advertising is enough?" was the first-generation offspring of this conflict. The threshold theory, as conceptualized in the Step Response Function and the S-Curve, is the next generation of offspring of this same inbred family of thinking. The S-Curve theory has been as difficult to prove as the Step Response Function theory. But that shouldn't surprise us; the S-Curve doesn't make a lot of sense when analyzed objectively.

Does Advertising Teach, or Does It Bring News?

The S-Curve, like its crude predecessor, the Step Response Function, is essentially a teaching curve. If the Step Response Function seems to have originated in observations of life at the parent-child level, the S-Curve seems to have originated in observations of life at the adult-teaching-adult level. Some of us need more repetitions than others to learn how to function as capable workers, spouses, participants in games and sports, and so on. A few among us are incredibly quick to learn (first- or second-exposure types). Most of us need repetitions to modify previous behavior (three- or four-exposure types). Is it possible that advertising works the same way? Doesn't advertising "instruct" us on how to live better by the acquisition of more products, or alternative products?

I'm sure we can find examples to prove that it does. As I've stated earlier, examples exist to prove anything you want to prove about advertising. But what is the dominant theory which drives the working of advertising? Is it really the teaching of the threshold curves? Is all of advertising's content a kind of "curriculum" through which consumers pass during their entire adult lives?

Or is effective advertising "news"? Many have said, and still contend, that only advertising that brings news to the consumer can hope to be effective. But we don't teach news. Conceptually, the ideas of "news" and "teaching" seem to be antithetical. The repetition of news changes its basic character from the new to the familiar. In other words, news can't be taught through repetition, because when repeated, it's no longer news.

In no way is this observation proof that product news, or a new product, can't benefit from repetition. All I'm really saying is that news and a teaching sequence of repetition are incompatible intellectual concepts. But if timing is a critical ingredient in how advertising works, the timing of the news may require repeating it to coincide with the consumer's state of readiness. In other words, what is new may be relevant news at this point in time for Eleanor, but irrelevant news at the same point in time for Carol. Without having experienced "the problem," Carol really can't be expected to perceive "the solution" as news. This final conclusion might not be true if the news were a product that cured cancer. But on the consumer's continuum of relevance × interest, most advertising news is closer to the end of the continuum, where we discover a new and improved toothpaste, detergent, or toilet paper.

Recognizing the News Curve
of Consumer Response

Researchers don't talk about the existence of a News Curve in their discussions of advertising theory. But they could, because one really does exist. They acknowledge its existence, but they call it by a different name. Actually, it has been called by several names (but never the News Curve): the Geometric Curve, the Convex Curve, and the Diminishing-Returns Curve. This curve is not only the most logical of all theoretical curves, but also the one that shows itself most often in communication research. (See figure 10–3.)

The News Curve implies that the first exposure to a brand's advertising stimulates greater consumer response than the second. It implies that the second exposure stimulates greater response than the third, the third a greater response than the fourth, and so on. In short, the News Curve implies diminishing returns for each succeeding exposure to a brand's advertising message. To paraphrase, *less* is better than *more*.

But this isn't the answer the advertising industry likes to hear to its fundamental question, "How much advertising is enough?" Advertising people want to hear just the opposite, that more is better than less! The answer provided by the News Curve seems more

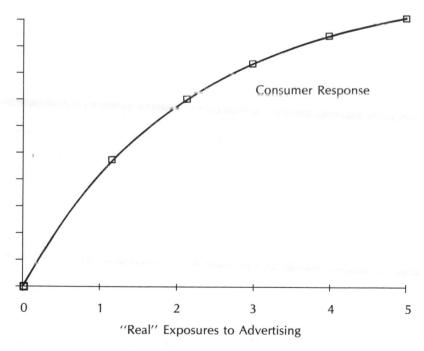

Figure 10–3. *The "News" Curve*

appropriate to the question that advertising works hard to ignore: "How much advertising is too much?" This curve has appeared in the results of communication research for decades, but it remains ignored. Why? Because it seems to give the wrong answer to the question most often posed by the industry. But it really doesn't. It gives the right answer. It's just that the question is wrong.

The News Curve has the configuration of a media-reach curve. As a brand buys more media exposures, it progressively reaches new consumers who have not already been reached. But as the percentage of consumers reached increases, so does the likelihood of the brand's recontacting some of these consumers. In other words, a brand that has already reached 50 percent of its target audience is more likely to duplicate a large part of this 50 percent with its next commercial than when it had reached only 10 percent of this audience. If each audience unit is of equal size, each unit added to a brand's schedule will add less to the net audience already reached. Each new purchase of advertising adds audience on a scale of diminishing returns.

The similarity between a media-reach curve and the News Curve that appears in the results of advertising research, suggests that relevant communication may take place more quickly than is generally thought. As consumers are reached by the advertising, they may be the ones who are responding positively in awareness research. The reach-like pattern of the News Curve implies that consumers are responding quickly, as they would to an element of news. For this reason, I think it's more correct to call the Geometric Curve a News Curve.

Six Years of Research Results
Support a News Curve

Between 1978 and 1984, I directed the interviewing of hundreds of thousands of consumers, to learn how and where these consumers responded to advertising campaigns. Their response was determined by an awareness measurement, but nothing as crude as brand or advertising awareness. Awareness of a name, with nothing attached to it, has questionable value, at best. Awareness of advertising gives an advertising agency a good feeling, but unless it imparts a consumer benefit to its sponsor brand, it may serve as little more than palatable entertainment for the consumer.

For my awareness criterion, I chose the link between the brand name and the consumer benefit offered by that brand name. To qualify as being "aware," the target consumer had to be aware of the benefit offered in the brand's advertising, and be able to link this benefit correctly to the sponsor brand. The benefit was asked on an "aided" basis, but the brand-linkage question was first unaided, then offered as a multiple choice, with the correct brand listed along with four incorrect ones. ("Have you heard of a toothpaste whose ability to reduce cavities has been endorsed by the American Dental Association? You have? What is the name of that toothpaste? You don't know? Here is a list of five toothpastes. Which do you think is the one whose ability to reduce cavities has been endorsed by the American Dental Association?")

Several hundred target consumers were questioned at frequent intervals during the exposure of each campaign. Sometimes there was a response to the advertising; sometimes there wasn't. When consumers responded, their response usually took the shape of a News Curve. For new brands of limited interest or differentiation, the curve rose only a short distance before flattening. For new brands of average interest and/or differentiation, the curve rose higher before flattening. For brands of high interest and differentiation, the curve rose accordingly. What was consistent was the convex, or geometric, shape of these curves. The point of diminishing returns was obvious.

Those Exceptions That Teach Us So Much

It is worth noting that a few linear responses to advertising were recorded during this six-year period. But linear response to advertising shouldn't exist! The advertising industry has tried to promote linear response for many years, because it encourages advertisers to spend more money. If an additional unit of spending for advertising produces an additional unit of sales, the burden of proof is on those who want to spend *less*, not on those who want to spend *more*. But the consistent failure of thousands of extra-spending tests has convincingly disproved linear response to advertising.

Knowing this, I was troubled by my encounter with the few, but real, linear responses to the advertising campaigns I measured. Then I discovered that the four linear-response patterns all had something in common, something which made them different from brands obtaining geometric response to their advertising. These linear-response brands all had an identifiable force working against the upward thrust of their advertising response.

For example, three of these brands were being repositioned as something different from what they had been before. So they were trying to do more than establish a brand-benefit closure in the mind of consumers. They were trying to undo the previous closure and establish a new one in its place. To visualize this on paper, we must show the geometric curving of the new position, but also show how consumers' prior understanding of the brand creates a downward force on the curve. Graphically, the result is a *flattened curve*, or a straight line, as shown in figure 10–4.

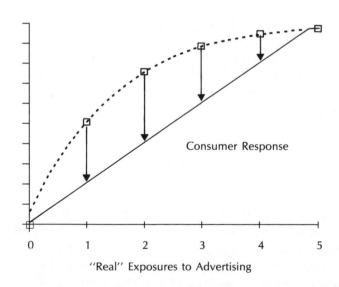

Consumer Response

0   1   2   3   4   5

"Real" Exposures to Advertising

Figure 10–4. *A Flattened News Curve*

The fourth brand was a new one, with no existing associations to overcome with its new advertising. This brand's linear response bothered me for a long time. It was the only new brand to record a linear response to its advertising during these six years of research. My hardworking subconscious took a long time to find a reason why this brand's response should not be geometric, like all the others. After all, this brand was bringing "news" to the category, and had no preconceptions to override. It should have had a News Curve! Why didn't it?

But it really did! Like the three repositioned brands, this new brand had something working against the rapid growth of its brand-benefit closure. Two competing brands were launched at an identical point in time, on the identical positioning. The consumer who became aware of the new benefit had the challenge of associating it with three new brands, instead of the usual one.

So, the advertising of our linear-response brand was driving its usual geometric curve, but the advertising of the other two new brands, which were competing for name/benefit association, was exerting a downward pressure on the curve, making it appear linear. In practical application, it *was* linear. This tells us that response to advertising will be slower when more than one new brand is claiming the same market positioning at the same point in time. But this is no great surprise, is it?

When we discover exceptions to advertising's News Curve, we can always expect to find a good reason to label it the exception that proves the general rule of geometric response to advertising. No S-Curve has ever shown itself in any of my research. However, I have always measured consumers' response to campaigns by using *tested* commercials and ads. It's theoretically possible for consumers not to understand a weak commercial on its first or second exposure, yet finally understand it on a subsequent exposure. I doubt that this occurs often enough to consider it more than a rare exception. My other testing experience has shown that consumers who fail to understand a commercial can't retrieve any of that commercial from their memory the very next day. How, then, can they build on some previous fragment of communication? And if there is no building process, there is no S-Curve. (From an economic viewpoint, it would be foolish to use a weak commercial or ad several times to get the same response that a good commercial could get on its first exposure.)

Northwestern's 1986 Symposium on Effective Frequency

Some of the best media-research minds in the business were convened at Northwestern University on April 26, 1986, to discuss the subject of effective frequency of advertising exposure. Their consensus, as reported in the *Journal of Media Planning*, was that "response curves should be convex, not S-shaped," which means that "advertising begins to work at the first exposure . . . continues to work from the first exposure on, but on a basis of diminishing returns."[1] I participated in this symposium, and was a contributing part of the consensus. But there is more on the subject of effective frequency that needs to be discussed, studied, and further researched before we consider ourselves knowledgeable enough to sit back and rest on our consensus.

Reconciling with Zielske's Classic Findings

Rarely are we certain of how many exposures a specific consumer has encountered when we interview her in our advertising research. We usually extrapolate an estimate out of the volume of total consumer contacts made by our advertising. More women are encountered for the second or third time during the second hundred GRPs than during the first hundred, more on the third hundred than on the second, and so on. But we never know if consumers who respond to our message are those receiving their first, second, or third exposure.

More than thirty years ago, Hugh Zielske, of FCB, led the initial attack on this problem with a beautifully controlled research experiment.[2] He took thirteen executions of a newspaper ad, for an ingredient food product, and mailed them to households in two different patterns of exposure. The first panel received a different ad each week for thirteen consecutive weeks. The other panel received the same ads once every four weeks, for a full year. Consumers were interviewed weekly, to measure their awareness of the advertising; to prevent research bias, no consumer was interviewed more than once during the twelve months. Zielske's findings are shown in figure 10–5, and are almost self-explanatory. Both of his curves are convex, but each of them seems to be growing more slowly, and are in need of more exposures, than my News Curve. This conflict must be addressed. If ever there was a well-executed advertising experiment it was Hugh Zielske's. The burden of reconciliation isn't on him; it's on those whose findings run counter to his. So I had better come up with an explanation, and I will.

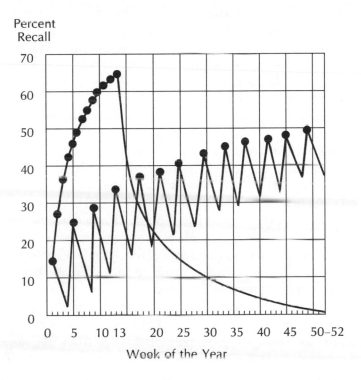

Source: Hubert A. Zielske, "The Remembering and Forgetting of Advertising," *Journal of Marketing*, January 1959, 239–43.

Figure 10–5. *Percent of Housewives Remembering the Advertising Each Week of the Year*

Zielske's curves are *learning* curves; my News Curve is a *discovery* curve. My point of departure is the assumption that advertising works when a consumer discovers something relevant for her in the advertising exposure she encounters. I'm not concerned with her recall of the advertising, or with the maintenance of advertising awareness. I certainly can't afford to keep tens of millions of consumers aware of my advertising for the long periods of time between their purchase occasions.

Zielske's chart has been used to illustrate the 1885 learning/forgetting findings of Ebbinghaus, who has been cited as the foremost contributor to the study of learning and forgetting. But Ebbinghaus intentionally used nonsense syllables in his research, so that his learning material would be "purified" of any biasing relevance to the subject of his experiment. When Mike Naples in his work mentioned in chapter 3, juxtaposed the work of these two researchers, he must not have been aware of the resulting inferrence, that is, that Zielske, like Ebbinghaus, was also teaching "nonsense" to his consumer subjects.[3]

I'm sure that's not what Naples intended to convey to us. But his inference is not wholly inaccurate. Note that after thirteen weekly contacts, more than a third of Zielske's sample still can't recall the advertising. And remember, this study was conducted before the explosion of third-class mail. It was much more of an event to receive a piece of mail in the late 1950s than it is today; there were days of the month when no mail was delivered to one's home. To receive a letter a week for thirteen consecutive weeks, from the same advertiser, was the highest level of "intrusiveness" imaginable. And after all this, more than a third of the sample still couldn't remember the advertising!

The intrusive effect of thirteen consecutive weekly exposures was quantified by their being able to raise the level of those "everawares" of the advertising 31 percent higher than the same ads mailed four weeks apart. The rapid drop in recall, once the weekly exposures were terminated, also supports my conclusion that the high level of recall was driven by the highly intrusive nature of the exposure pattern, rather than by broad consumer interest in the content of the advertising. So Naples was partially correct in his unintentional inference that Zielske, like Ebbinghaus, was measuring the learning/forgetting effect of repeated nonsense on his subjects. Perhaps irrelevant advertising and nonsense syllables have enough in common to justify their being used interchangeably in a teaching experiment. If so, we can agree with Naples when he concludes that a frequency of one is "inadequate." One exposure is obviously inadequate to teach nonsense syllables (equated with irrelevant advertising) to the majority of the population.

But can this conclusion be broadly translated into the real world of consumer marketing? I doubt it. Anyone who resists learning about a new brand, or a new brand idea, through many exposures of its advertising, is not likely to purchase this brand in place of what she's already using. On the other hand, any brand that has nothing relevent to say to consumers in its advertising will find multiple exposures no more effective than the first one. Irrelevance and non-sense both carry a consumer value of zero. Multiply any number (of exposures) by zero and you get the same response—nothing.

Can Our Magic Number Be *One*?

If we are unsure of how many exposures each of our interviewed consumers has really seen, we may be misreading what we are being told by the convex shape of the News Curve. I said earlier that a media-reach curve is convex in shape, and looks very similar to the shape of the News Curve. Could it be that almost all actionable communication takes place when a consumer is reached by his or her *first* exposure to relevant advertising, *at any specific point in time?*

Multiple exposures are usually offered as a means of assuring understanding, or of overcoming established thinking about brands in current use. But if a commercial or ad is not understood on its first encounter, why should it be understood the next time the consumer sees or hears it? Likewise, if material in the commercial or ad fails to overcome established thinking on its first exposure, why should the same material have a different effect on the second, third, or subsequent exposure at that specific point in time?

If the *consumer* changes in some way, (if he has a new problem, if his current brand fails to live up to expectations), a subsequent exposure of the same advertising might perform in a way that earlier ones didn't. But this wouldn't be a function of his seeing the magic third exposure. Its new performance would be a function of his being a different consumer, encountering his *first* exposure of the advertising in his new role.

It's very possible that the answer to advertising's question of how much is enough is the magic number *one*! Then, it's equally possible that the answer to the neglected question of how much advertising is too much is *anything more than one*! These would appear to be traumatic answers for the advertising industry to accept. And they are, but only for brands that are financially able to indulge in the excesses of advertising waste. For brands with effective advertising, accepting these answers would not necessarily mean canceling most of their media. But it could mean *rearranging* it.

Implications of the Timed Single Exposure

One exposure, at any point in time, should certainly be enough to allow an uninterested consumer to reject a brand on the basis of its advertising. One exposure, at the right time, may also be enough to allow an *interested* consumer to accept a brand on the basis of its advertising. If this is correct, the only function of what we know as "frequency" is to provide this one exposure often enough to reach all potential accepters at the right point in time.

I can hear a collective sigh of relief from advertising agency management. For a moment, they might have thought that their economic foundation was about to be swept away by a flood of logic. But it isn't, at least not as a result of this particular logic. (Other good reasons exist for eliminating much of the advertising that does little more than subsidize an inefficient industry, one whose productivity is taken for granted.) A frequency of *more than one* is probably needed if a brand's advertising is to be effective in exploiting the full potential of its benefit to the consumer.

The problem is that the word *frequency* is misunderstood by most of its users. A frequency of *three* is not the same as the frequency of *one* which is repeated twice. To the media person who doesn't plan according to advertising theory but according to traditional advertising practice, a frequency of *three* is just that, nothing more. But if a brand needs a frequency of *three* for effectively teaching, these three exposures will be scheduled in relation to each other, in order to perform a teaching function.

On the other hand, if a single exposure is effective for part of a brand's potential audience, this single exposure needs to be scheduled in a way that relates to a pattern of activity in the life of the consumer, not to the brand's other advertising exposures. This brand's advertising exposures work independently of each other. Each of them is like a campaign in itself.

If a single exposure is effective at the right time, this is the answer to the basic question that advertising has tried to ignore: *More than one exposure at the "right time" is too much advertising.* Most brands don't have enough money to reach all the right consumers at the right time, even if it is with a single exposure. Just as *reach* is given up for *frequency*, so do we give up effective single exposures, at the right time, in order to cluster multiple exposures that serve no purpose.

If the "right time" is considered to be the last exposure to advertising immediately prior to a consumer purchase in this product category, the brand probably wants to reach as many prospects just once, at this precise time. If the "right time" is immediately following a problem (seeing your first cockroach of the year, or third cockroach of the day, or being handed a cockroach by your two-year-old son), the brand wants to reach you just once, and as quickly as possible—before you go to the store and buy the first roach killer that you find there. Multiple exposures do nothing more than waste money faster when they reach a consumer who has already made her only purchase of the month, or of the quarter, or perhaps even of the season.

Before going any further into the implications of the timed single exposure, I should probably address the negative response that can be anticipated from some people in the advertising industry. It's easy to continue to cite the conflict of interest created by their commission system of compensation. But let's look instead at what will be their standard objection, and see how it fails to take into consideration the role of timing and its effect on frequency of exposure.

In response to my line of reasoning, an advertising person will most often comment: "One exposure may be enough for some consumers, but certainly not for all of them!" This person's bias in favor of "teaching" is obvious. He thinks that a consumer needs multiple exposures to understand the advertising. Or perhaps his thinking is influenced by the "power" bias; this is the person who claims that his agency's advertising will "convince" consumers, or "make them believe" the claims of his brand. He thinks that the consumer needs multiple exposures to "drum out" positive attitudes toward the consumer's current brand. Conditioned by this power bias, he can't understand that it's possible that a single exposure, the last exposure a consumer encounters, may be the only one that "works." He can't understand how the earlier exposures of his brand's advertising may have had no building effect whatsoever. For him, frequency is frequency. He probably doesn't believe that anyone is ever motivated by a single exposure.

Evidence Supporting Response to a Single Exposure

But we have evidence that consumers do respond to a single exposure. Here is a quote from a sales manager's weekly report to the home office:

> Just to cite an example of what an impact the Mrs. Jenkes' commercial can make, District Account Manager Paul Rich was shocked when he walked into Fleming Wholesale in Oklahoma City to present Befresh, and the buyer, head buyer, and sales manager confront him as to why he was so late in making the presentation. As it turns out, we ran one of Mrs. Jenkes' spots in Oklahoma City on Sunday evening as a test, and on Monday morning Fleming had calls from nine store managers advising headquarters that customers were asking for Befresh. Needless to say, when Paul informed them that he just received the program, they were all impressed with the response just one commercial can make.

I mentioned earlier that Duncan Hines Deluxe Cake Mix became the number-one seller in the Albany test market before its advertising began. This may not sound like it has anything to do with advertising's frequency of exposure, but it does. Advertising is only one form of communication. In-store communication from a package to its consumer is as much "advertising" as we are smart enough to make it be. Cake-mix users saw Duncan Hines Deluxe mixes on their next visit to the supermarket shelf. For many of them, one visit, one purchase.

There are other examples. It's not unusual for a new brand to run a coupon ad early during its introduction, often before regular advertising is scheduled to begin. This early timing is intended to push the retail trade to rush to stock their new brand. Store managers don't want customers coming into their stores with coupons for a product that still sits in the warehouse. For these new brands, if they're not total failures, there is usually a significant response to these coupons, even when other advertising has not yet begun, and when the number of exposures is still unequivocally just *one*.

A few years ago, I tracked the brand-benefit closure of a new hair-care brand. My first postadvertising wave of interviewing was done a week after the initial coupon ad appeared in a Sunday newspaper supplement, but before any other advertising had appeared. The response curve had climbed to 60 percent of its stabilized peak level, despite the ad's being followed by an expensive sampling program, and the expenditure of millions of dollars in TV advertising.

To deny the effectiveness of a single exposure of relevant advertising content to an interested consumer is to fail to understand how a great deal of our advertising works. All of us have been led to purchase something by a single advertising exposure. All of us have ignored multiple exposures of the advertising of something that we eventually purchased because *one exposure suddenly became relevant and meaningful*. Rarely has the cumulative number of exposures been important to our ultimate action; more often, it has been the timing of the single motivating exposure.

Some of what is currently being done in the advertising business pays homage to the theory of timing. Much more could be done, and will be, if and when the thinking of the advertising industry is freed from the intellectual bias of the commission system. In the next chapter, I'll show how timing leads to some unconventional, but very effective, media usage.

11
Timing the Effective Exposure

The temperature outside is ten below zero. The windchill gives it the effect of minus forty-five degrees. Cars are being jump-started everywhere. Weak old batteries in other cars have been given the coup de grace by the razor sharpness of this latest cold wave. Cars are towed away. Other cars are abandoned until warmer weather. But it will be three days before warmer weather comes.

I'm reading the Sunday paper in the warmth and comfort of my living room. My car sits in the unheated garage, which still keeps our cars warm enough to start without fail. But I'm thinking about going to work tomorrow, about leaving my car sitting in the parking lot all day, about having to go out and start it at lunchtime so it doesn't fail to start at the end of the day.

I'm also thinking that I should have something in my gas tank to prevent fuel-line freeze-up. I remember having seen store ads for these products, more than once during the past several weeks. But I didn't pay any attention. The weather was warmer than usual. I had thought more about cleaning the garage than preparing for the cold that hadn't yet come.

Reading through the newspaper insert for a local mass-merchandiser, I discover a price feature for Isoheet, one of the gasoline additives used to prevent fuel-line freeze up. An hour later, I'm in the store buying half a dozen of them for our two cars. The display shelves have been substantially depleted by others like me, reacting to the effective *timing* of this one ad. Was it luck or careful planning that the ad coincided with the coldest weather of the year? No matter. The advertising was effective, because it was *timed* right.

The earlier ads had been much less effective, because the weather hadn't cooperated with the advertising.

How Radio Can Time Effective Exposures

This simple anecdote demonstrates how timing can influence the effectiveness of an advertising exposure. Earlier in the book, I cited other obvious examples. A tired working mother, on her way home from work, hears a fast-food commercial on her car radio, and stops to buy food to take home that evening. A young woman is using the family toilet early in the morning. She's listening to the news on her radio. An air-freshener commercial tells her how it eliminates odors, and leaves her bathroom a fresher place (for her husband to use after her). On her next visit to the supermarket, she buys a can of this brand's air freshener.

More examples easily come to mind. A young man in the act of shaving hears a shaving cream commercial tell him that he can get a more comfortable shave from this brand's patented superior lubrication. The young man is using an old razor blade which pulls his beard as it cuts. He notes the name of the shaving cream, and will buy it the next time he shops for this kind of product, which, luckily, is the following weekend.

Another young man is in his car, driving to the record shop to pick up an album. As usual, he's listening to his car radio. A commercial asks him to check what happens to drops of water on the hood of his car. Coincidentally, rain is falling at that very moment. At the next traffic light, the young man follows the commercial's suggestion, and observes that the rainwater is sheeting, not beading, which means that there's no protective coat of wax on his car. Two stores down from the record shop is an auto-supply store. The young man goes in and discovers the advertised brand of car wax featured on display. He buys it.

So far, all my examples have involved the use of radio advertising. This is no surprise. Radio listening is usually a shared activity. This splitting of a consumer's attention is, on one hand, a disadvantage that radio suffers relative to television and print media. Consumers' other activities are limited when TV or print engages their vision. Thus, television commercials and print ads exercise greater control over the attention of the consumer than does radio.

But what radio gives up in the control of consumers' undivided attention it recaptures by its frequent ability to time its message about a brand so that it coincides with the consumer's need for that brand. This strategy was the cornerstone of Procter & Gamble's use of daytime radio serials during the two decades before mass TV audiences were available. P&G wanted women to hear about the benefits of its laundry products while they were in the process of doing their laundry. They wanted to reach women who could see, right there in front of them, the problems they were having with their laundry. They wanted to tell these women how a P&G product would solve their laundry problems.

Even TV Messages Can Be Timed Effectively

Television can't often hope to match radio in its ability to time the promise of a product benefit to coincide with activities involving the precise need for that benefit. But it can try. During certain times of the evening, viewers get thirsty, or hungry, or both. Food and beverage commercials can be timed for these opportunities. There are times of the year when many consumers can be asked to feel their skin to discover dryness that a skin-care product will correct. There are times of the day, and week, when women are most likely to leave for the supermarket to do their weekly grocery shopping. Those who view TV immediately before leaving the house provide brands with an opportunity to be the last one in their product category to speak to these consumers (unless they hear a radio commercial on the way to the store). What better time to find a consumer receptive to a mosquito-repellent commercial than when she's been forced to come indoors by the repeated biting of mosquitos? What better time to find a woman receptive to a commercial that attempts to involve her in an intimate fantasy than when she's watching TV alone, late at night?

Getting in the Last Word
Before a Purchase

Some advertisers have become creative in timing their message to coincide with the consumer's best opportunity to react. In-store advertising has become an important advertising medium in the 1980s. Many advertisers are getting in "the last word" to consumers as they approach the shelf to make a purchase. There consumers see a mini-billboard for one of the brands in a particular category. Where possible, a creative in-store advertiser will use the key illustration, or copy headline, that appeared in its print advertising, or perhaps even in its TV commercial. If the message had registered positively with the consumer when she was exposed to the ad or the commercial, the mini-billboard should evoke that message at the shelf, and make the sale happen. For the consumer with no strong orientation to any brand, the last word may, on its own, be a compelling stimulus.

Having the Product Itself Deliver
a Timed Exposure

But the product itself, on the shelf, or even in the home, can deliver an effective advertising exposure to consumers. The Procter & Gamble Co. test-marketed a toilet tissue, with lotion added to improve the cleansing effectiveness of the paper. The test was terminated, presumably when P&G found insufficient consumer interest in this premium tissue to warrant expanding the product nationally. However, they are still selling it in the test market, which happens to be where I live.

My wife and I think that this product, originally called Certain, now sold under the Charmin Care trademark, is an excellent one. We continue to buy it in preference to other tissue. When first using it, I discovered that the cardboard core, on which Certain was rolled, had printing on it. This printing showed users the Certain trademark (the brand's stylized floral design) and the benefit inherent in the product form: "Cleansing Bathroom Tissue." P&G

had decided to incur the expense of printing something on the tissue core, a piece of cardboard which couldn't be seen until the entire roll of tissue was used up. This core can never be seen until the moment it's removed and thrown away. And P&G paid money to print on every one of these throwaways! Why?

They wouldn't tell us if we asked them, so we have to guess. But it doesn't make any difference whether we're right or wrong, so long as we find good advertising logic behind the printing on the core of Certain cleansing bathroom tissue. And we can. Satisfied triers of Certain, when they finished their roll, were told the name of the brand that satisfied them. And they were also told *why* they were satisfied: because Certain is a *cleansing* bathroom tissue. Great advertising! It won't win an industry award for so-called creativity. But if there were awards given for advertising creatively timed to be effective, Certain would win one.

Contrast this with an example of a missed opportunity to do the same kind of timed advertising. We introduced a plastic toilet-tissue roller which contained beads impregnated with air freshener. The roller therefore provided an invisible source of continuous air freshener for the bathroom. Even better, it gave off extra fragrance when the roller was spun by the action of removing some of the toilet tissue. The product, called Spinfresh, was sold in individual packages, sealed to keep the fragrance inside, and fresh.

When the consumer removed Spinfresh from its package, he discarded the packaging materials, and was left with the roller. But the roller was made of white plastic, with nothing on it to identify the brand! Every time the user put a new role of toilet tissue on the Spinfresh roller, an advertising exposure was made available to the brand—free! But it wasn't used. The cost of buying this many contacts with the user of Spinfresh, using conventional advertising media, would have far exceeded the brand's advertising budget. Yes, the small cost of printing on the roller would have given the brand millions of advertising contacts with its users, but the opportunity was missed. A multitude of similar opportunities are missed by advertisers, especially those who can't visualize an obscure part of their product as an important advertising medium.

Using the Cereal Box to Communicate

Marketers of breakfast cereals have, for many years, made extensive use of their packaging as an advertising medium. I occasionally find coupons mixed in with my cereal. I assume that the function of these coupons is to do what coupons usually do. But I'm surprised that more efforts aren't made to get the coupon on the *inside bottom* of the box, where it would be discovered at the time the consumer needs to buy more cereal. Not being very adventuresome in trying new cereals, I don't know that clever things aren't already being done by their marketers. But I wonder if many, or any, of them are using the inside bottom of the box to time a critical message to their users. It seems like a great opportunity.

Cereal manufacturers certainly haven't neglected the outside of their packaging as a means of delivering timed messages to the consumer. The front of the box often serves as a selling billboard. Sometimes it evokes the brand's television campaign. On a box of Wheaties, there usually is a picture of a currently famous sports personality, one who recently has been seen performing on TV in his or her sport. The picture captures our attention at the supermarket shelf, as we shop for cereal. In our homes, it continues to evoke the athletic image, every time we take the box from our cupboard.

The back of the cereal box has been used creatively for a long time. When the morning paper is late, some of us read the back of our cereal box while eating breakfast. We learn how to use more of this cereal by adding it to recipes for cookies, or as a topping for dinner meals. We read the cereal's nutritional benefits, which make us feel good about eating it. All this is efficient, well-timed media usage, even though most advertising people don't think of packaging as a major advertising medium. But it is.

Finding Timed Opportunities to Communicate

One way to look for timing opportunities is to pose the question negatively. When are we reasonably certain that advertising *won't* be effective? Maybe we can say that a bad time to deliver a Wheaties coupon or product message is when a new jumbo box has just been opened. At this point in time, the consumer is as far removed from her next purchase occasion as possible. Perhaps we should avoid putting the message/coupon near the inside *top* of the box.

When we launch a new brand, we don't want to time our advertising exposures so that they reach consumers in this product category the day after they've purchased a new container of their current brand. This timing would put exposure to our brand as far away from a purchase occasion as possible. Reverse our thinking, and we'll try to reach each consumer in this category just before she makes her next purchase. If our message is clear and relevant, it will probably communicate effectively with her. And the message won't be required to last weeks or months while the current brand is being used up. Neither will there be much opportunity for other brands to insert a persuasive message between ours and her next purchase occasion.

If the purchase cycle in this product category is eight weeks, we might try to reach as many target consumers once each week for these eight weeks. This pattern of exposures gives our new brand the maximum opportunity to make contact at the best time for its advertising to be effective. If competitors have used some sort of defensive product-loading device, which has taken a significant number of consumers out of the market during our introductory cycle, our brand may have to use the next eight-week cycle. Anyone who knows media costs won't have to be told that the cost of reaching the majority of consumers once a week, even for only eight weeks, will be in the millions of dollars. Many new brands can't afford this ideal timing of their exposures.

But perhaps their advertising doesn't really need this much contact with their potential consumers. Repeated exposure to this advertising may have a cumulative effect that slows the rate at which the influence of each exposure decays. The second exposure may well be required in the second week, but perhaps the effect of exposures one plus two allows the third exposure to take place in the fourth week instead of the third. Perhaps the next can be placed in the sixth, the next in the ninth, or at the beginning of the purchase cycle which follows the one in which the brand began its pattern of communication.

All exposure patterns that deviate from the ideal timing are speculative, and only theoretically effective in how they work. But so, too, is the ideal pattern theoretical until proved effective, and failure to reach all consumers quickly will probably only delay trial of the brand, not prevent it. Response to advertising is ruled by the law of diminishing returns. Advertisers of a new brand are more likely to be wrong by doing *more* than by doing *less*. Moreover, if the advertiser can't afford the ideal timing of its exposures, he has to settle for next best. To build a retreat plan backwards from the ideal is the only way I know to get to whatever is next best.

Timing Can Increase a Brand's Price/Value Dimension

Now let's suppose that our brand isn't of significant interest to consumers. "Then it shouldn't be introduced," you say. And you may be right. But in many product categories, manufacturers today are finding it difficult to achieve a technological advantage over competitors. This manufacturing parity leaves the consumer with relatively indistinct preferences for individual products in many categories. Product promotions are often asked to help sway consumers. But a timed advertising exposure may be able to help.

All brands have a price/value dimension in the minds of the consumers who purchase them, or who reject them after considering these brands for purchase. A brand of high quality and low cost (when promoted, for example) has a large price/value dimension; a brand of average quality and cost has a much smaller dimension. The advertiser of each brand tries to increase the size of its price/value dimension by enhancing the consumer's perception of its quality, through advertising, packaging, and product performance. It also lowers its price from time to time, but judiciously, as an alternative way of increasing its price/value dimension as much as possible. (To reduce the price can work against the consumer's perception of quality, if overdone.)

Promotional pricing often is an attempt by advertisers to enlarge their brand's price/value dimension over that of brands, which may be seen by consumers as being no different. Promotional pricing often is effective as a tie-breaker among these "no-difference" brands. The effect of the lower price is to enlarge the brand's price/value dimension from the pricing end only. An advertising exposure—which does anything to increase the perception of the quality of the brand at the time of the price promotion—will further enlarge the price/value dimension, and, presumably, will break more ties.

The Timing of Movie Commercials Is Great, but Are They Advertising?

First-run movie advertising on TV is worth thinking about for a moment. The timing aspect of this advertising is obvious. The movie has just begun its showing in local theaters. Newspapers are advertising the availability of this movie at these theaters. The PR mill is grinding out interviews with the stars, or the producer, on TV news and talk shows. Then the advertising of the movie appears on prime-time TV. It must be very effective, because it happens in the same way, over and over again.

But is it really advertising? Stop to think about it for a moment. What we see as a movie commercial on TV is really *sampling*, not advertising as we know it. We're given a piece of the movie to taste. No copywriter needs to be hired to think up something persuasive to say about the movie. Snip, snip. They cut out some pieces, splice them together, and get us to take a taste, without any overt effort on our part. If movie advertising on TV is as effective as I think it is, the reason is that movie studios are indulging in low-cost sampling, not in high-priced advertising.

We often confuse advertising with other forms of communication from a brand to its consumers (whether potential or acheived). Coupons, for example, are classified as "promotion activity," not as advertising. But sometimes they do exactly what we expect advertising to do. Let's examine what a coupon can do to help advertise a new brand.

How a Coupon Helps Bad Advertising
for a Good Brand

Sometimes a new brand has outstanding advertising copy, as good
as any agency could develop to help it get the consumer's attention and interest. But more often than not, a new brand's advertising copy is far below the quality it deserves. Agencies usually
focus on making a great commercial, or a great ad. Many times,
they even lose sight of the brand, and what it has to say to its consumers, in the process of trying to make the advertising look good,
not the brand.

Also, a new brand often gives an agency too little time to go
far enough through the process of trial and error to develop the
best commercial or ad. For good reasons, agencies don't like to
admit that the path to effective advertising copy is a long zigzag
through weak, bad, or even off-strategy creative efforts. And in
fairness to agencies, the zigzag may even include backtracking to
a piece of advertising that had once been rejected by an indecisive
client. If you can look back over the development of dozens of
campaigns, as I have, you may recall that a new brand's advertising becomes clearer and better as the people working on it learn
what it is they are trying to communicate about the new brand.

Now consider what a coupon does for a new brand whose copy
doesn't attract and interest consumers as much as it should.
Nobody likes to pass up an offer of money, which is what a coupon
is. Neither you nor I are likely to turn the page, and reject a high-
value coupon, without knowing what it is we're rejecting. We don't
reject the fifty cents. We reject buying the brand that wants to give
us fifty cents for buying it.

But how can we reject something we don't know anything
about, or don't understand? The answer is that we can't. The
coupon has become an integral part of the introductory *advertising*. It replaces, and improves on, the headline of the ad. It makes
some of us read and learn—at least enough to accept or reject the
fifty cents.

Several years ago, this forced-learning process was demonstrated
dramatically in the test market of a new hair-care brand. After
about a month of substantial advertising, consumers' awareness

of the brand, and their ability to make name-benefit closure with it, reached a plateau at about 50 percent and 25 percent, respectively. Monthly bursts of additional advertising (which would cost about two million dollars each, in 1989 dollars) did nothing to increase consumer awareness. Then the brand ran a Sunday newspaper supplement ad, with a fifty-cent coupon in it.

Six days later, research was conducted for the next measurement of awareness levels. Total brand awareness had leaped from 50 percent to 80 percent! Brand-benefit closure also soared, from 25 percent to 45 percent! Nobody ever expected that the translation of the brand's magazine copy into a newspaper ad would cause such increases. But the ad itself didn't make it happen; the ad had run before, without the coupon. The coupon had forced the attention of consumers who had previously ignored the advertising, which had been exposed to them in the same way as the coupon ad. The coupon had improved the headline of the ad, and also had improved it over the awareness-building of the TV commercials. The coupon ad had become better advertising than the original advertising.

That was the good news. The bad news was that all those consumers who had become aware of the brand, and those who had become newly aware of the benefit it offered, were not really interested in the brand itself. They learned only enough about it so they could decide whether to accept or reject the fifty cents. We discovered this five weeks later, when the next wave of research showed that awareness had fallen to pre-coupon levels. Everything gained by the coupon was lost—except for the insight it gave us on the ability of a coupon to draw consumers' attention to a brand about which they don't yet know very much.

Whether you label these paths of communication from a brand to its consumers "advertising," or whether you label them couponing, sampling, packaging, or whatever, they are all exposures of what a brand has to say to consumers. If timing is the most critical decision in putting together a media plan, if timing is the key issue in the effectiveness of actionable advertising, we can't ignore the value of these many well-timed opportunities to communicate. Among them we may even find that elusive exposure—"effective frequency."

12
Finding Media Insights
Where Least Expected

O ne of my recurring themes is the belief that advertising people know so little about their business because they think
they know so much. They spend little or no time seriously trying
to learn. They seem to think that effective and efficient communication to a mass consumer audience is an easy task for any advertising agency skilled in the conventional disciplines of its business.
But it isn't easy. At best, it's difficult; at worst, it can be impossible. We know far too little about how the communication process
works, or what we need do to lead a consumer to take action at
the supermarket shelf. If the industry knew how to create the most
effective advertising campaign at the lowest cost to the advertiser,
it wouldn't need to cover up its ignorance with the wishful thinking as evidenced in the verbal narcotics I've mentioned—*impact,
synergy, competitive presence*, and so on.

I'm painfully aware of how little I really know about the
business I've worked in for thirty-seven years. I don't need to be
reminded of how important it is to keep my eyes open at all times,
looking closely at everything that goes into the advertising process, trying to find a new clue that will allow me to replace a bad
guess with a good one, or at least a better one. I've often asked
questions about copy and research, questions that media people
aren't supposed to ask, because they didn't deal with media. That
is, the questions didn't deal with media in the opinion of others,
those who believe that media people are media specialists, and
shouldn't ask embarrassing questions about copy or research. I've
always believed that anyone who tells me to close my eyes, and

not try to learn something about the nonmedia areas of advertising, is someone trying to protect his personal turf; that person is not trying to advance his company's business. I've never taken advice from such people, and never will. Nor should anyone else.

Wonderfully productive things can be learned when a person wanders outside the boundaries of his own discipline with open eyes, and, even more importantly, with an open mind. By doing this, I've discovered some of my most useful media insights, and where I least expected to find them. I'll share a few of these with you. I'm going to reach back about twenty-five years for the first example, because I think it best demonstrates how a casual statement, by a nonmedia person, can lead to innovation in media usage.

Of Course, 120 Divides More Ways Than 60!

In the early sixties, television advertisers were moving from 60-second commercials to shorter lengths. The movement began as piggybacking two commercials in the standard minute of time. Most of these fractional commercials were thirty seconds long. However, some were 40/20 splits, rather than 30/30. The problem with 40/20 splits was that if a brand needed more than thirty seconds for its commercial, it had to find another brand that needed less than thirty seconds. Since the creative trend was to reduce commercials from sixty seconds downward, it was easier to find a brand with 40-second commercials than one with 20-second commercials.

I was working at Procter & Gamble when all this occurred. P&G could usually reduce its slice-of-life commercials to 40 seconds. But 20-second commercials required a totally different format. Consequently, there were few of them to partner with the many 40-second commercials that had been produced. I was explaining this problem to a young associate brand manager in the Toiletries Division. (I emphasize his job level to establish that he was not the beneficiary of years of marketing and advertising experience.) He wanted to use his brand's new 40-second commercial, and I was telling him that he would have problems because of the shortage of partners. I explained that the networks sold time only in 60-second blocks, and that we probably wouldn't be able to find enough 20-second partners for all P&G's 40-second needs. He looked at me quizzically and said, "Then why don't you just buy two minutes? You can divide 120 seconds more ways than you can divide 60 seconds."

Just like that! A matter-of-fact solution to a simple arithmetic problem! I was embarrassed because I hadn't seen the solution myself. I guess I was a little jealous, too. But I wasn't going to pass up the opportunity to use this brilliant insight. It deserves being called brilliant because nobody else was doing it. Nobody else had ever thought of it. I left P&G at about that time, and never had the opportunity to make productive use of this creative thinking while I was still there. But I did later, for the brands of S.C. Johnson & Son. These brands were also cutting their 60-second commercials to 40-second lengths, and suddenly it was discovered that they needed three times as many forties as they could partner with twenties. That's when I began buying two-minute blocks from the networks. Instead of putting four thirties in these two minutes, we scheduled three forties. As my P&G associate had observed, the longer block of time could be divided in more ways than the standard one-minute block. We even scheduled 40/40/30/10 lengths in these longer blocks, after we discovered that we had inadvertently created a place for our 10-second commercials on network television, and for the first time.

However, we encountered an obstacle to our creative scheduling in half-hour TV programs. These programs were formatted with three commercial breaks, each sixty seconds long, at the beginning, middle, and end of the program. But now the solution was simple. I went to the networks, and asked them to sell me their opening and middle minutes on the half-hour shows we wanted. But I also said that we needed the first commercial break shortened to forty seconds, and the middle one lengthened to eighty seconds, so we could run our 40-second commercials without 20-second partners. I guessed that the networks would instinctively reject any request to reformat their popular half-hour shows, so I included some self-interest thinking for them. "If you shorten the first commercial break, you get viewers back to the entertainment quicker at the beginning of the show, while they're still deciding whether to stay with it or switch channels. And they probably won't even know that the middle break is twenty seconds longer than usual." It worked. Old monitoring reports show that 40-second commercials for our brands routinely opened half-hour programs on all three networks. And all this creative media usage originated with the observation of a nonmedia person. But only because someone listened to him.

Media Insights from Copy-Testing Results

Copy-testing results have also provided me with insights which, subsequently, I have been able to use in media planning. For fifteen years, I set up all the on-air recall tests of our finished TV commercials. As I became familiar with the testing technique, and the kind of responses it obtained from its standard questions, I became curious about what would happen if additional questions were asked at the end of each interview. So I added a few. One of them was asked of only those who could accurately remember something from the test commercial. It went as follows: "Was there anything confusing or unclear in the commercial you saw for Raid (or Pledge, or Glade) last night?"

After asking this question as part of almost a hundred recall tests, I discovered that consumers gave me an almost unanimous negative response for each commercial tested. There was usually one consumer who said yes; sometimes there were two, sometimes none. What I found curious was that the response was the same for failed commercials as well as for the most successful. This bothered me. I felt, instinctively, that a weak commercial would be less clear, more confusing than a strong one. But my information seemed to be saying that it wasn't. I was wrong, however.

The question was being asked of only those consumers who could, after twenty-four hours, remember something about the commercial. The obvious conclusion to be drawn was that anyone who could remember part of the commercial the day after seeing it hadn't been confused by this commercial. Turn the sentence around, and the conclusion now reads: "Anyone who is confused by a commercial, or who finds something unclear in it, can't remember anything about that commercial the next day." Logical, isn't it? Isn't this what happened to us in school? What we didn't understand was hard to remember when we took an exam on it. "Well, that's interesting," you might say. "But it isn't media planning. It's a creative problem. The answer is don't make confusing commercials. The consumer doesn't put confusion in her memory bank, so she can't retrieve it. But it's not a media issue. Talk to the creative people about it."

Ah, but it is a media issue. It may be the most important insight affecting your media planning. It may totally change your perception of how advertising works. It may even put your thinking about effective frequency in the garbage can.

Let's talk about effective frequency once again, and the subject of response functions. Most advertising people assume that many, if not all, consumers need an exposure frequency of more than one to understand, evaluate, and react to a TV commercial. Their feeling is that the second exposure builds on the first one, which by itself can't provide consumers with a full understanding of what the advertising is trying to accomplish, and that a third exposure often is needed to build on the second. In short, the belief is widely held that a consumer carries fragments of commercials in his or her head, and that these fragments make it possible for a succeeding exposure to combine with them to culminate in a completed exposure, or in what most advertising people call "effective frequency."

But my copy-testing experience has told me that incomplete communication can't be remembered the next day. How then can it be built on by a second exposure two days later, a week later, or whenever later? If communication isn't stored in the consumer's accessible memory unless it can be hooked there by an intellectual or emotional understanding, there can't be pieces of commercials waiting to be built up into something complete. If it is accessible in the consumer's memory, and can be built on, each commercial exposure seems obliged to communicate something *in its entirety*.

If this assumption is correct, each individual exposure seems obliged to be understood, either at the intellectual or emotional level. Each individual exposure needs to be effective every time it is encountered by the consumer. If this effective exposure doesn't lead to action at the shelf, it's probably because the *consumer* wasn't ready, not the advertising. The advertising worked, but the consumer's portion of the two-ingredient chemistry was missing. Now, do you still think it's only a creative problem? Suddenly, what was a casual look at an exhibit of research numbers from copy tests has become a new insight into the basic workings of a media plan.

Understanding Psychological Time

My third and last example of discovering media-planning insights outside the media department involves the psychological perception of time. Several years ago, I tracked the growth of a new brand's awareness (measuring brand-benefit closure) over a long period of time. This brand had been sampled when it was introduced, so at the end of each interview we asked respondents if they remembered having received a sample. Results of each survey were tabulated to show the difference in awareness between those who claimed to have received the sample and those who didn't. (Awareness was very much higher among those who claimed to have received the sample.)

An interesting finding, and a logical one, was that the percentage of women claiming to have received the sample declined over time. The decline was slower than most people expected, but it was consistent—a gentle downward slope. Then a survey that came in showed a sharp vertical drop. Had we reached the end of the consumer's memory capability for retrieving these samples? No, the next few surveys showed the same gentle slope that had preceded the sharp drop.

The sharp drop had occurred in a survey conducted early in January. What had happened between this survey and the previous one? Christmas happened. That's what I told people. They thought I was crazy. How could Christmas change the shape of a curve that had started four months earlier, and resumed for three months afterward? Perhaps it was only an aberration. No, it wasn't an aberration. It was Christmas. Let's consider our psychological, or subjective, perception of time.

We measure time subjectively—less by the calendar than by the events that have occurred during the time our mind is measuring. To use an exaggerated example: Suppose there is a guru who resides on the side of a mountain, high in the wilderness of Tibet. If only one person has visited the guru this year, and that was eight months ago, it won't seem like eight months ago to the guru. The time will seem much shorter. He will even remember that person's name, because not much has happened to the guru since their meeting. The previous year, the guru had received twenty visitors in twenty days. At the end of the twenty days, the guru couldn't remember the name of the first person to have visited him. The guru couldn't remember anything about that first person. It seemed like a long time since that first person had climbed the mountain to see him.

The guru, like all of us, perceives time retrospectively, in terms of *events*. The more events, the longer the time. The fewer the events, the shorter the time. When we have done many things during a week, the interval seems longer than a week. When we have done little, our perception is that the time was shorter than a week.

Let's go back to what happened to the consumer's memory after having received a sample. The percentage of consumers remembering the sample was declining at a constant rate over time, which suggests that the further removed in time from when the sample was received, the less likely the consumer was to recall having received it. This means that time was eroding her memory of the sample. But Christmas accelerated this decline. Christmas *added time* to the consumer's memory. Christmas is a period of many events compressed into a short time.

"All this is very interesting," you say, "but what does it have to do with media planning?" Quite a bit, actually. It tells me that the effect of a commercial or an ad encountered by the consumer *before* Christmas will have a shorter life in her memory (or will become inaccessible more quickly) than one encountered *after* Christmas. All other factors, such as cost and seasonality, being equal, I would choose to deliver my message to consumers after Christmas rather than before. The gain in advertising effect might be a small one, but I think it would be a real one. And real gains aren't easy to come by in this business.

External Media Insights Don't Come Easy

The vigorous interaction with marketing people in the process of media planning has provided new media insights, even in this fourth decade of my media career. However, the accolades for this source of media insights need to be qualified. The marketing people in these meetings have been willing to commit themselves to full and honest disclosure of their thinking process, without regard for embarrassment or loss of face for not being able to answer the basic strategic questions of their business. From an intellectual point of view, they washed windows and cleaned toilets, without regard for rank or personal prestige. These people, in the kinds of meetings that ask for an important contribution to media thinking from them, are the only marketing people who can give you new insights.

Copy testing has always seemed to me to be a wonderful source of ideas and insight into better media planning. Copy is tested, quite logically, by exposing it to consumers. Media plans work by exposing commercials and ads to consumers. Copy is tested by exposing it in different ways, and/or a different number of times, to consumers. A media plan works by exposing ads and commercials to consumers in different ways, a different number of times. Most advertising people don't see any relationship. But most of them aren't looking for one. That's why they know so little about how to create and schedule effective and efficient advertising campaigns.

Research people don't help the cause. They don't want media people mucking around in their copy research, or in their campaign research, either. Copy testing has never stopped being painfully controversial. Inviting media people into this intellectual scrimmage would be asking researchers to inflict another source of pain on themselves. The same is true of campaign research. Advertising campaigns are not being researched adequately, or at all. Researchers are not likely to welcome the intrusion of media people whose professional development is being frustrated by the absence of good campaign research.

I was lucky to be privileged to violate the sacred halls of copy testing and campaign research. Many years ago, our marketing vice president lost confidence in his marketing research director, and asked him to leave. Although I had no research credentials, I was named to replace the research director. I learned a lot about advertising research, but I was not welcomed by the internal research group. In the absence of a corporate mission to develop effective and efficient advertising, everyone involved in the advertising process becomes a staunch defender of turf, not an unselfish member of a dedicated team. (I'll bet that the reader of this page, if actively involved in the advertising process, is right now ducking arrows in one of these tribal wars.)

How to Improve Advertising Insights

The solution to all this divisive activity, which blocks new insights, rather than encouraging them, is cooperation. We put men on the moon through the cooperative effort of a small army of dedicated people. We developed an incredibly productive economy during World War II because we united to cooperate at our highest level of dedication. Most important human achievements have required cooperation. So will advertising insights. But getting individualistic human beings to cooperate with each other requires leadership, and a mission drafted or mandated by this leadership. The business of advertising has no mission to learn how advertising works. It has no leader to provide or mandate a mission that would inspire individuals in advertising to work together in order to learn what they need to know to make advertising more effective.

For reasons given elsewhere in this book, I see little likelihood that anyone working in the advertising business will draft such an industry mission. By default, then, it must be the advertiser's corporate management which assumes this leadership role. Corporate management must provide their own mission to achieve effective and efficient advertising through internal and external cooperation between the different functions that make up the advertising process.

The question is, can they handle this leadership role without understanding advertising? They obviously don't understand it, or they wouldn't put up with its irresponsible activities, both internal and external. Perhaps too many of them can still afford the waste that accompanies ineffective or inefficient advertising. Perhaps they haven't had to understand advertising enough to worry about it. Too bad. We really need their leadership before any progress can be made.

13
Word of Mouth

The most persuasive advertising I can remember didn't reach me on a TV screen, or on a page in my favorite magazine, or on the radio, or in my morning newspaper. This advertising came to me across my back fence, from the mouth of my neighbor. He told me about a movie he had seen the night before. His reaction to the movie was so compelling that I decided, on the spot, that I was going to see that movie myself.

Something similar happened to my wife. One day she brought home a hand lotion whose compelling advertising had reached her across the sink in a washroom at work. Moosehead Beer was only a whimsical name to my brother-in-law until somebody he met at lunch told him that it was "a real good beer." My sister-in-law is reading a book that a friend at work told her she "should definitely read."

No advertising medium is more powerful than words from the mouth of a friend who has had a good experience with a product. I doubt that many people would disagree with this observation. However, even those who agree will generally dismiss the observation as being nonactionable. An agency can buy magazine or newspaper space for any product. An agency can buy TV or radio time for most products. But an agency can't buy praise from the mouths of our friends, or relatives, for any of these products.

An agency can, however, learn what makes word-of-mouth advertising so effective. Once this is learned, the agency can create advertising that incorporates some of the benefits of word-of-mouth communication from a friend. At least it can avoid incorporating, in its advertising, the *antithesis* of the benefits which seem to be associated with successful communication from one person to another.

For example, if I'm a typical mainstream-American consumer, none of my friends talks with an accent that I can't understand. But I've listened to a radio commercial which was spoken in such an exaggerated British accent that I couldn't understand what was being said. I've watched a TV commercial for a new shampoo, which began with a woman speaking in such a heavy French accent, that I couldn't understand the first two sentences. During the rest of that commercial, I spent so much time trying to understand what had been said during the first few seconds that I never grasped what the brand was trying to tell me.

A multitude of products have tried to tell me that they were a new "concept" in something or other: floor care, oven cleaning, driving comfort, stereo sound, retirement living, and so on. My friends, whether talking to me across the back fence, at the lunch table, or in the washroom, have never used the word *concept* to describe something they've enjoyed using, or something they've experienced with pleasure.

"Concept" is an abstraction from intrabusiness language. It isn't "plain-folk talk." Why, then, do brands use it in advertising directed at us plain folks? Business people use different language in their business and personal lives. They have different vocabularies for the boardroom, the bedroom, the locker room, the church social, and so on. They don't talk like business people in the bedroom or in the locker room, but they often do in their advertising.

My neighbors dress much the way I do. Their homes may be unique, but they aren't very different from mine. I don't feel strange and uncomfortable when I visit their homes. But when viewing TV, I've felt uncomfortable when watching a woman in a cocktail dress polish her furniture. When watching TV, I've been uncomfortable in many ultramodern interiors, where I've spent a lot of time watching out for the sharp corners of the furniture but payed little attention to the product that was being advertised.

And perhaps most important, when my friend talks to me across the back fence, he stands still when he talks. His mouth doesn't zoom into and away from my face. He doesn't leap back and forth across the fence while he talks to me. He doesn't disappear behind trees and bushes, reappear, disappear, reappear. I have no trouble concentrating on what he's telling me. I can really understand him. He doesn't entertain me. He certainly doesn't amaze me. But he does communicate what he wants to say.

TV commercials impress me much more than my neighbor. Many of them actually amaze me. But I find that it's rarely the *product* that amazes me. Only the commercial. In the old days, we used to call "amazing" commercials like these "vampire video." Today we call them "intrusive, contemporary commercials." In the old days, we were cautioned to avoid them. Today, the self-designated experts counsel us to pursue them at any production cost.

Most of my friends are well educated. But the language they use when talking to me across the fence is pretty basic. They don't use sweeping metaphors, enigmatic symbols, or contrived inferences. They may or may not use their own colorful language. Their words sometimes exaggerate or understate. But one way or another, they act out a conviction that communicates to me across the fence. Why does so much advertising fail to do as well?

The advertising business claims that it tries to communicate. With one hand, it gives us a multitude of commercials to show us how hard it's trying. With the other hand, it whisks them away to be aired on TV before we can challenge their effectiveness. Let us examine one of them more closely. This is a shampoo commercial that wants to communicate "clean" to its viewers. The agency has used the word *clean* eleven times in thirty seconds. Well there, doesn't that prove the agency is trying hard to communicate?

Nope. They couldn't resist having three Betty Boop actresses, dressed in sailor outfits, mug through thirty seconds of quick-cut singing and dancing. When this commercial was researched the day after it was shown on a prime-time TV program, only 1 percent of the women who saw it used the word *clean* when describing what they had seen. The meaning of clean was given no *visual* support, despite universal knowledge that (1) television is a visual medium, (2) the human brain receives 90 percent of its information through the sense of sight, and (3) for decades, advertising research has been consistent in telling us that what is *shown* is likely to be communicated, but what is *said* is not. The agency was so determined to put on a good show in their commercial, that they relegated the commercial's most important sales point to the audio track, where research data would have assured them that it would fail to communicate. And so it did.

But even when the advertising is understood by the consumer, it usually fails to make something positive happen. Is it that we don't trust advertising as much as we trust our neighbor's judgment? However, I don't always trust my neighbor's judgment. We vote for opposing political candidates, as often as not. He likes coffee, but I prefer tea. He likes chocolate ice cream, but I don't like it very much. I like butter pecan ice cream. He doesn't. Yet each of us is more likely to believe the other's opinion of a product than we'd believe a TV commercial. At a bar, he and I are more likely to believe a stranger than the TV commercial the three of us are watching while we drink our Moosehead beer. Why can't more advertising capture the conviction of the common man who sells us from the adjoining bar stool? Is it even trying?

Advertising agencies use well-known personalities to attract attention to their commercial, and perhaps to build trust in its content. But the agency that selected Carol Channing as the best spokeswoman for a floor wax wasn't looking for someone with whom women could identify across the back fence. The selection of Bill Cosby (the most popular personality of the late 1980s) for your spokesman sounds like a good decision. And it may well be— for the first advertiser who uses Mr. Cosby. But when he appears every day on your television tube, talking to you about many different products, the neighborly Mr. Cosby seems to be taking on the image of a persistent salesman, rather than a friend talking across the fence. At least he has for me, and for others I have heard talk about his presence in so many commercials.

But do I digress? Is the subject of gaining insight from word-of-mouth advertising exclusively the domain of creative people, account managers, marketing and corporate management? Is there a sign that says: Media People Keep Out? Unfortunately, there is. People trained in a discipline are expected to restrict their business activity to this discipline. We who know what we're doing in media are asked to stick to media, and leave creative problems for the people who know what they're doing in this discipline. But, ah, there's the rub. Who knows what he's doing in the creative area? Who has been well-trained, and what constitutes "training?"

A product manager, responsible for developing a new commercial for his brand, may have participated in the development of fewer than half a dozen commercials prior to a new assignment. His first few commercials were probably tested by one or more questionable techniques, which may have given him the scores he needed for getting approval to air them, but this didn't *teach* him how to make an effective commercial. It's possible that none of the testing techniques he's used can discriminate between an effective and ineffective commercial. And it's almost certain that the product manager has seen little or no campaign research that could teach him the difference between what works and what doesn't.

One might expect that the creative people in advertising agencies would know a good commercial from a bad one. But they don't. Because of the absence of good, coordinated testing experience, their knowledge is limited. They may have worked on more commercials than the product manager, but nobody told them which ones were effective and which ones were not. Their experience, therefore, has been in the physical making of commercials, not in discriminating between the effective and ineffective ones.

Insightful media people have been kept too long in the background because they are thought to be deficient in the expertise needed for them to participate in developing the creative product. But since there is no substantiated expertise in the creative part of the advertising business, media people can, and probably should, bring insights to the creative process, just as copy testing brings new insights to the media process. If they do, the creative process will have better direction, and the final creative product will communicate more effectively.

For example, a media person knew that while the managers of the original creative execution for Lemon Pledge were constructing elaborate TV fantasies, the brand's primary competitor (Behold) was allowing Ruth Lyons, a TV show host, to talk to viewers about it in her own words ("woman talk"). Ruth had a large, loyal following in the Dayton, Cincinnati, and Columbus area. The ratings proved it. So did the business results for Behold. The brand had twice the share of market in this area than it had nationally.

A media person can alert a creative team about the environment for which they create their commercials. Commercials seem to be created without regard for the environment in which the consumer will see them. I've never seen a new commercial screened for approval under conditions comparable to what this commercial will encounter in the real world. The screening TV set is big, expensive, and kept in perfect working condition. The screening room is kept silent while the new commercial is being shown. No other commercial is shown before or after it. If anyone coughs or sneezes during a screening, the commercial is shown again, so it can be seen under perfect viewing conditions.

A media person can describe the real environment in which consumers view commercials. It isn't perfect. It's on a set of average size, of average quality, and in "working order." Reception isn't always good. Conversation in the room where TV is viewed is never hushed by anyone when the commercials come on. Someone coughes, someone sneezes. The phone rings. Or the doorbell. The dog barks to be let out to relieve himself. Kids fight on the floor in front of the TV set. Mr. Advertiser, your commercial is running while all this takes place! And it's running just once!

Even worse, somebody else's commercial ran just before yours. Yes it did! Believe me, it did. I know you've never seen another commercial run in front of yours. You'd fire anyone who interfered with the perfect showing of your new commercial in the viewing room. But there was this ugly, ugly commercial for something unmentionable, just before your beautiful new commercial was run.

And that's not all the bad news. Following your commercial, there was another commercial. Yes there was! And you know, it looked an awful lot like yours. People were dancing, and jumping, and splashing water all over themselves. If you like your commercial, I bet you'll like theirs, and a lot of others very much like it; theirs look just like yours, too.

We media people know little about making TV commercials. Like the creative people, we can't discriminate between an effective one, and one that makes nothing positive happen for its brand. So we can't help you in this area of creativity. But what we can do is bring a sense of reality and responsibility into this fantasyland where creative people often lose sight of what their commercial is supposed to do. We can ask them questions that require clearly thought-out answers. These questions may inhibit some of their creativity, but creativity that does nothing for the advertised product *should* be inhibited, shouldn't it? We might even cut in half the high cost of developing new advertising. The focusing of the creative execution doesn't mean diminishing its quality. Ravel wrote a piano concerto for his friend who had only one arm. The sonnet is the most disciplined form of poetry, but Shakespeare wrote a book of them.

A media person is good at gathering numbers, and in putting them into meaningful clusters of numbers we call statistics. He can collect all the published spending data for the brands that have used the kind of commercials the creative people want to use for your brand. He can show you how much money has been spent (sometimes with no effect) on a brand's sales volume. He can show you how the advertising world *demands* a postevaluation of his media buys, and how this leads to better media buys. He may point out to you that almost *nobody* asks for a postevaluation of the creative execution's effect on a brand's business. If you let him, his next words will probably be: "Creative people would probably be able to create better copy if their predecessors had been asked for a postevaluation of their creative work."

For seeing things in context, media people are better than others in advertising. Their battles take place in advertising's trenches, hills, and fields of mud—the real world of communicating with consumers. Others in the business sit comfortably in a paneled strategy room, talking about a romantic war, an abstract war. Most of them wouldn't know a bullet from a billet. But they don't need to. You, Mr. Advertiser, have given them a lifetime pass to fantasyland. And the rides are on you.

They have such beautiful, theoretical ideas about their creative execution. They need a specific quality of reproduction for their ads, which only certain magazines can provide. Or their TV commercial needs to be showcased within the boundaries of a glossy TV program. But an ordinary media person can disabuse them of these theoretical concepts by showing them the test-market activity of our most successful trademarks. The media people stuffed the TV commercials of these brands into whatever nondescript slots they could find on the stations in the test markets. They often translated their brand's slick-magazine copy into local newspaper supplements. Media people probably could prove that the success of these brands could be traced to the *content* of the advertising, rather than to the style or quality of its execution.

Word-of-mouth may have no "style," but it does have content. Its content, pure and simple, is *believable consumer satisfaction*. Media people are the grunts of this business of advertising, and from their low angle of view in the trenches, they can see what makes word-of-mouth so effective. Perhaps you should listen more to your media people. They're on your side, you know. You may not be able to win the war without them.

14
Television: Our Best Friend,
but Worst Enemy

If I were to tell you that television commercials dilute the vital essences of advertising and marketing people, you would write me off as being of unsound mind. So, obviously, I won't tell you that it does. I'll let you draw this conclusion yourself.

A television presentation is undeniably the most effective way for advertisers to communicate with most people. A television commercial can hold the attention of people who have absolutely no interest in the product being advertised. This product can be on the bottom of the totem pole of consumer interest; but if its TV commercial sings, dances, or dazzles the senses, the uninterested viewer will sit still and watch, listen, and be sincerely impressed.

This isn't an expression of my opinion. This is a consensus belief held by just about everybody involved in the advertising process. If you haven't already heard them, you'll soon hear words like these: "We have a low-interest product with no real news to use in our advertising. The only way we can break through to the consumer is by concentrating all our advertising in TV. The magazine reader is going to turn the page on us. The radio listener is going to tune us out. We need the sight, sound, motion, and drama of TV to have any impact on our consumer."

What this consensus is telling us is that an advertiser, who has nothing to say to uninterested consumers, is ready to sing, dance, or dazzle millions of people with something other than his product. This advertiser is about to sell his consumers *television entertainment*, not the product he manufactures. His commercials won't sponsor the programs on which they appear; his brand will sponsor *the commercials* in which they appear. His brand will be much like those corporations that sponsor programs on noncommercial public television. "These thirty seconds of entertainment are brought to you by Zephyr air freshener."

Supporters of this consensus thinking argue that this is the only way to keep the brand name in the forefront of the consumer's mind. If a brand has nothing "salable" to communicate to consumers, they're probably right. This is one way to keep a brand's name in the forefront of the consumer's mind. But exactly what is this worth? We know what it's worth to the advertising agency: spending, commissions, revenue to the agency. But what is the value of a name, without any meaning for the consumer, to the brand who has sponsored a commercial of TV entertainment? Not much, in my opinion. But don't accept my opinion. Take the opinion of all those advertisers who have shifted advertising dollars into promotion budgets. No intelligent advertiser likes to discount the price of his brand. The role of advertising, in its broadest meaning, is to raise the quality of a brand in the consumer's mind. Discounting a brand's price works against the elevation of quality. Advertisers want to use promotions as little as possible. Yet they are using price promotions more and more. Why?

Well, to put as much consumer perception of value between quality and price, they must either raise quality through advertising or lower price through promotion. Shifting money from advertising to promotion betrays a belief in their inability to succeed in their first choice, that is, to raise quality through advertising. People in the business of advertising, who know what advertising can do for a brand, deplore the shifting of dollars from advertising to promotion. But they're also deploring, at the same time, the shifting of dollars from their pocket to someone else's. The smart marketer, who has nothing salable to say to consumers in his advertising, can put these dollars into promotion until he finds something worthwhile to say in his advertising.

But others keep their money in advertising. They may have nothing to say, but they can make TV commercials that get them a lot of attention. Most of this attention is confined to within the industry. But some of it does come from consumers. You can hear consumers talk about these commercials: "You know, TV commercials are better than some of the shows themselves." But how are they better? Not in helping the consumer make a better choice of detergent, deodorant, shampoo, or toilet-bowl cleaner. The commercials being talked about in this way are seen as better *entertainment* than some of the shows that carry them.

Making a better product than your competitors is far more difficult than making a better TV commercial than the last one you made for your brand. To provide a consumer benefit by offering a new marketing idea, as Mop & Glo did, is far more difficult than making a new TV commercial. Electricity, and most advertisers, take the path of least resistance. Many brands improve the quality of the entertainment they sponsor in their TV commercials. Far fewer are able to improve the quality of their product enough so that consumers begin to buy it in preference to another brand they've been using. Far fewer are able to discover a new marketing idea that can capture the self-serving interest of consumers.

"Doing something better" is the perennial goal of marketing people. Making a better TV commercial is often a substitute for doing something that makes "something positive happen" in the mind of the consumers. An exciting TV commercial can win an industry award. It can impress the company's management, and help the career of the people responsible for the exciting commercial. It can impress consumers, who watch it at home on their TV sets. It can even make something positive happen in these consumers. But it may not be positive for the brand. It may be positive only for the *commercial*.

Exciting TV commercials often become end-result goals in themselves, not just for advertising agencies, where these commercials serve an important economic function, but for the advertiser who chooses the path of least resistance. If product improvement is thought to be impossible, if no new marketing idea has surfaced in years, an advertiser can "do something better" by making an exciting TV commercial. But if this commercial does nothing for his brand's business, it has prevented him from tackling a difficult task (improving the product), and has allowed him to label this task "impossible." All this, because he has what he thinks is a constructive alternative. If he knew that the only way to help his brand's business was to improve the product itself, or find productive new ways to use his existing formulas, he'd find a way to do it. Almost nothing is impossible until we say it is.

One of my discussions with a marketing manager will illustrate the point I'm trying to make. This marketing manager said, in effect, that he couldn't argue with my theories, acknowledging that I had spent many years thinking them out, and he hadn't found a way to refute their logic. In explaining why he was advertising, he said that his brand was in a declining category, and had nothing to say that will turn the market around. He wasn't even sure that what it said had any effect on the user of competitive brands. Then he asked me if the brand wasn't better off by advertising, than by not advertising. After all, he said, *something* was better than *nothing*. The brand couldn't be better off by not advertising.

My answer was something to this effect: Yes, the brand can be better off if it doesn't advertise than if it does. If it doesn't advertise, you're going to put the highest priority on doing something real for this brand, which you can then advertise, which you can then expect to make something positive happen in the consumer's mind. If you can't find anything to say that will raise the consumer's perception of your brand's quality, you'll scramble until you can find a constructive way to give it more value through promotions, or other marketing means. If you continue to advertise, you'll think the brand is doing something tangible to help itself, when it really isn't.

This marketing manager has moved on to bigger and better things, but his brand, still without anything important to say to consumers, is still advertising, still trying to make better TV commercials. The brand's product category continues to decline. The brands within this product category exchange a few share points from time to time. Most, perhaps all, of these involuntary trades are stimulated by price promotions. No sense of crisis exists. There is always an advertising budget. Money is always there to make a new TV commercial. Like the Las Vegas gambler, a product manager is probably thinking, "One of these days, I'm really going to hit it big."

Like the glitter of Las Vegas, the production values of today's TV commercials can start a person's head spinning. TV commercials use the latest and best production techniques. No expense is spared in the production of these commercials. Their cost per second averages more than four thousand dollars. Many cost twice this much. Some cost even more than that. At the average price per second of a TV commercial, a two-hour movie would cost about thirty million dollars. It's not surprising, then, that consumers find many commercials more impressive than some of the programs that carry them.

But being impressed by a TV commercial is not the same as being helped to a new course of action by relevant product information. The TV commercial that successfully introduced Bounce fabric softener was not an impressive commercial. Neither was the commercial that tripled the market share of Crest toothpaste, nor was the commercial that enabled Mop & Glo to take over leadership of the floor-wax business. Many other unimpressive TV commercials introduced a multitude of other successful products. Without knowing what happened in the marketplace, no agency would have put any of these proved successes on the tape they use when soliciting new business. They may have been successful, but as TV commercials, they weren't impressive at all.

TV commercials are *functional* instruments of communication. TV commercials are as functional for communication as knives, forks, and spoons are for eating. Man has always had the impulse to embellish his functional instruments, and these instruments have continued to perform their intended functions, even though embellished by man's creative instincts. But there are limits. When embellishments interfere with functionality, the instruments become purely *decorative*, and often are no longer functional. We look at embellished cutlery in museums. We look at TV commercials on Clio-award reels. We begin to enjoy them more as decorative objects than as functional instruments.

Television commercials can be an advertiser's best friend, so long as they remain functional instruments of communication—from his products to their consumers. But TV commercials become an advertiser's worst enemy when they become decorative objects, used to hide gaps in his marketing program, gaps left by his having nothing worthwhile to say to consumers. TV commercials can be made attractive enough to hide, or distract us from, the biggest hole in a brand's marketing program. But they can't fill that hole. Many marketers don't want to believe this. Like the Las Vegas gambler, they continue to hope. I guess we shouldn't be surprised. Hope is always easier than hard work.

15
How to Obtain Good Advertising Research

G ood advertising research is obtained in the same way you obtain anything else in life. The process is simple:

1. You decide you *want* it.
2. You *figure out how* to obtain it.
3. *Resources are allocated* for it.
4. You go out and *do* it.

Most people in advertising, especially those in the research areas, are likely to dismiss this sequence as oversimplified. They're likely to give you a long discourse on why the research is difficult, if not impossible, to perform. Everyone who is failing to perform a task critical to the success of his profession, obviously sees this task as difficult or impossible to perform. But sending men through space to walk on the moon wasn't impossible. Yet, good advertising research seems to be. Why?

Let's look at the difference between the two tasks. First, the moon project. President Kennedy decided that he *wanted* to put an American on the moon by a predetermined date. He was satisfied that the task was theoretically possible; someone had *figured out how* to do it. He *allocated the resources* needed to develop the project to its execution phase. A task force of competent people went out and *did it*. Two men walked on the moon.

Now consider advertising research. But let's be more specific than "advertising" research. There is media research, copy research, campaign research, and so on. Media research can be further broken down into research done by its suppliers and research done by its users. Media research done by its suppliers is different from all other advertising research. In this area, we are rarely told that the research is difficult or impossible. To the contrary, we are given more good media (audience) research than we have good theories to make use of this research. Suppliers *want* to do this research; it makes it easier to sell their media. They find out how to do new or improved audience research, allocate the resources to do it, and then do this research as often as needed to keep advertisers using their media. They don't say "can't." Their pattern of decisions and activity parallels, on a small scale, what it took to put two men on the moon.

Other advertising research doesn't have the same pattern of decisions and activity working for it. President Kennedy may not have made a good decision in commiting so many resources to putting two men on the moon. This may have been a terrible waste. But an "impossible" job got done, because Kennedy, and the rest of the country, *wanted it done.* Very little good advertising research is done for or by the user of advertising, because the user often doesn't want it done. When you don't want something, you don't make a real effort to find out how to do it. You don't commit the resources to do it. Which means you can't do the research.

Let's look next at copy research. Most creative people don't want their work researched. These people are usually convinced that their work is good advertising. They honestly believe that any research technique that shows their work to be less than good is a bad research technique. They may be right, in that copy-research techniques are often the wrong technique to measure the value of the copy being tested. But bad test results from a bad research technique don't prove that their copy is good. They're more likely to be reassured, by a bad technique, that their copy is good, when it really isn't.

Good Reasons for Testing
TV Commercials on-Air

The primary function of a TV commercial is to communicate. You can argue about what needs to be communicated, whether it should be rational copy points or emotions. But you can't argue that a commercial should or shouldn't communicate. It must. In 1988, for example, it had to communicate in an environment where movement from commercial to commercial was being accelerated by the continued infusion of 15-second commercials. As I mentioned earlier, additional commercials don't "clutter" their selling environment, because clutter doesn't exist, except as a red herring to distract us from the inadequacies of advertising. But 15-second commercials do move viewers more quickly through commercial breaks.

Contemporary commercials are formatted to move viewers at a more rapid pace than ever before. Rapid cuts from one visual element to the next are shorter than ever. The viewer is almost challenged to keep pace with commercials, which seem to be trying to lose and confuse, rather than communicating. But, say their creators, these commercials are striving for a "total impression." No individual piece of them needs to be understood or retained for the commercials to be successful in conveying a benefit, usually a "higher-order benefit," for the brand being advertised.

But many brands that appeal to a particular target audience, even though in different product categories, now have commercials, side by side on the same program, that look pretty much alike to the tired TV viewer. You can see consecutive commercials, pairing beer and jeans, or a soft drink and jeans, with formats that are so alike as to be interchangeable. Snip out the few seconds where the brand is shown in these commercials, throw the snips in a hat, pick them out at random and reinsert them at random. What do you have? The same commercials that the casual viewer thinks he's seen before you took them apart, and randomly reconstructed them.

Put these factors together: more commercials, which creates a faster-moving environment; faster-moving commercials, many implicit in their mode of communication; and the sequential proximity of more similar commercials. Now, isn't it more of a challenge to communicate on TV than ever before? I think so. Then why have many advertisers, who previously tested commercials on the air (the environment in which they must communicate to be successful), shifted to *off-air*, or laboratory testing, of their new TV commercials? If the on-air testing of commercials was ever of any value, *now* is the time of its greatest value.

Advertisers and their agencies say they want to measure more than communication. They want to measure "persuasion." But earlier in this book, I showed that my experience with persuasion scores found them to be sample variances, far more often more than they signaled real differences in pre-post shifts of choice between brands. If my experience is broadly applicable, advertisers have traded away the best measurement of how well their commercials communicate in the real world, at a time when real-world communication is more difficult than ever before, in return for what may be a handful of sample variances. Sounds like a bad trade, doesn't it? But maybe it isn't. Maybe there's a *good* reason for testing outside the real world of a harsh television environment.

I also mentioned earlier that certain kinds of TV commercials test higher in forced-viewing research than they do when tested in the real world. My experience has shown these to be the implicit commercials, which appear to have increased in number where on-air testing of commercials has decreased. The more "beautiful" or "exciting" a commercial is, the more likely it is to blend in with the TV entertainment before and after it. It can be viewed as being not a commercial, but part of the flow of entertainment. A tired or casual viewer of television—which most people are at most times—may let these beautiful, exciting commercials flow over him with the rest of the TV entertainment. A consumer is less likely to let this happen if he participates in a recruited research session for this same commercial. I've never seen one of these commercials perform better on the air than in their forced-viewing research. I've usually seen them perform at *lower* levels than they have in forced viewing.

A "Good" Reason for Not Testing on Air

Perhaps this is our "good" reason for testing commercials today under forced-viewing conditions. The scores are higher. Advertisers and their agencies probably get better scores for the kind of commercials they want to use if they *don't* test them on the air. Does this seem to be self-destructive behavior? Not really. Remember, a lot of people in the advertising business use copy research only because someone, or some policy, requires them to do so. Many of them can't get approval to put their TV commercial on the air without a "score" of some sort, usually a "good" score. If forced-viewing gives them a higher percentage of good scores for their commercials than on-air testing, they'll have fewer "failures" if they test via forced viewing. That's productivity! Well, at least it's productive for the people who have responsibility for approving and making these commercials, if not for the brands who ultimately use them.

Perhaps this explains why many agency account managers, and many marketing managers, also would avoid testing their commercials if they had the choice. Some of them believe, like their creative people, that the advertising is good, and that any research that tells them otherwise is bad research. Others are not as sure of their advertising, but are convinced that the research technique imposed on them by corporate research policy is worthless. These people accept the researching of their commercials because they have no choice: they need a score to get the commercial approved for airing. These people have more important career battles to fight than arguing about which "black box" to use for testing their commercials.

Advertising Gets the Kind of Research It Wants

The advertising industry gets the kind of research it *wants*. Advertising people *work to develop* the techniques they want. Advertising management *allocates resources* for the techniques it wants. And finally, the advertising industry *does* the kind of research it wants. If it wants self-serving research rather than truly evaluative research, that's what the industry gets. Perhaps that's why so much advertising looks alike, and that's why so little is known about how to make a good commercial. Perhaps that's why there is so much wasteful trial and error needed to develop approved advertising copy.

If those responsible for making commercials want nothing more than abstract numbers that relate positively to a research norm, for no purpose other than getting their commercial approved and on the air, that's what they get. This process should be expeditious as well as efficient, even though the result may secure approval for airing the wrong commercials. Often, even the process isn't handled expeditiously. Countless hours of managerial time are spent debating whether a test score, which is numerically but not statistically below the norm, is really average or not. Conversely, when the approval guideline is an above-average test score, managerial time is wasted in the debate about what is or isn't "above average."

Nobody Seems Sure of What Copy Research to Want

But do advertising and brand-management people really know what they want from copy research? Do the marketing researchers who issue guidelines, approve techniques, and conduct this copy research, really know how to give advertising and brand-management people what they think they want? Much evidence exists to say that these researchers don't. We shall look first at general, and then at specific, examples which suggest that the research community either doesn't know what it wants from copy research, or if it does, doesn't know how to get it.

First the generality. Every change in the management of a marketing research department is likely to result in a change of techniques to measure the effectiveness of advertising copy. When I moved from Procter & Gamble to S.C. Johnson & Son, I found that my new employer was using a different copy-testing technique. And during my last twenty-four years of work, five changes in the management of marketing research resulted in four changes in copy-testing techniques. (The technique was held constant only once, when promotion to the management position came from within.) Most of these changes were not to "new and better" techniques, but were back and forth between on-air and forced-viewing techniques. The point to be made: For decades, there has been basic disagreement within the research community on how to test TV commercials.

Three Examples of Confused Copy Testing

Now for the specifics. A package-goods brand, a leader in its category, had been directing its advertising at nonusers, in an attempt to increase trial. Marketing intelligence discovered that two new brands were about to enter this category, each claiming to provide the benefit of the leading brand, but offering themselves to consumers at a much lower price. The leading brand quickly changed its advertising strategy to direct its advertising to its current users. The copy demonstrated how ingredients in its formula provided a high level of performance. The intention was to sensitize current users to this high level of performance, which they were already obtaining from use of the brand, and relate this performance to the ingredients in its formula.

The finished commercial was tested by one of the forced-exposure testing services, because the score provided by this service was the one needed for approval to air the commercial. The commercial's recall score was in line with the norm, but it was noted that the pre-post shift from other brands to the testing brand was on the low side of average.

Have you already detected the dissonance in what I've just written? The brand wasn't trying to influence its nonusers. The target of its advertising was exclusively *its own user base*. A measurement of pre-post shift in brand choice was totally irrelevant and unnecessary. What was needed was a measure of the response of the brand's *users* to this new advertising. But there was none, because the sub-sample was too small, and the cost of augmenting it was said to be prohibitive.

What the brand did get from this weakly targeted research sample was a communication measure. But it was communication in a forced-exposure situation. The commercial was very contemporary, very high tech in its execution. It was, without doubt, a high-risk commercial. It was so good that it moved into the class of commercials that are easily enjoyed by consumers for their visual reward to the senses. Since the only valid measure of effectiveness that could have been obtained in the research was a *good* measure of communication, the brand should have tested for this communication in the harsh world of television viewing, not in the pampered environment of a forced-viewing laboratory.

Here is another specific example to show why copy research can't expect us to take it seriously. This brand is in a category segmented to a major degree by price. There is a low-price segment, a "value" segment (just above this one), a medium-price segment, and on the top of the category, the premium brands.

This brand competes in the value segment. Brands in this segment must offer consumers something more than low price. They must communicate a perception of quality. But this quality doesn't need to be as high, or as explicit, as for brands in the higher-priced segments.

This brand made a series of rough commercials, and tested them in the forced-viewing technique used to weed out the probable successes from the failures. If you're not familiar with it, this technique offers consumers in the research sample a gift in return for their participation. This gift is a choice of any brand in the category being tested. The offer is made to women before and after exposure to the test commercial. The degree to which they change their choice of brands, after seeing the commercial, becomes the persuasion score. Need I go further, or have you already discovered the dissonance in this test? The flaw should be apparent.

Where is the pricing segmentation that works with the advertising to influence consumer choice among the brands? It isn't there. All the brands—from which the consumers in the research sample get to choose—are free! The research technique, whether intrinsically good or bad, was totally inappropriate as it was used for this brand.

The final example concerns a long-established brand which had dominated its category at the time. It had by far the highest market share. More than 80 percent of category users claimed to have tried the brand at one time or another. Awareness of the brand was close to 100 percent of these category users. Like most successful package-goods brands, this one created its new commercials according to a continuing creative strategy. In other words, it kept constant the consumer benefit that it offered in its advertising. Only the executions of this creative strategy were changed, to "freshen" them, to improve them in some way.

The first time this brand tested one of its new commercials in a forced-viewing session, it was greeted with a *negative* score of minus 2 percent (which is really a statistical zero, since the scores were claimed to be accurate only in the range of plus or minus 2 percent). You might expect everyone involved with this brand's commercial to be quite upset by this score. And they were. But I wasn't. I expected it. And I explained why to the product manager.

Everyone in the research sample was aware of the brand and the benefit it offered to consumers. Prior to showing the test commercial, when consumers in the research sample were offered their choice of brands in the category, everyone interested in this brand asked for it, obviously. Then a commercial was shown, one which was written to the same creative strategy, one which offered these consumers nothing new. They learned nothing that could influence them to switch to the testing brand. Most of them already had real experience with the brand (probably more than 80 percent), which meant that a commercial, *with no news*, was trying to add something to what the product itself had already communicated to consumers as they used it.

The product manager understood what I was saying, and seemed to agree with its logic. But the technique had been recommended to him by his company's marketing research department, and he didn't know what else to do. Moreover, the logical conclusion to be drawn, after understanding the situation, was not that a new research technique was needed. He understood that he couldn't hope to switch lost consumers without having something new to tell them. It was his *strategy*, not his executions, that needed to be freshened.

What happened next is what too often happens in today's consumer-product marketing organizations. Product managers underwent their biannual rotation of brand assignments. This leading brand got a new product manager, who stepped forward to "try harder" to accomplish what the previous manager had failed to do. New TV commercials were soon developed, *using the same creative strategy* that had been used by the previous product manager.

Undaunted, the marketing research department offered their usual reflex-action recommendation—a persuasion test for the best of the batch. They didn't accept my logic as to why this test would also give back a score of plus or minus zero. I wasn't a professional market researcher, and marketing research management always assumes that only their own kind can find fault with a research technique. The new product manager was unable, emotionally, to accept my prediction of absolute failure for *every* commercial produced to the long-term creative strategy. So the test went ahead as scheduled. Results: another negative number, identical with that of the earlier test—another statistical zero.

Something constructive might have resulted from this second piece of evidence in favor of logic and against the reflex action of using testing techniques. However, the same brand then came under threat from a major new competitor. It chose to modify its creative strategy by claiming the benefit of the new competitor. The testing for this latest advertising concerned itself with whether or not it had a *negative* effect on any of the brand's large user-base.

But when the dust of this skirmish settled, and when there was yet another product manager directing our leading brand, the old strategy was back in force, and a new commercial was again ready to be tested. The researchers, who never seemed to learn, were again recommending their favorite persuasion test. I went through my logic for the third time, with this third product manager. She was skeptical. I couldn't understand why. Not only was my logic the same, but there were now two examples in support of it. Then I remembered. She had begun her marketing career in research. She too may have been taught not to believe anything negative said about research by anyone outside the research community.

They decided to go ahead with the test. But this time, I decided I was going to drive a stake through the heart of this monster, "Ignorance." I told the product manager I was going to predict the test results. I told her that her persuasion score was going to be a *plus* 2 percent which was, of course, a statistical zero. But in this case, I was even predicting the *direction* of the variance. I figured that after two negative variances, there was a good chance for the next one to come up positive. And I really had nothing to lose; nobody was paying attention to me.

I was lucky. The test score was precisely as I had predicted. I knew it couldn't have been anything other than a statistical zero, but it could have been a negative variance, like the others. I felt great! There I was, finally about to score a point for logic, for *thinking* rather than for the reflexive use of "the best TV-testing technique available today."

But nothing constructive happened. All I did was create a new set of anxieties for those who already had more than they could handle. The same persuasion testing is being done years later, for the same kinds of brands; and no real switching can take place in the marketplace as a result of their commercials, because they're telling the consumer nothing she doesn't already know. The only place that some of these brands get consumers to switch to them is in the forced-exposure situation of the testing laboratory, where a level of awareness (100 percent) is created. This hasn't yet happened to any of them, and never will happen to most of them, not in the real world.

Sham Research Leads Us to Sham Advertising

How can media planning be taken seriously by its practitioners after they've gained insight into some of these sham tests of their agency's creative product? It can't. Media planning becomes a cynical exercise in the manipulation of data. When those responsible for the creative product don't know how to measure the quality of the product, or don't care whether or not they measure it, media planning itself becomes a sham. The almost universal unwillingness to measure the success or failure of multimillion-dollar media plans confirms this.

Most marketing research people don't understand advertising. But that's not surprising. Most of the people in advertising don't either, as I've tried to illustrate in this book. But advertising people don't need to understand it in order to make commercials and ads, or to write media plans. They merely have to make commercials and ads that look like the commercials and ads that everyone else in the business is making, without benefit of any understanding. They must make commercials and ads that get the approval of their clients, who also don't understand advertising. Media planners merely have to write media plans that look like everyone else's media plans, and get them approved by clients who don't understand media planning.

Consider what the researchers of advertising are supposed to be doing. They're supposed to measure whether commercials and ads are really good advertising. Research people are charged with learning whether anything will happen as a result of using a certain commercial or ad, and if so, which of them is more effective. These researchers are charged with finding out who is playing games with the making of commercials, ads, and media plans, and who isn't.

But they don't. They can't, because they don't understand advertising any better than the people who provide them with the commercials, ads, and media plans to research. So they do what the advertising community does. They do what others around them (in the research community) do. Everyone's doing recall testing, so they do recall testing. Everyone's doing persuasion testing, so they do persuasion testing. Everyone's measuring brand awareness, so they measure brand awareness. Everyone's experimenting with a new technique or two, so they experiment with a new technique or two. None of them knows how advertising works, and none of them asks. But they test the advertising. They fill in the blanks with magic numbers, just like their advertising counterparts do. They may say, "In order to be able to measure the results of a media weight test, you must increase your advertising by at least 50 percent in the test cell." (If media-weight tests, unaccompanied by product news, have virtually always failed, where did the research community come up with their magic 50 percent increment?)

We wouldn't be so ignorant about advertising today if we had measured the results of only 10 percent of the ad campaigns that have been run during the last twenty years. Neither would we be as ignorant about how to make a successful commercial if we had researched commercials consistently and accurately during these past two decades. But we haven't measured the results of campaigns, and we haven't researched commercials and ads in a way that leaves us any more knowledgeable about how to make a good one today than we were two decades ago. How much longer will we give research techniques the opportunity to prove themselves? When will they begin trying.

Using Cost as an Excuse to Avoid Research

The allocation of resources is a key step toward getting something done, and, even more important, in doing it *right*. This argument is put forth routinely: Better advertising research will cost too much money; nobody will pay for it. And I've heard this said many times; "We haven't got the money to track the results of our advertising. We need all (four million dollars) we have for media, just to stay competitive." Or this: "We've already spent thirty-five thousand researching these commercials. You can waste all your media money testing commercials, if you're not careful." A comment similar to the latter was made by a product manager for a brand that planned to spend "only" three million dollars on media for it's commercial. A 5 percent improvement in a commercial is too small to be measured using available testing techniques, yet an improvement of this magnitude would be worth $150 thousand to this brand. The product manager's concern with spending a small percentage of this potential increase in value betrays his lack of confidence in the research technique. Yet he is willing to gamble his company's money on commercials that have been inadequately tested, rather than insist that his research staff develop effective testing techniques.

Until the people responsible for commercials, ads, and media plans want good advertising research, whatever research is done will continue to be mostly the mechanical decision-aids (or should we say decision-excuses?) they are today. When those in the business of advertising are sincere in their professed desire for an accurate report card on their efforts, they'll get it. They'll get good research, because methods of doing this research will be discovered. Managers will insist that resources be allocated for this research.

The United States put men on the moon. Perhaps advertising research will put good numbers on paper someday. It sounds too good to be true. Maybe it is.

16

The Iron Fist
of Judgment

G ood judgment is a capability that all of us want to possess.
The phrase "good judgment" might make us think of history's
wise men, those who have been called sages. Good judgment is
that which earns a wise man the respect of others. This wise man,
our sage, weaves new thoughts into the rich fabric of his experience
and gives us answers to questions that we cannot answer using
the knowledge we have.

People who come to a wise man for advice usually need to
make decisions they themselves can't make. The good judgment
of this wise man helps them make an otherwise difficult or impossible decision. But the judgments he offers must be proved
good, over time, if he is to be known as a sage. Many people
have been elevated to positions of power, even though they
themselves were not powerful. Many people have been elevated
to positions of honor, even though they themselves were not
honorable. But no one is elevated to the position of sage without
having earned it.

Some among us claim to possess good judgment without having proved that their judgment is indeed good. Most of them are
pretenders, who delude themselves (but not others); they believe
that because they have the *power* to make judgments and decisions, this automatically makes these decisions and judgments good
ones. Where the value of these judgments is impossible to prove,
they simply assume that their judgments are good. When they have
power over others, they can force their subordinates to accept their
decisions and judgments.

If I have the hierarchal power that merits a corner office with a view, and you have an inside office, without windows, our disputes over the unknown are easily settled. You have "your opinion," and I have "good judgment." I don't need to earn the title of business sage. It comes with my office, along with the leather desk accessories and expensive calendar clock. Ultimately, my lack of good judgment may be revealed. But by then, I'll have been promoted to a higher position, and I won't give a damn what you think of my judgment. Or I'll be retired, living off the efforts of those who have had to work a little harder to make up for my irresponsible exercise of power.

This, then, is what "judgment" reveals itself to be in a knowledge-poor environment: *Power*. Advertising is, without argument, a knowledge-poor environment. The people in it admit that they don't know how, when, or why it works. Its effectiveness is almost never measured. As a consequence, advertising judgments and decisions are most likely to be the opinions of people unqualified to make good judgments. But these opinions are thrust upon others with the iron fist of hierarchal power.

The executive in the corner office says that these three TV shows are "quality" programs. He can justify paying a high price for his commercials on these programs because of their quality. His judgment ignores the higher cost per thousand (CPM) and authorizes their purchase. How do we know that his decision is good? Because it comes from the corner office. By definition, all judgments that come from this corner office are good. Everything else in this office is good: the furniture, the accessories, the art on the wall. Why not the judgment?

A laundry product's commercial tested well. It scored high above the norm, and communicated its main selling idea clearly to most of the test subjects. The marketing people liked it for the way in which the strong female character attacked her laundry problems, and solved them, using their brand. The commercial began its run on TV. But someone on the management committee, after seeing it, judged it to be a little "hard," and out of character with the "charming" advertising used by the brand for many years. The marketing group was asked to have the advertising agency work on a new execution of the old advertising. This "hard" commercial had a short life on TV. The iron fist of "good judgment" was too strong for the weak opinion of marketing people.

In media planning, the use of judgment is said to play an important role. Someone will caution us not to accept a value ranking of media vehicles on their CPM alone. He will tell us that we must use judgment to override numerical decisions: "Cost per thousand isn't everything. You have to look for the judgmental values." Certainly we do. Then, after applying a judgment value to some of our choices, we can reindex all our CPMs, and develop an adjusted numerical ranking. But those who suggest that we use judgment (usually theirs, not ours), often don't want the media choices to be renumbered by a judgmental value-index. Why not? Because whenever they give their choice a numerical value, it usually fails to qualify for selection by responsible media people. Usually, their selection must be allowed to remain a nonquantified "judgment call," if it is to be chosen over alternatives that have been assigned a numerical value for their intangibles.

Marketing men and women often feel compelled to offer their "good judgment" to resolve a media-planning unknown. I remember one who was convinced that he had the only accurate insight into the effective frequency needed for his brand's advertising. This brand had three million dollars to spend on advertising, and was in a category where annual advertising totaled an awesome two hundred million dollars. The "competitive pressure" convinced this marketing manager that consumers needed to see at least six real exposures of his brand's advertising, in four weeks, before anything happened. His judgment also told him that the effect of his brand's advertising decayed very quickly—almost instantly.

I pointed out to him that a sequence of six exposures wasn't possible if the effect of each exposure decayed almost instantly. If the effect of exposure number one decays before number two is shown, exposure two, in effect, never exists. The second exposure becomes a *new first exposure*. So does the third, and the fourth, and the fifth, and so on. But good judgment can, of course, overcome this kind of flaw in the design of a communication structure. Bang! An iron fist comes down on the table. Six exposures it is! When the brand is shown to receive an effective reach of zero, the agency is asked to look at unadjusted household GRPs, which give appropriately high reach and frequency numbers. Good judgment conquers all. Even intelligent media planning.

Often, poor judgment is substituted for good research into the needs and wants of consumers, which is why thousands of new products that enter the market each year are doomed to failure. Poor judgment is substituted for systematic learning in the creation of commercials, which is why so many bad ones are screened out by the weakest testing methods, and why so many others get through—to waste our time and our advertising budgets. Poor judgment is substituted for accountability research, and for testing the thousands of media plans that run each year. And this is why, today, we know no more about how to construct an effective media plan than we did three decades ago.

The iron fist of power throttles any attempt by the curious to learn what they need to know to become truly professional. Power is retained by limiting the amount of knowledge available to those subject to this power. The iron fist must keep shut all doors that lead to new knowledge and understanding for the weak and powerless. While the sage offers his judgment with an open hand, the powerful impose theirs with a closed, iron fist. This is why there is little new learning in a profitable power structure. This is why advertising is as it is today, and as it has been for decades, and as it may continue to be for decades into the future. The only way it can change is to destroy itself, and rise reborn from its own ashes. But is advertising ready for self-immolation? Who has the match? Is he willing to strike it?

17
The Reluctant Future
of Media Planning

The Need for Accountability

Most people involved in the media planning process show no signs of wanting to perform significantly better in the future than they do today, or have done in the past. And if they did, how would they do it? There's only one way. That's by making advertising accountable. By measuring results. Without measuring results, media planning, and everything else in this business of advertising, can be made to *look better*, but not to *be* better.

Little more than this has happened in the last quarter of this century. Commercials look much better than they did twenty-five years ago. But there's no evidence to prove that they *sell* any better. Nobody can prove that today's commercials even sell as well as the crude black and white executions of the late fifties and early sixties. Granted that they probably have less to sell to consumers than their ancient counterparts, but the observation doesn't change. Commercials and ads are supposed to be *functional*, not *decorative art*.

Media plans also look better than they used to. They have access to far more data on the audiences of media vehicles. Computers can manipulate these data more ways than a media planner could ever have dreamed of doing on crude calculators twenty-five years ago. But there's no evidence that a media plan of today is any more efficient at using media productively than it did decades earlier, when media planners had available only a small fraction of today's data base. Like their creative counterpart, current media plans look so much better than media plans once did that everybody takes for granted that the plans must be more effective, more efficient. But there's not one shred of evidence to prove it, because nobody has bothered, during the last quarter century, to figure out how to get this evidence. Perhaps nobody really *wants* to get it. Perhaps everyone can advance his career without doing anything *real* to improve his advertising.

To measure the successes and failures of advertising campaigns will cost something. People involved in the advertising process will pay for these measurements. And not just with research money. For the failures they measure, they will pay in lost or deferred revenue. Many who have acquired an undeserved reputation for good advertising will lose that reputation when their failures are revealed. But not measuring the success or failure of advertising campaigns also costs something. Many of the brands that fail to measure results will continue to spend unproductively, not knowing that they need to change something in order to make their advertising work, or work more efficiently. Men and women in the advertising business will continue to work as novices rather than as experts in their profession, because they will be denied the knowledge they need.

The advertising business remains enormously profitable, even though no one measures its effect on sales. So long as it is profitable, there will be no incentive to measure success and failure. So long as advertising's success can be inferred by the absence of bad news, why risk measuring it? Why be accountable when little or no gain is offered in return for the risk of discovering failure?

Ineffective advertising can escape accountability as long as advertisers can pass its economic waste through to consumers in the form of higher prices. Or these advertisers can continue to afford to advertise ineffectively by reducing expenses through early retirement programs and hiring freezes. But it's foolish to think that advertisers will cut all the flesh off their organizations and continue to allow the flag of advertising to fly from their skeletons. Under competitive pressures these advertisers never had to contend with before, they began butchering their organizations in the mid-eighties. It's no longer a question of will it happen? The question is, when will the blade of the knife encounter advertising?

Eliminate the Commission Compensation System

Nobody does anything in life without some kind of incentive. Rewarding good conduct usually stimulates good conduct; rewarding bad conduct usually stimulates bad conduct. Rewarding advertising people for wasting money usually stimulates them to waste more money. Therefore, rewarding advertising people for *not* wasting money should stimulate them to waste less money. I use the word *should* only because this point is still theoretical. I don't know of anyone who has begun to reward advertising people for spending less money. I don't know anyone who has begun to reward advertising people for spending no more than is needed for a brand in order for it to achieve its maximum level of long-term profitability. I don't even know how they could do this. If nobody knows how, why, or when advertising works, it's virtually impossible to make it work at peak efficiency.

But no progress will be made, not even a directional improvement in the margin of error, until advertisers stop rewarding their agencies for the unproductive spending of more and more advertising monies. If an agency knows that an advertiser with four million dollars to spend on advertising on a brand has nothing important to say in this advertising, nothing that will make something positive happen in consumers, the agency shouldn't be asked to give up six-hundred thousand dollars in commissions for telling its client the truth. Under the commission system, if the brand spends nothing, the agency generally gets nothing.

If the same advertiser lost a sack containing four million dollars from the open door of its payroll truck, and if a street bum found and returned the four million, the bum would be rewarded with some money. The bum would be rewarded, but for providing the equivalent service, the advertising agency won't. We expect to get what we pay for in life. If we pay nothing, we get nothing. If we pay something, we get something in return. But in advertising, we pay someone for losing our money (allowing us to spend it unproductively), but not for finding it (advising us not to waste it when we have nothing to say). A strange kind of incentive, indeed!

Men and women involved in the advertising process, both agencies and advertisers, should be paid for the quality of their work, not for how much money they spend. People in advertising should be paid more when they get a job done for *less* money than when they spend *more* to accomplish the same job. Incentive money should motivate *efficiency*, not waste. The current system of compensation works backwards. Until it's turned around by 180 degrees, *advertising* and *waste* will continue to be interchangeable words.

Advertising Must Kick Its Verbal-Narcotic Habit

Even if advertising begins to measure the success and failure of all its campaigns, even if the commission compensation system is replaced with a financial incentive that will encourage advertising people to become efficient producers, advertising will make little progress until it kicks its verbal-narcotic habit. Language is the most important tool used in the building of new understanding. The sharper the tool, the faster the building of new knowledge. The blunter the tool, the slower the progress. Verbal narcotics make the cutting edge of advertising language so fuzzy that it generally builds nothing more substantial than daydreams. How can we take seriously anyone who admits he doesn't know how TV advertising works, or how radio advertising works, yet who supports his recommendation to use radio advertising by saying that "it works synergistically with the brand's TV advertising?" The answer is that we can't take him seriously. Nor can we expect him to be capable of adding to the little we know now about media planning and the advertising functions related to it.

Nor can we expect progress when phrases like these are used: a media plan that will create "a meaningful competitive presence." This language isn't compatible with accountability. How can we hold someone accountable for delivering something that we can't understand or define? With what instrument shall we measure the "impact" of this media plan?

Scientists didn't learn to split the atom by sitting around impressing each other with the scientific equivalent of verbal narcotics. Medical researchers won't discover a cure for cancer by strutting in front of each other spouting meaningless medical jargon.

Nobody struggles through the powerful membrane of ignorance, into new understanding, relaxed by his own verbal Valium. To move even one step forward into new understanding, advertising people must throw away the crutch of verbal narcotics, which is their daily language. To become professionals, they must begin to act like professionals. To begin to act like professionals, they must begin communicating in professional (meaningful) language.

Few drug users step forward and voluntarily give up the habit that makes them feel good. Users of advertising's verbal narcotics are no different. Their use must be denied by someone in authority, probably someone in the advertiser's chain of command. When a recommendation is supported with words such as *impact, presence, synergy, intrusiveness, continuity*, and the like, the responsible manager should pencil them out, send back the recommendation, and ask that these verbal narcotics be replaced with meaningful words, words which convey real meaning. Once the crutch has been pulled out from under the user, he'll learn how to create better media plans. If he can't, he'll fall on his face, and someone more capable will step forward to try to do it better. It may not be comfortable, but progress rarely is.

Advertising Must Confess Its Ignorance

All of us have clear vision into the problems of others, but most of us are frequently blind to our own. We all know that an alcoholic who denies his alcoholism can't be cured of it. We have equally good insight into the problems of people addicted to hard drugs, and those with other kinds of emotional problems. We also know that people who refuse to let go of their problem have given themselves what they think are good reasons for holding on. And most of us know someone who has overcome his problem once he accepted the fact that he had a problem.

Ignorance is also a problem that requires acknowledgement of that problem, with the expectation of a cure once it has been admitted, accepted, and attacked as a problem. The difference is that ignorance *isn't* socially unacceptable. Like childhood, ignorance is recognized as a part of life. Ignorance is the first stage in every intellectual growth process. It's human, it's normal, and it's constructive when it's accepted as a challenge to be overcome.

The denial of our ignorance leaves us in the helpless state of the alcoholic who refuses to accept his condition. He uses rationalizations to support the denial of his condition. This is what advertising does. Like the alcoholic, advertising doesn't want to believe it has a problem. Ignorance is denied. Complex rationalizations support the denial. The language of verbal narcotics supports it. The self-serving theories of advertising support it. The excuses for not measuring results support it. Clio awards support it. The Advertising Hall of Fame supports it. Advertising people who, with their pretense of knowledge, support it most effectively, are compensated with much prestige and money. Prognosis for a cure is not good at all.

If the advertising industry is to have a better future, and not just a continued extension of its inadequate past, all this must change. Unless advertising people stand up in front of their peers and confess their ignorance, accept their ignorance, and attempt to work their way out of this ignorance, the advertising industry's inadequte present will continue indefinitely. There will be no real growth in the stunted understanding that advertising people have of their own profession. There will be no better future for the advertising industry.

Advertisers Must Stop Taking the Easy Way Out

As Lincoln said, in an 1858 speech, "You can fool all of the people some of the time, and some of the people all of the time, but you cannot fool all the people all the time." However, advertisers can fool themselves as often, and for as long as, they choose. They may think that they are "adding value" to their product with better advertising, but they're not. It's illegal to say something is in a product that isn't in it. Advertising can highlight the best in a product, or can point out everything of value in the product. Advertising can enable a product to live up to its fullest selling potential, but it is against the law to deceive consumers by saying something is in a product that isn't.

So, advertisers must stop trying, with advertising, to make products look better than they really are. These efforts rarely work, anyway. Advertisers must start doing it the old-fashioned way, the hard way. They have to start making better *products*. Really better. Not legalistic "new-and-improved" products, but really better products. Or they have to show consumers better ways to use them. Really better ways. (The key word is *really* better, not seemingly better.)

Advertisers can add value to their commercials by making them more enjoyable to watch. Many of them already do. But this improvement in the entertainment value of their commercials usually isn't the same as improving their product. To like the commercials for Tide isn't the same as liking the cleaning performance of Tide. If you like the commercials for Raid, this doesn't mean you like the bug-killing performance of Raid. A brand's improved commercial makes for better entertainment, but that's not what the consumer pays for when she buys the product. Entertainment is what the consumer expects to get on her TV set—free. When she pays money for a product, she wants clean wash and dead bugs.

Just as media planners must think of consumers as individual, flesh-and-blood people, rather than demographic abstractions, so must advertisers think of people as consumers of products, not as consumers who watch or listen to commercials merely for their entertainment value. When they do, they will improve their products and will leave it to the entertainment industry to satisfy the consumer's entertainment needs.

As I've said, verbal narcotics are the crutches used by advertising people to avoid the hard work of doing their job as it should be done. Making "better" commercials is the crutch used by many advertisers to avoid the hard work of doing their marketing job as it should be done. Advertising agencies and their advertising can't make better products. That's the advertiser's job. If he does it well, he'll probably have good advertising. Better products usually make better advertising.

We are all consumers. All business ultimately serves people, who are consumers. Business that serves us well is rewarded. Business that doesn't is punished. Not always immediately, but sooner or later. Much of today's advertising doesn't serve us well.

I think it will, sooner or later. Probably much later. Not until after advertisers and their agencies have been punished for not having served us, the consumers, as well as they should have—as well as they could have.

I'd like to end my career and my book more optimistically than this. But I can't. Reason controls my emotions too much. Reason says that too many indicators point in the wrong direction for the advertising business to want to redeem itself for its lack of professionalism, certainly not in the near future. Emotion would like to be able to hope for a better outcome. Our economy, more and more involved in global competition, needs all the help it can get. It needs more from advertising than another entertaining soft-shoe dance.

The thousands of good advertising men and women who dedicate their lives to this irresponsible business deserve more than fair wages and good working conditions. They deserve to be trained with facts and knowledge, not with folklore that has little more substance than Santa Claus, the Easter Bunny, and the Tooth Fairy. These men and women deserve the opportunity to become truly professional. Emotion wishes it for them. But reason says it won't happen. Not without a lot of painful trauma, which most of them don't deserve, and for which they will never be compensated.

Emotion hopes that reason is wrong this time. But it usually isn't.

Notes

Chapter 1

1. Dick Vaughn, *How Advertising Works: An FCB Strategy Planning Model*, 1979. Published for internal use.

Chapter 3

1. Unpublished research findings, provided to the author over many years, and quoted with permission from Burke Marketing Research, Inc.
2. Herbert E. Krugman, "Why Three Exposures May Be Enough," *Journal of Advertising Research*, December 1972.
3. Colin McDonald, "What Is the Short-Term Effect of Advertising?" Marketing Science Institute, Special Report No. 71-112, February, 1971.
4. Michael J. Naples, *Effective Frequency: The Relationship Between Frequency and Advertising Effectiveness*, Association of National Advertisers, 1979.
5. *Related Recall Norms for Day After Recall Tests of Television Commercials*, Cincinnati: Burke Marketing Research, 1983.
6. "Effect of Program Involvement On Related Recall Scores" (Technical Paper). Cincinnati: Burke Marketing Research, 1981.

Chapter 6

1. Herbert E. Krugman, "Why Three Exposures May Be Enough," *Journal of Advertising Research*, December, 1972.

Chapter 10

1. Jack Z. Sissors, "Advice to Media Planners on How to Use Effective Frequency," *Journal of Media Planning*, Fall 1986, p. 7.
2. Hubert A. Zielske, "The Remembering and Forgetting of Advertising," *Journal of Marketing*, January, 1959, 239–243.
3. Michael J. Naples, *Effective Fequency: The Relationship Between Frequency and Advertising Effectiveness*. Association of National Advertisers, 1979.

Index

About the Author

Gus Priemer completed his liberal arts education with a year at the Sorbonne, and a year in Aix-en-Provence as a Fulbright scholar. In 1952, he began his advertising career in the media department of the Procter & Gamble Co. In 1964, he joined S.C. Johnson & Son as director of media, a position he held, and to which were added other staff responsibilities, until his retirement in 1987. Since then, he has done consulting work for S.C. Johnson & Son and other companies while preparing this book.

From 1973 to 1976, Mr. Priemer was chairman of the Television Committee of the Association of National Advertisers, a committee on which he served for twenty-two years. In 1977, he was appointed to the National Advertising Review Board (NARB), an organization formed to render judgments on individual matters of truth and accuracy in advertising. During his tenure on the NARB, he chaired a consultative panel that produced the 1981 white paper, "Advertising Self-Regulation and Its Interaction With Consumers." In 1987 he was honored by Northwestern University's Medill School of Journalism for his contribution to media planning.